THE WAX PACK

THE
WAX
PACK

On the Open Road
in Search of
Baseball's Afterlife

BRAD BALUKJIAN

University of Nebraska Press | Lincoln

Library of Congress Cataloging-in-Publication Data
Names: Balukjian, Brad, author.
Title: The wax pack: on the open road in search of baseball's afterlife / Brad Balukjian.
Description: Lincoln: University of Nebraska Press, 2020. | Includes bibliographical references.
Identifiers: LCCN 2019032953
ISBN 9781496218742 (hardback)
ISBN 9781496221506 (epub)
ISBN 9781496221513 (mobi)
ISBN 9781496221520 (pdf)
Subjects: LCSH: Baseball players—United States—Biography. | Baseball—United States—History—20th century. | Baseball cards—United States. | Balukjian, Brad—Travel—United States.
Classification: LCC GV865.A1 B3235 2020 | DDC 796.357092 [B]—dc23
LC record available at https://lccn.loc.gov/2019032953

Set in Minion Pro by Laura Ebbeka.

Baseball is very much a game about fathers and sons, as the following pages attest. My gratitude to my dad will hopefully speak for itself, but I want to use this space to thank my mom. For every game my dad took me to, my mom took me to a baseball card shop in some converted garage or basement in rural Rhode Island to indulge my passion. Thank you, Mom, for always giving me the confidence to be me. I love you.

Security is mostly a superstition. It does not exist in nature, nor do the children of men as a whole experience it. Avoiding danger is no safer in the long run than outright exposure. Life is a daring adventure, or nothing.

HELEN KELLER

CONTENTS

AUTHOR'S NOTE

This is a work of literary nonfiction, and as such, I have played with the chronology of events in some instances for the benefit of the narrative and ultimately the reader. The only composite events take place in chapter 2, when two visits to Visalia (an initial scouting visit for the road trip and the visit on the trip itself) are combined into one. All quotes are accurate, as I tape-recorded my conversations with players and took contemporaneous notes. There are also no composite characters in the book; on occasion I have changed the names of certain people to protect their identities.

PROLOGUE

Mary Lou Gula knows it's going to be a long day.

Since starting her job on the floor of the Topps factory fourteen years ago, she's worked on every part of the baseball card manufacturing process: card cutting, general help, the DF line, day coding. She even played Santa at the company Christmas party.

The two-story factory sprawls among the hills of Duryea, outside Scranton in eastern Pennsylvania's coal country. Duryea has long been a town of miners and factory workers, first from the silk and cigar industries and now baseball cards. These 2.5-inch-by-3.5-inch slices of cardboard, initially included as giveaways in packs of cigarettes in the 1880s, have produced a collecting craze across the country. By 1992 sales will reach $1.5 billion, and soon after that, a confluence of forces—oversaturation of product, waning interest in baseball, the advent of the internet—will burst the bubble, sending baseball cards back to the dugout. But we're getting ahead of ourselves. Right now, in late 1985, Topps is the flagship, and Duryea the flagship's home.

The DF line, where Mary Lou is scheduled today, is especially grueling. No one even knows what the *D* and *F* stand for—they just know that the process of cracking twenty-five-pound loaves of cold pink bubblegum into individual sticks, loading them into the chutes of the DF machine, and stacking the finished packs of cards in boxes, all at a breakneck pace, mean sore feet and an achy back by the time happy hour rolls around.

Lowering herself into her car to drive the two blocks to the factory, Mary Lou's mind jumps ahead eight hours, when she and her coworkers will clock out, walk through the factory doors, and make a critical decision for happy hour: turn right and walk half a mile to Town Tavern, or turn left and go half a mile to Litzi's Lounge. Litzi's will cash their checks at the bar, and, being a Thursday, it's also payday. While Mary Lou has the masochistic habit of working doubles (*can't argue with the pay!*), today she has first shift, the prime shift, and will be off by 3:30 p.m.

Arriving a few minutes early, Mary Lou pushes open the double doors of the factory. The scent of sugar immediately assaults her nostrils, sending a pang through her jaw. In another part of the building known as Hell's Kitchen, latex, wax, rosin, calcium, and sugar are all mixed together in giant cauldrons to make one-ton batches of the famous bubblegum.

She waves to the security guard and walks down the long hallway of administrative offices, a tunnel of calm before emerging into the chaos of the open factory floor. A small but sturdy woman, she steels herself for the grind of the next eight hours. Yet a smile creeps across her face. This is, literally, her family: twelve of her relatives work here. It's tough work, yeah, but it's a collective struggle. When she was pregnant with each of her now-teenage kids, she worked right up until the day they were born.

Just like the players on the cards she manufactures, Mary Lou wears a uniform, except hers is stained with sugar instead of grass. Snapping the buttons on her knee-length white smock, the red italicized lettering of the Topps logo emblazoned in front, she thinks about hitting her target of 170 packs per minute, near the maximum capacity of a DF machine. She pulls on her red Topps baseball hat and walks from the locker room onto the cavernous factory floor, where she finds her post and greets Mona, her partner for the day.

Six weeks from now, these cards will sit under millions of Christmas trees, fifteen players per pack wrapped in red-white-and-blue wax paper, a slice of Americana and source of instant delight to the kids who will tear them open, hoping for a hometown player or superstar.

Mona stands at one end of the DF machine, one of twenty on the factory floor, and switches it on. It hums to life.

"Is it three thirty yet?" she asks as Mary Lou positions herself at the other end, ready to load.

"We're hitting 170 packs today," Mary Lou replies, glancing at the meter that measures their productivity.

She grabs a small pile of cards, feeding them into the machine's A chute, and in a blur of muscle memory and coordination loads a stick of gum in the B chute almost simultaneously.

The machine combines all the elements of the pack—cards, sticks of gum, and special inserts—into a little stack and then pushes it onto an elevator, where a machine folds a sheet of wax paper around it. A heater melts the wax to seal the pack, which then slides along the conveyor to Mona, who places it in a box to be packed for shipment to the world.

As the wax paper wraps around that first set of cards, Mary Lou has no way of knowing that that pack holds any more significance than the thousands of others she has fed into DF machines over the years. She has no idea that rather than being unwrapped under a Christmas tree six weeks from now, it will remain sealed in storage, a forgotten time capsule waiting to be excavated. She has no idea that almost thirty years later, a sports archaeologist with a penchant for underdogs will come along and discover that time capsule, open it up, and then set off on a daring adventure to track down every player inside.

And she has no idea that one day she will meet that sports archaeologist in a smoky casino near Duryea and that that archaeologist will be me.

THE WAX PACK

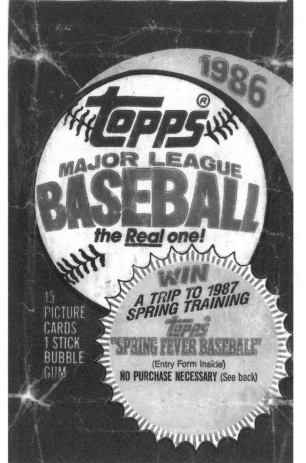

1986

topps ®

MAJOR LEAGUE

BASEBALL

the Real one!

15
PICTURE
CARDS
1 STICK
BUBBLE
GUM

WIN

A TRIP TO 1987
SPRING TRAINING

topps ®

"SPRING FEVER BASEBALL"

(Entry Form Inside)

NO PURCHASE NECESSARY (See back)

WARMING UP

Are you ready to grow up?
—*All my ex-girlfriends, ever*

SUMMER 2014

I have always gravitated toward the obscure, the unknown, the unsung.

In 1984 I was one of only two kids to vote for Bert over Ernie in the Greenville Nursery School's version of the presidential election (*Sesame Street* providing a more compelling choice than Ronald Reagan or Walter Mondale). I liked that Bert collected bottle caps and kept Ernie, who always seemed to be causing mischief, in line. As I grew, so too did my love of underdogs: my favorite insects were stinkbugs; my favorite New Kid on the Block was the reclusive Jon Knight; I even had a favorite railroad track at the Providence Train Station (track 5, remote and little used).

While I liked bugs and boy bands and train stations just fine, far and away my biggest passion was baseball. And true to form, my childhood heroes were the journeymen and benchwarmers, the underdog fringe players who needed to work like mad just to stay in place.

Always outside the mainstream, I identified as an underdog myself. A natural introvert, I was a late bloomer in everything from school to puberty to sex. I faced a good deal of middle-class adversity growing up, going through six years of speech therapy to treat a debilitating stutter, enduring another six years of orthodontics to tackle a dental situation that baffled my own father (who himself was a dentist), and struggling with obsessive-compulsive disorder. I've never forgotten what it feels like to stand alone in the corner of the room.

Now thirty-four, I am still putting bugs in jars, still listening to eighties music on cassette tapes, and still loving baseball. And so it's probably no coincidence that I am also still single, living on a shoestring adjunct professor's salary while renting a room from a lawyer in Oakland, California. In my early twenties I thought I'd met "the One" and was ready for what you're supposed to do next—marriage, kids, etc. But I was wrong.

Expectations can be a dangerous thing.

Oakland is an underdog in its own right, its skyline no match for the glitz and gloss of its counterpart, San Francisco, across the bay. I prefer the grit of Oakland, a difference symbolized best by the differences in the cities' baseball stadiums. The crowd at the Giants' AT&T Park resembles a corporate happy hour, with tech hipsters swiping on their phones, their bodies turned away from the field in animated conversation, the game a mere backdrop for socializing. The Oakland Coliseum, on the other hand, is a postapocalyptic crater ringed with hot dog stands. Opened in 1966 on the flank of the I-880 freeway, the eyesore has been decaying for years, its plumbing regularly failing and leading to major sewage problems in the clubhouse.

But the Coliseum is my church and the upper deck my pew. One lazy summer day in 2014, I plop down fifteen dollars and have an entire section to myself, stretching out across three seats. I share my perch overlooking the first baseline with brazen seagulls squawking and jousting for food scraps, unfazed by my presence. The Jumbotron displays the teams' lineups and players' statistics, and just beyond, the tops of the Oakland hills glow in a sea of golden light. Even from these nosebleed seats, the freshly watered green of the outfield grass and reddish brown of the infield dirt radiate like a tropical rain forest with a buzz cut.

As the A's leadoff hitter swaggers to home plate in that way only baseball players can—thick haunches pumping up and down with each stride like the coupling rod of a locomotive—I hover my pencil a couple of inches above my scorebook, ready to record the action.

I glance at the scoreboard and scan the names, suddenly aware of how few I actually recognize. While I still follow baseball, my knowledge of players peaked around age ten, when shoeboxes brimming with baseball cards covered my shelves. Those cards were like little monuments to my heroes, the backs of them crammed with statistics in squint-inducing fonts. And while I appreciated, even obsessed over, those numbers (I can still recite the career stats of my favorite player, Don Carman), gaudy statistics did not impress me. Rather, I was drawn to those players who for some reason resonated with my quirky personality—I liked Spike Owen because of his funny name, Marty Barrett because I thought he was handsome, and Felix Fermin because his initials were both *F* (which, for no apparent reason, was my favorite letter). I curated a baseball card album of all these players, whose only other common thread was that they were underdogs.

Every week, I marched my fifty-cent allowance to the Greenville Pharmacy to buy a wax pack of these cards, complete with a chalky stick of gum that snapped like a twig when you bit into it. Each pack was a kid's version of a scratch-off ticket, a chance to find a favorite player waiting inside.

But even at that young age I was not content to just let my cards sit in an album. I wanted, *needed*, to know everything I could about the players themselves, to connect with them in some way.

When my parents purchased our first computer in 1992, I immediately opened the word processor (remember Notepad?) and typed up a biography of Marty Barrett and his complete statistics, which I printed out and pressed to my nose, inhaling the scent of fresh ink. Somehow writing down those numbers and printing them out made them real and tangible in a way that mere thoughts never could. But again, it wasn't enough to just print them—I then had to track down Barrett in person, finding him at a car dealership where he was signing autographs so I could present the report to him. I wanted to study him, to see what he looked like in normal street clothes, to simply know if he was a nice guy. (He was.)

As I got older, my pathological need to scrutinize and document only grew. I became a scientist (specifically, an entomologist), a profession demanding meticulous observation, research, and record-keeping. And the right side of my brain kept up with the left: my other passion was writing, particularly writing about people, and so, struggling to choose between science and journalism (my commitment issues extending to all facets of my life), I resolved to do both.

Back in my nosebleed seats at the Coliseum, I think more about the benchwarmers and journeymen of my childhood, the figurines of my

Toy Story, whose cards are now locked away in a storage unit in my mother's condo. (Thank you for not tossing them, Mom!) I picture the vessel that those cards came in, the wax pack, wondering if they even make them anymore, a smile spreading across my face as I recall the thrill of opening one. Each pack held fifteen individual surprises. And then I experience a wonderful moment of inspiration bubbling from the subconscious, that ever-elusive visit from the muse: What if I could open a pack *just one more time*? Not a new pack, but one that had been kept sealed by some hoarder in the vain hope that it would one day be worth something, one that—and this is the key—would almost certainly contain many of the very underdog types I once idolized (the contents of a pack being random and underdogs being more numerous; most teams only have a few star players).

Completely forgetting the game in front of me, I begin scribbling ideas and questions in my scorebook. What happened to the underdogs of my childhood after the spotlight faded? How do they feel the game has changed? And what can I learn from them about what lies ahead for me? Pencil in hand, I realize that at thirty-four I am now the same age that most of them were when they retired, their bodies betraying them. In what other profession are you washed up for good in your midthirties? Most would be content to let this daydream evaporate into the summer sky. But not me. Not having saved any wax packs from childhood (the idea of *not* opening one as a kid was heretical), I take out my phone, log on to eBay, and order a pack of 1986 Topps, the first year I remember collecting.

When the Pack (now a proper noun) arrives a few days later, I cradle its still-shiny wax paper, admiring the sunbursts of gaudy color and nonsensical slogan ("the Real one!"), noticing the way the horizontal bar of the lowercase *t* in "topps" extends farther than it should.[1] I remove the calcified stick of gum with the caution of a bomb expert, place it in my mouth, and clench down on its powdered surface, splintering it into a thousand crumbs, which instantly dissolve on my tongue. It's delightfully gross.

I draw out the unveiling process as long as possible, slowly revealing each player while cherishing the mustiness of neglect. It is a tantalizing mix of greatness and mediocrity, fourteen Wax Packers in all (card 15 is a checklist, a card that is literally a list of other cards). Of course, for me, it's not enough to just open the Pack. Now I need to find the players inside it. And write a book about it.

I do some research online and find the Wax Packers are spread out across the country, from California to Massachusetts. The fourteen players played a combined 201 seasons for twenty-three different teams; only the Minnesota Twins, Atlanta Braves, and San Francisco Giants are not represented. I also luck out on their longevity: while the average big-league career lasts only 5.6 years, all but one player in the Pack (Jaime Cocanower) played at least 10. In addition, all but one is still alive: Google informs me that Al Cowens, best known for his days with the Kansas City Royals in the 1970s, succumbed to a heart attack in 2002.

Baseball being a game played largely on the road, I decide the best way to tackle this project would be to take one mother of all summer road trips, a zigzag route that, when drawn on a map of the United States, looks like someone passed out with a Sharpie in hand. My unemployed status (in between semesters teaching biology at Laney College) gives me the luxury of time (but certainly not money; unlike literary quests like *Eat, Pray, Love*, the only advance I have is the warning that Vince Coleman might be a dick). This journey would, of course, require condensing a year's worth of driving into seven weeks, which raises two serious concerns: (1) my tendency to get immediately drowsy behind the wheel (I've been known to nod off driving the Bay Bridge between Oakland and San Francisco) and (2) the steed for my odyssey would be a 2002 Honda Accord, already with 154,029 miles on the odometer, the automotive equivalent of asking a forty-year-old pitcher to throw a complete game.

I circle June of next year on the calendar as my departure date, giving me nine months to try and locate thirteen ex-ballplayers (and the ghost of a fourteenth) and convince them to talk to me. But here's the thing: I have no special connections, no rich uncle who was golf buddies with George Steinbrenner. I don't even have a sports-writing pedigree to give me legitimacy, having focused almost exclusively on science in my freelance writing career. So I resort to good old-fashioned stalking. My methods vary according to the player—some are only a Google search away (Rance Mulliniks's Century 21 Realtor web page instantly pops up, including his cell phone number), while the more famous players, like Carlton Fisk and Doc Gooden, are much harder to contact.

I have a narrow window in which to pull off this road trip—forty-nine days, leaving June 19 and returning home August 6, with only one buffer day in case I have car trouble or get arrested trying to ambush Carlton Fisk. Time is tight because on August 8 I have a plane ticket to fly back across the country for the wedding of one of my college buddies, an event I can't miss.

When I encounter each new Wax Packer, I will hand him a thick manila folder, a collection of all the articles written about him in the sports media.

I will say, "This is my file on you. I've read it all, and I still feel like I know nothing about you."

He will smile and chuckle, impressed that I am willing to call him out on the well-known fact that players are trained to say nothing of substance to journalists.

"What do you want to know?" he will ask.

You're about to find out.

BLUE JAYS

RANCE MULLINIKS

2

HAPPY MEALS

Control what you can control.
—*Rance Mulliniks*

Days 1–2
June 19–20, 2015
Miles driven: 303
Cups of coffee: 3
Oakland CA to Visalia CA

Twenty-five miles outside the city limits, I get my first whiff of Visalia.

Nose crinkling, I hit scan on the Accord's radio, ping-ponging between Christian rock and mariachi, then finally resort to the AM dial. More Christians, talking this time.

What do you do if you need to perform a baptism and there's no water available? asks the host.

"What the fuck?" snaps Jesse from the back seat, his dark brown eyes flashing.

For the first leg of the trip, driving east from Oakland and then south along the spine of California's Central Valley, I've brought along my two best friends, Adam and Jesse Brouillard, figuring the company would be nice before I strike out on my own. I met the Brouillard brothers right after college, in 2002, when I moved to Santa Barbara. Our parents, who were acquaintances back in our home state of Rhode Island, had arranged a play date for us at a local bar, something that, ninety-nine times out of a hundred, doesn't result in a sequel. Fresh from a shift at their family restaurant, the Brouillards, who pride themselves on being blue collar, took one look at the literal blue collar of my starched polo shirt and flat-front khakis and checked the clock. But it turned out we had a lot in common: Jesse and I both loved baseball, were terrified of power tools, and used Caps Lock instead of the Shift key for capitalization; Adam (whom we call the Kid, even though he's technically a few months older than me) hated baseball, but we bonded over our love of obscure *Star Wars* characters. And the brothers couldn't have been more different from each other, Jesse a loud-talking, cymbal-crashing force of charming neurosis and mercurial pride, Adam a sensitive free spirit and ex-bartender ready to nest with his fiancée, Ali.

The radio voice in my car continues: *The book of baptism rules states that if no water is available, certain "doubtful matter," such as saliva, tears, or light beer, can be substituted for the baptism.*

"How much longer, dude? I could use some doubtful matter right now!" Jesse says. "I'm thinking Heineken," he adds, leaning so far forward he's almost in the front seat.

"And some chicken tenders," the Kid says, shutting off the radio sermon. Riding shotgun, he shifts his feet and yanks on his black hoodie from the Kona Club, a bar back in Oakland where he used to sling fruity cocktails.

If San Francisco and Los Angeles are California's showrooms, then this, the Central Valley, is the boiler room. The carefully gridded quilt of ranches and farms bears little resemblance to the land once roamed for centuries by the Yokut tribe of Native Americans. Gold-seekers flocked here in the early 1850s, and when they didn't find the bounty they expected, they transformed the grassland into an agricultural hub. Pistachio, walnut, and orange orchards stretch to the horizon, interspersed with cattle stalls.

"So who is this guy again? Lance Mullinks?" the Kid asks, fishing out the 1986 baseball cards that inspired the trip. Jesse rolls his eyes.

"Jesus Christ, Kid, it's Rance Mull-i-niks!" he replies, dragging out each syllable. I smirk at Jesse's frustration—we've only been on the road three hours, and I've already refereed half a dozen spats, headlined by an epic debate over the food at IHOP versus Marie Callender's (the edge going to the latter, based on their free blueberry banana loaf).

Rance is the perfect leadoff hitter for this journey, wonderfully pedestrian as a player but phonetically unforgettable. He epitomizes the underdogs I idolized as a kid, a scrappy overachiever with the physique of a librarian who managed to play sixteen seasons in the big leagues. In newspaper accounts from his career, the same adjectives come up over and over: "smart," "mild-mannered," "hard-nosed." He was a perpetual part-timer who got by on guile and hustle, a line-drive hitter whose career ended in Hollywood fashion, winning a World Series with the Toronto Blue Jays in 1992. He had not been hard to find: his cell phone number was listed online, and when I called him and explained the gist of the project, he seemed genuinely interested, almost bashful. In our very first conversation, he said, "I'd be happy to show you around. The small town I'm from, Woodville [located right outside Visalia], I'm not sure how interesting you'll find it."

"Rance wanted to come back *here*?" the Kid says, billboards streaking by as we enter Visalia proper.

If abortion was my right, why do I feel so wrong? reads one.

Rance came home and now works as a residential Realtor, which raises this very important question: What the hell is a World Series champion doing hosting open houses in a place that smells like cow shit?

—

Getting marital advice from Rance Mulliniks was definitely not on the itinerary.

I stare at the shiny gold rock clamped on the fourth finger of his left hand, a symbol of his one true love. The Toronto Blue Jays logo sits front and center in the ring, a sparkling diamond in the bird's eye, commemorating the Jays' 1992 World Series victory.

"Lord knows I'm not an expert on marriage, but I got married at twenty-two. And I tell my older children, until you're thirty, don't even think about it," he says.

Jesse and I glance over at the Kid. Rance arches an eyebrow.

"What?" the Kid protests. "I'm thirty-four. I know what I'm doing."

Rance is wearing a black polo shirt and black plaid shorts, and his graying hair, a bit thinner now than it was during his playing days, is slicked straight back. His bushy mustache is still there, but with a lot more salt than pepper now. He casts a figure bigger than his six feet, with a late middle-age leanness belied only by settling around the midsection that says fatherhood. His face is florid and his features are a bit avian, with a weak chin and warm bluish eyes. He is a relaxed fifty-eight, still spry enough that if a ground ball came screeching his way, he could instinctively crouch down and snuff it.

Rance has suggested a homecoming tour, visiting all the places where he crafted the hitting stroke that brought him to baseball's promised land. We've gathered behind the fence at Monache High School's baseball field, a padlock on the gate keeping us from standing in the spot where a teenage Rance once crushed it. A life-size cardboard cut-out of his likeness looms down the right-field line above the outfield fence, a tribute put up by the school when they retired his jersey (number 4) last year.

After this tour of Rance's alma mater, we'll visit the tiny town of Woodville, too small to have a high school of its own, and then watch him give a hitting lesson at his baseball academy. But right now, Rance is in mentor mode, having been informed of the Kid's recent engagement to Ali.

"You've got to work at it. It doesn't just naturally flow, because at some point the shine's gonna wear off, and now it becomes a day-to-day thing," he says.

He's talking marriage in his measured baritone, but he could just as easily be discussing baseball and its grueling 162-game schedule.

Rance speaks from experience—he was forced to grow up way too quickly while playing a child's game for a living. Although he had scholarship offers from USC, Arizona State, and other schools, he spurned them for a $32,500 signing bonus from the California Angels, a reward for signing in the third round of the 1974 amateur draft. Two years later, he met his first wife, Jeannie, while playing in the Minor Leagues in El Paso, Texas, and the year after that, at only twenty-one years old, Rance got the call that every Little Leaguer dreams of: you're going to the Major Leagues to be the Angels' starting shortstop. Even forty years later, he can recall his exact statistics the day he was called up: eleven home runs and fifty-one runs batted in.

The next sixteen years were a blur away from home. And three years after his career ended in 1992, so too did the marriage.

"What happened?" I ask, fully aware of how nosy I'm being.

Rance stares out to center field, his hair matted with sweat at the edges, his face still.

"I don't really know what happened. It just got to a point where I wasn't willing to do it the rest of my life. My ex, Jeannie, she would always say, 'I know you must have a woman,' but I just laughed. There was no other woman."

I don't press beyond that, and he doesn't offer a further explanation. Although he and Jeannie haven't talked in years, they're forever linked through their three adult children, Ryan, Merissa, and Whitney, who all live elsewhere.

"I can honestly say that I wasn't the giving father that I should have been," he volunteers. "I don't want to give the wrong impression. I wasn't hanging out and partying all the time and doing those kinds of things, but when I was home during the off-season, I didn't spend the time that I should have with my children." I'm surprised by his candor. He's already shown us more vulnerability than he did in sixteen seasons with reporters.

"And as a husband, I wasn't a bad guy or anything, but I was so dedicated and into what I was doing that I could have done better," he says, his ring flashing as he talks with his hands.

"You can be home and a mile away," he adds.

I think about how opposite my relationship with my father was, the countless games of catch, the way he taught me how to read box scores and batting averages.

"Where does Ryan live?" Jesse asks.

"Seattle. He works for the U.S. Postal Service. Used to be in the navy, served on a nuclear submarine."

A job that will take you as far away from home as you want to go.

"Was he not into baseball?" I ask, knowing how common it is for players' sons to try and follow in their dads' footsteps.

Rance shakes his head, then blinks, holding the fence.

"Well, he liked to play. He was a very good athlete, well-coordinated. I coached him a couple years, and I could put him anywhere on the field and he could play. But I don't know, because I didn't spend the time with him that I should have. If I had, maybe he would have really taken to it."

He pats the dirt with the toe of his sneaker, carving a small mound.

I look over at the Kid, who has been listening intently this entire time. Baseball has never seemed so interesting to him.

We pile into Rance's white Toyota Avalon to drive to Woodville, the tiny town next door and site of the original Mulliniks homestead.

"That 1985 team was underrated, wasn't it?" Jesse asks from the backseat, unable to resist talking directly about baseball any longer. He was every bit as obsessive and fastidious a fan as I was growing up in the eighties.

Rance smiles. For Blue Jays fans, 1985 is the moment you lost your virginity: bittersweet, wonderfully flawed, but unforgettable. That year, only eight years removed from their inception as a pitiful expansion team, the Jays won ninety-nine games and their first division title.

"I think that '85 team was the most talented team I ever played on," Rance replies, easing the Avalon down flat county roads, shifting his body occasionally to relieve the sciatica that has plagued him since running out a bunt hit in 1978.

Despite being favored, the Blue Jays lost that year in the playoffs to the Kansas City Royals, who went on to become champions.

"Winning a world championship [in 1992] was a great thing, but the overall experience in '85 was greater," he says.

Woodville's misfortune lurks behind the ubiquitous chain-link fences walling off homes from the sidewalk. It's a squat, dusty town, the houses packed in close, devoid of restaurants or other commerce. We park at the elementary school, and after a cheery greeting from the principal ("When's your mom going to bring more of those pies around?"), we walk past a group of kids playing pickup basketball behind the school, barbed wire lining the top of the fence. Striding quickly toward the baseball field, Rance says the town has changed considerably, although his childhood home and his grandparents' house still stand.

On this field many years ago, his dad, Harvey, had seen the future: Rance would succeed where Harvey had failed. Once a prospect himself, Harvey had had a live arm, a cannon, and was signed in the 1950s with high hopes as a pitcher by the Yankees. He was born in Oklahoma, his family moving to California with the hundreds of thousands of other southwesterners (nicknamed "Okies") during the Great Depression in search of literal greener pastures. He met Rance's mom, Ganell, on a school bus at age fifteen in nearby Porterville, devoted himself to baseball, and, when he blew out his arm, settled into a career as a finance and loan businessman and later a county assessor.

With the help of Rance's brother, Dana, Harvey threw batting practice to Rance on this field deep into the twilight every single day after school beginning in February, when the cold plains air stung every bit of exposed skin. Rance swung until his hands were raw, his muscles being programmed with each subsequent pitch. His talent was obvious as he blew past his peers, but most impressive was his quiet confidence and resolve. When he had stitches removed from a deep gash on the bottom of his foot right before his first Little League game, he wrapped it up and, against the protests of his mom, declared he would play, no matter the pain. When he broke into the Major Leagues with the Angels in 1977 and slumped horribly, he didn't flinch, telling the *Sporting News*: "At no time did I think I was over-matched. They don't throw any harder up here than they do in the Minors and their breaking pitches aren't any better."[1]

Harvey was there every step of the way, driving the family to Oakland whenever the Angels came up to play the A's and demanding they arrive two hours before the first pitch just to watch Rance take batting practice. They invested in a satellite dish in the 1980s so they could watch him on TV, long before the advent of cable channels that broadcast every game. And in Rance's last season, when the team reached the 1992 World Series against the Atlanta Braves and were on the verge of clinching, Harvey and Ganell were so nervous that they got in their car and drove around listening to the game on the radio for the last several innings.

We huddle around the slab of wood peeking through the grass on the pitcher's mound, the sun beating down on us, the air a soupy mix of dust and moisture.

Rance glances at a large tree near the backstop. "Right over there is where he would pitch to me, starting every February through the summer," he says, his hands tucked in his shorts, his blue eyes watering. "My childhood, growing up out here in Woodville, I wouldn't trade that for anything."

He presses his sneakers into the dry grass of the pitcher's mound. The leaves of that solitary tree sway behind the backstop.

"Dad was a very emotional guy, but he wouldn't necessarily show it. He would hear singing in church and cry," he says.

Harvey passed away from liver cancer in 2001 after an otherwise healthy life. It was then that Rance, still living in El Paso and now with his second wife, Lori, heard the call to come home.

⸻

I want to get the Wax Packers on the field to see what it feels like to face Doc Gooden or to play catch with Lee Mazzilli. And now, on day 1, that wish has already come true: I'm about to get a hitting lesson from Rance Mulliniks.

We're standing in an airplane hangar in Visalia, a space serving as Rance's new baseball academy. From the outside, nothing indicates this is where a world champion trains the next generation of ballplayers. The closest sign of any kind is located in a lot across the street, a faded Romney/Ryan campaign poster. Inside the hangar, the decor is simple: a sock of black netting to simulate a batting cage, with a carpet of green turf.

For seventy dollars an hour Rance gives private lessons to local kids. Today's charge is Jonathan, a senior at Porterville High with college baseball aspirations. Jonathan is short and has limited natural ability, but he's a hard worker. He nods to the three of us gathered around the sock, probably wondering why he suddenly has an audience.

They start with some soft toss, Rance crouching a few feet away, lobbing the ball underhand to let Jonathan find his stroke. He struggles, hacking off-balance, and although Rance does not seem pleased, he remains patient, offering a constant patter of advice and encouragement. When he starts throwing overhand and harder to simulate real pitching, Jonathan flails and seems uncomfortable, verbally annotating all of his swings with apologies and explanations.

Rance throws him a few pitches, struggling to find his location. Jonathan swings wildly and misses.

"If it's not a strike, don't swing at it!" Rance admonishes.

"You throw pretty well for a guy your age," Jonathan says, not trying to be funny.

"Thanks," Rance replies dryly. "Eye on the ball now."

Jonathan starts to find his stroke, and they then move on to fielding. Jonathan's a second baseman, and while Rance played very little at that position (he was mostly a third baseman), he knows his way around an infield. They specifically work on turning the double play—receiving the throw from the left side of the infield, turning, and firing to first. Rance asks to borrow my glove, the same glove I used in Little League, which I've brought just in case there's an opportunity for some catch. He puts it on his left hand and scowls.

"You call this a glove?" he teases.

He straddles second base and asks Jonathan to throw him the ball so he can demonstrate the proper technique.

"It's nothing but a dance move, that's all it is," he says. "The right foot's leading the dance."

He starts a couple of steps behind the base, charges forward and POP!! receives the ball, right foot down, left foot down, and then throws to first. It's a spectacular blur of coordination as Rance sheds years with each muscle's contraction, his legs suddenly appearing nimble below the line of his shorts.

Switching spots, he throws a few to Jonathan, who, try as he might, has nowhere near the grace of the former Major Leaguer.

"Just be athletic," Rance says, trying not to plead.

After Jonathan leaves, we hang out and take turns hitting off a tee so Rance can critique our swings.

Rance twirls and half-swings a bat as he talks, explaining his approach to hitting. I look over at Jesse and smile, knowing he appreciates this as much as I do. Rance's face bristles with concentration, his body taut and attentive.

"Hal McRae is the one who really taught me a lot," Rance says of his former Kansas City Royals teammate.

"It's a cat-and-mouse game. Some people call it being a guess hitter," he says, a Jedi with his lightsaber.

"But it's not really guessing. I would try to wait for my pitch to hit and predict what he's [the pitcher] going to throw. Most of the time you look for a fastball. And if they don't throw the pitch you are looking for, you don't swing. Unless, of course, there's two strikes, and then you've got to shorten up the swing, go the other way [hit to the opposite field] or up the middle," he explains.

"I stood about this far from the plate, slightly open," he says, lining up his feet a little less than two feet off the plate, his right toes slightly more angled toward first base.

"I would have been just about like this," he adds, holding the bat above his left shoulder parallel to the ground. "I would take a little step back like that and then go." His front foot taps back ever so slightly before striding forward toward third base, his arms violently bringing the bat forward like a helicopter blade slicing the air. It is a swing of pure beauty, the geometric precision of the chunk of wood hurtling forward toward an imaginary ball.

He hands the weapon over to us, moving the act from gold record to karaoke.

Jesse has the most experience, having played high school baseball. I peaked in Little League, and the Kid once swung at ball 4 after it had hit the catcher's glove, forcing a befuddled umpire to change his call to strike 3.

But it turns out the Kid may be the most natural athlete of us all. While I whiff on my first swing (off a tee!), he connects on several line drives.

"He's got some pop!" Rance says.

———

I'm thirsty.

I prop my elbows on the bar at Rookies Sports Bar and Grill and lean over to try to get the bartender's attention.

"Let me guess. Sex on the beach?" Jesse says, sipping a glass of Jameson on the rocks.

"Mai tai," I say proudly, playfully shoving my best friend. Chasing women at a bar is *our* batting practice, a routine we've indulged in since meeting all those years ago in Santa Barbara. Although we now live far apart and rarely have the opportunity, we quickly fall into old habits, posting up on the sidelines and scanning the room, hoping to make eye contact with a prospect. Rance is probably fast asleep next to his wife, Lori, by now, having tucked in their kids. But the day has me fired up, riding high on such a successful mission with the first of the fourteen Wax Packers and craving a release. That hedonistic need to double down on the thrill is something I have a hard time squaring with the careful, methodical aspects of my personality, making me wonder at times which is the "real" me.

"Where's the Kid?" I ask.

"Outside on his phone, talking to his wife," Jesse says with a slight eye roll.

Rookies is a sports pub in downtown Visalia, and because the city is equidistant from the nearest major sports markets, Los Angeles and San Francisco, neither city's team dominates the local fan base. Instead, Rookies has settled on safe, generic alternatives—John Elway, Dan Marino, and Emmitt Smith jerseys.

We pay the five-dollar cover charge to see Mr. Rude, who everyone tells us is a "must-see" cover band. The crowd is a diverse mix of Latinx and white, representing the Central Valley's profile of third-generation Okies and migrant Central Americans.

Over the croons of Mr. Rude (*Oh-oh-oh-oh sweet child of mine*), I turn to the girl seated next to me, a fetching Latina, and ask her if the device she's holding is the world's largest cell phone or the smallest computer. She laughs at my lame joke and tells me her name is Jasmine and that she grew up in Visalia. I tell her about my book project and hand her Rance's baseball card to see if she knows the town's prodigal son. But like everyone else I ask in the bar, I'm disappointed to find that she does not recognize him. She drags me onto the dance floor, where I flail like a plastic bag in a tornado long enough to earn a tongue-filled kiss, despite my half Filipino / quarter Armenian / quarter Euro rhythm, clearly less than the sum of my parts.

I'm lost in the distraction, all too happy to switch off my brain and indulge. The next morning, when my brain feels like a gong being struck by a frying pan, I will think back to Rance's discussion of life on the road and how this very scene played out time and again over six long months every baseball season, except unlike me, the players often had wives and toddlers back home.

The Kid bails from the bar early, walking back to our motel, while I lose track of Jasmine and in my drunken stupor get separated from Jesse and end up wandering in the wrong direction after the bar closes.

With my phone dead, my wrist scratched from a fall I barely remember, and my wits dashed, I end up curling up on the side of the freeway in a patch of dewy ice plant whose succulent tendrils suddenly look like thousand-thread-count Egyptian cotton sheets. At some point predawn, I manage to stumble my way back toward the motel, collapsing in a fully dressed heap at the foot of my bed, too exhausted to be bothered by Adam and Jesse's snoring duet.

I just had one of the most exciting days of my life.

I am a mess.

⹀

Stirring four fitful hours later, I do a quick scan of the room in full shame spiral. Clinging to my drool-drenched pillow, I play back the night's events, trying to fit and order the fuzzy fragments. It's like watching a game of Tetris with someone else's glasses on.

All traces of the Kid and Jesse are gone, and I remember that they had to leave on an early train to get back to Santa Barbara. At one point we had planned on taking this whole adventure together, but Jesse chose the stability afforded by a new job, and the Kid was settling into his new partnered life with Ali. Neither one had seven weeks to fritter away on thirty-year-old baseball cards.

I stagger to my feet, grabbing the dresser for support. I dump out the contents of my toiletry bag in search of Advil, take a shower so short I barely get wet, and slug whatever lukewarm coffee is left in the lobby. I've got another date with Rance, and I can't be late.

Jesus Christ, I might still be drunk. What is Rance going to think?

I speed over to the baseball academy (which for me means going five miles over the limit), where I find a fresh Rance finishing up with another student, chatting with the boy's father. The jackhammer in my head is made worse by the pounding of the first-day-of-summer sun, but I do my best to rub the hangover out of my eyes and smile.

While Rance crouches over a cooler and gathers his equipment, his cell phone starts chiming with text messages.

"This woman wears me out," he says with a huge grin as he scrolls through his messages from his wife. "She's so energetic, I can't keep up.

She runs half marathons," he says proudly, then pauses to look at me more carefully.

"Are you okay?" he asks. I show him some of the cuts on my wrist.

"I woke up with this," I say meekly.

"I won't ask," he replies.

We have a list of errands to run—the grocery store, a McDonald's stop for Lori and the kids, and then a stop at their church rummage sale.

I glance at my phone—already 84 degrees, with a high today of 101. I offer to help pay for the groceries we're buying for dinner, but Rance refuses. When I push, he says to give the money to his son, Seth, for his church youth group trip to Kentucky.

Pulling into the drive-thru under the golden arches, Rance turns to me.

"If I can remember this order, I'll be in good shape," he says.

Facing Roger Clemens is a piece of cake compared to keeping this straight: two regular hamburgers with pickles and ketchup only, one hamburger with no onions, a four-piece Chicken McNugget Happy Meal with fries and ketchup, and three bottles of water.

He's sitting on the fastball, but the voice from the drive-thru throws a curve. "Would you like the Nerf toy or the Rebelle with the Happy Meal?" the voice asks.

Rance freezes.

"Jiminy Christmas," he says, exasperated.

Sensing his doubt, the voice offers some help: "The Rebelle is more for girls."

A look of relief crosses his face. "The Rebella I guess," he says, mispronouncing the toy's name.

The world champ comes through in the clutch, just like old times.

In the hallway of the Mulliniks home, tucked in a suburban development of Visalia, hangs a framed quote from Teddy Roosevelt: "It is not the critic who counts; not the man who points out how the strong man stumbles, or where the doer of deeds could have done better. The credit belongs to the man who is actually in the arena, whose face is marred by dust and sweat and blood, who strives valiantly . . . and who at the worst, if he fails, at least he fails while daring greatly."

From his struggles early in his career with the Angels and Royals to losing in five postseasons before finally snagging a gold ring, Rance learned the lessons of failure early and often.

"I saw guys that were bigger, faster, stronger," he tells me in his living room, sipping a Tanqueray and tonic while the family cat, Thumbs, basks in a corner.

Always forced to compete for playing time, he was never afforded the luxury of feeling comfortable. But he also never felt resentful of those trying to take his spot.

"I never really thought about who I was competing against on my team. I said, the one thing I can control is that I can outwork everyone. Control what you can control."

Much like Teddy Roosevelt, Rance walked softly and carried a big stick. Several of them are on display in his office, which doubles as a shrine to his career, assembled by Lori (Rance would never be so self-indulgent). His preferred bat, with "Mulliniks" stamped on the barrel, was the Genuine P72 Louisville Slugger. Three racks, each holding six bats, line one wall below several framed pictures, including one of Rance with George H. W. Bush. Various accolades, milestone baseballs (his first hit, his first home run), and even an original seat from Comiskey Park in Chicago (Americans were *definitely* smaller a hundred years ago) round out the room.

Perhaps the greatest struggle every professional athlete faces is knowing when to hang it up. Starting the 1992 season two years older than I am now, Rance knew he didn't have too many more sunsets left on the baseball diamond. But he was excited by what lay ahead—the Blue Jays had added stars Jack Morris and Dave Winfield in the off-season and were poised for a World Series run.

But before the season even started, his balky back seized up, landing him on the disabled list. It kicked off a miserable season in which he would only come to the plate twice all year. Mentally, he was never better—the student of the game had become the master, able to predict sequences of pitches with ease. But his body was giving out. Ever the loyal soldier, he called a meeting in August with general manager Pat Gillick and team president Paul Beeston.

"I told them, 'I'm injured and I'm not gonna really be able to help the club. I'm gonna shut it down and go home,'" he recalls, taking another sip of his drink.

But the brass would have none of it. For eleven seasons Rance had been the model player. He wasn't big, he wasn't brash, but he was reliable, and he was smart. The Jays were streaking toward history, and Rance deserved a ticket. They convinced him to fly back to El Paso to think it over; Rance changed his mind and rejoined the team a few days later. He was there when Joe Carter recorded the final out of the World Series.

The city was planning a giant parade in downtown Toronto, but on the plane ride back, he told the team he wouldn't be there: his mother-in-law was sick with ALS, and his family needed him.

Figuring there was nowhere higher to go in his career and badly needing rest, Rance retired. The following spring, *Toronto Star* writer Dave Perkins caught up with him, asking about his new life on the sidelines.

"Retirement feels good. I don't miss baseball at all," he told Perkins.

"He's kind of lost right now," his wife, Jeannie, said in the same article.[2]

The ride over, reality set in, and they divorced two years later.

And then opportunity knocked. A second chance. He met Lori on a blind date in 1995. She had no clue he was a baseball player, and when she mentioned his name to coworkers following the date, she came back to find her desk plastered with Rance Mulliniks baseball cards. They got married in 1998, adopting Shaylee and Seth soon after.

The front door swings open.

"I hear trouble!" Rance says as Shaylee bounds into the room, cradling a fake cell phone that she uses to send and receive pretend texts. She's all spirit and spunk, her head a riot of brown hair.

Seth, on the other hand, is understated and calm, almost delicate. He's got a black belt in karate and makes wallets out of duct tape for fun. I instantly like him.

Rance is invigorated by the kids' presence.

"Everything is awesome!" he half sings from *The Lego Movie.*

While Rance and Lori set up dinner and Shaylee plays in the backyard swimming pool, I challenge Seth to a game of ping pong. I like the kid's serious countenance, his precociousness. He's got his dad's good sense of humor, maybe a little drier. We rally back and forth, me pressing him, not wanting to let him win just because he's a kid.

"Who's more talkative, your mom or your dad?" I ask, pushing him deep into the corner of the table.

He returns the ball to my backhand.

"My dad talks a lot when it's about sports or something he likes to talk about. Otherwise he's pretty quiet," he says.

I laugh. "A lot of dads are like that," I say.

About fifteen minutes of ping pong in the ninety-degree heat and we're both soaked. I walk inside to a fully set dinner table and feel like one of Seth's playmates, half expecting Lori to tell me to wash my hands before eating.

A delicious meal of corn, steak, salad, and potatoes awaits, and I bow my head with the rest of the family and listen to Shaylee say grace. I silently thank the Lord that this wholesome family has no idea that I was passed out on the side of the freeway a little more than twelve hours prior.

Before long Shaylee's up and out of her chair, twirling and dancing to a song playing in her head, offering me a party hat, which I gladly don, while Seth sits by dutifully.

Following the meal, I sense family time dawning (tomorrow is Father's Day, after all) and gather my things. Rance walks me outside to my car, parked on the street.

This tony suburb, an oasis of potted palms and in-ground pools and church rummage sales, is where Rance belongs. He's happy here. But you can still remember, without attachment, where you've been. And it's not the strategy, or the home runs, or the lefty/righty matchups that Rance misses most about baseball.

"If someone said, 'Rance, you can go four to four with a couple of doubles and a home run tomorrow, or you can spend the day with some great friends and just experience that camaraderie,' it's an easy decision for me," he says.

I nod. I get it. Anyone who has spent a day on a sports team, whether it's the Toronto Blue Jays or my beer-league ice hockey team, the Sofa Kings, gets it.

"I didn't know coming in how this was gonna go, but it's been a great experience for me," he says. "I'd love moving forward to have the opportunity to get together again or just reconnect, talk on the phone to stay connected." He asks me if I have Facebook.

I feel giddy, and not just because my hangover is finally gone. A few days ago Rance was another hero from my childhood, and now he wants to be pen pals.

Later that night I lie in my boxers in an Airbnb that smells of sweat and garlic, the heat so oppressive that each movement takes twice the effort. I pull out the Wax Pack, shuffling to Steve Yeager, whom I will visit next in Los Angeles. Yeager promises to be an entirely different animal from Rance. While the newspaper accounts repeatedly describe Rance as steady and quiet, the rap on Yeager is the opposite. "A cocksure guy with a Type A personality," wrote the *Dayton Daily News*; "one of the more spirited belters in the neon league, where games have been known to go all night," said the *Atlanta Constitution*.[3] His exploits off the field were always colorful, posing for *Playgirl* in 1982 (in a pair of Daisy Dukes that needs to be seen to be believed) and teaching Charlie Sheen how to pitch for *Major League* (Yeager played pitching coach Duke Temple). Via a series of text messages we have tentatively planned to meet on Monday, and I'm already excited by the thought of exploring the Hollywood nightlife with the Dodgers' longtime catcher.

I put the cards away and open the YouTube video of the last out of the 1992 World Series, Rance's last breath as a player. Otis Nixon of the Atlanta Braves drops a bunt down the first-base line; pitcher Mike Timlin scrambles over to field it and throws to Joe Carter at first, clinching the Series. The Jays dugout empties, a melee of mustaches and mullets, ending with a pig pile on the mound.

And at the bottom of that pile, hidden from the TV cameras, is a thirty-six-year-old kid from Woodville, his face marred by dust and sweat (but probably not blood), shedding failure, daring greatly.

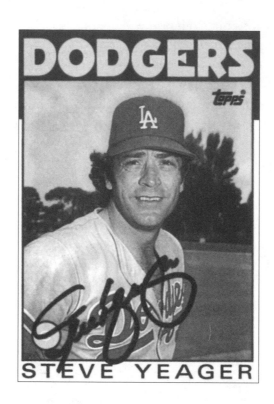

3

YEAGER BOMBS

Between the lines, when the game
started, you were going to war.
—*Steve Yeager*

Days 3–5
June 21–23, 2015
Miles driven: 640
Cups of coffee: 9
Visalia CA to Los Angeles CA

In a properly functioning human brain, thoughts operate much like the scan button on a car radio. The same way the radio pauses for a few seconds on each station before moving to the next, thoughts typically arise and just as quickly dissipate.

The OCD brain is different. Instead of the radio skipping along from station to station, imagine getting stuck on Nickelback's "Rockstar" and never moving off. When an irrational, intrusive thought emerges, it sticks, and the more you try to get rid of it and "change the station" (through some kind of compulsive mental or physical behavior), the worse the anxiety gets.

I was first diagnosed with OCD during my senior year of college. It started with some physical tics, having to pick my nose or shift my pants a certain number of times before I could start studying, and then worsened during a biostatistics midterm. When the professor handed me the exam, my brain immediately began running through a checklist of mental compulsions as I desperately tried to neutralize the obsessive fear that I had left the iron on in my dorm room. I would later learn that the content of the obsessive thought doesn't really matter. People with OCD tend to be scrupulous individuals to begin with, and the disorder often attacks with whatever fear the person finds most morally reprehensible: the deeply religious obsess over the fear that they are Satan worshippers; antiviolence pacifists fret they will stab their child with a butcher knife; I apparently couldn't stand the idea of appearing rumpled in public and burning the dorm down as a result. But I couldn't even begin to calculate the standard deviations in front of me until I had run through the list one more time: *Yes, I definitely remember turning off the iron. I saw the red light switch off. I even unplugged it!* The more I tried to convince myself, the more the fear grew.

I flunked the exam.

A therapist at the college counseling center stitched together my bizarre symptoms and gave me my official diagnosis, which actually came as a great relief (knowing what you are dealing with is half the battle). He prescribed me some antidepressants, the symptoms subsided, and I moved to Santa Barbara following graduation to begin my adult life.

Three years later, my OCD roared back with a vengeance right here in the City of Angels, the adopted hometown of the next Wax Packer, Steve Yeager.

Los Angeles is a perfect match for Yeager, known to his teammates as Boomer for his big personality. The Hollywood lights have nurtured him since signing with the Dodgers out of Meadowdale High School in Dayton, Ohio, in 1967, only the third year of the baseball draft's existence (before then, owners simply scouted and signed players at will). The consummate Dodger, Boomer rose through the Minor League ranks, playing for five years in towns like Ogden, Utah, and Dubuque, Iowa, before cracking into the big leagues in 1972. Much like Rance, for most of his fifteen-year career (all but one with the Dodgers), Boomer had to compete for a starting job, accumulating his share of splinters while riding the bench. But every time the team tried to replace him with someone younger, stronger, and shinier, Boomer proved them wrong.

He was ahead of his time. He played catcher, the most grueling position in baseball, which he fell into as a high school freshman when all the prospective players lined up by desired position at tryouts; dozens of players congregated at each infield position, while only one stood behind home plate. Doing the math, Boomer joined that player and never looked back. In the 1970s and 1980s, before the *Moneyball* revolution replaced traditional statistics (batting average, runs batted in) with newer metrics that better measured a player's true value, Yeager's paltry offensive numbers undersold his true worth, which was bolstered by his defensive prowess. Had it not been for a guy named Johnny Bench, Boomer would have won multiple Gold Gloves. And he wasn't afraid to let you know it.

"Defensively, we're even in one respect. We both have strong throwing arms," he told the *Los Angeles Times* in 1975. "Otherwise I think I'm a better defensive catcher than Bench. Maybe I shouldn't say it, but as long as I feel that way, I will."[1]

As I drive the freeways of the gleaming fortress of LA, I think back to one newspaper quote about Yeager that stuck out from the rest: "Steve Yeager is not a complex man," wrote the *Los Angeles Times* in 1981, the year the Dodgers won the World Series for which Yeager shared the Most Valuable Player Award.[2]

I don't believe it. I've read too much about his life—three marriages, Hollywood aspirations, returning to the low Minor Leagues to manage after his playing career ended—to believe that his story is that simple.

Crawling through traffic on Route 405 with the San Gabriel Mountains in the distance, my thoughts flicker back to my battle with OCD as I see the exit for my old psychologist Tom Corboy's office, putting me right back on his sofa, where I sat ten years ago, face in hands, peering through the spaces between my fingers while he calmly explained why I absolutely under no circumstances should take my ninth HIV test in the past two weeks. I was living in LA with my girlfriend, Kay, a pixieish brunette with soulful brown eyes, killing time before starting graduate school. I had fallen hopelessly in love the day I met her in the *Islands* magazine office in Santa Barbara, immediately declaring her "the One" despite our significant age difference (she was thirteen years older).

In early 2005 I left my job at *Islands*, taking a leap of faith to write the biography of my favorite professional wrestler, the Iron Sheik (a failed experiment that ended with a drug-addled Sheik threatening to kill me in his living room), and then retreating to LA, where Kay was in culinary school.[3] Then things really went sideways. Stress exacerbates

OCD, and as I sat in our tiny Pasadena apartment copying and pasting my résumé, my mental illness came roaring back to life, hijacking my brain. Kay was my life raft as I floundered in a sea of depression and self-doubt, unable to land a job even at the local Blockbuster Video.

I was a shell of myself. During a trip to the beach in Rhode Island that summer, I slunk away as often as I could just so I could go through my mental rituals of reassurance seeking. On the outside, I was just another curious beachcomber, but inside my head, I was refereeing a civil war. I have never been that scared in my life—scared not of dying but of never getting the light back in my eyes.

Kay remained steadfast and compassionate, even when the OCD dial in my brain started flickering all over the map, from fears of leaving the stove on to the fear that I had contracted HIV and would now give it to Kay. I spent hours researching HIV online trying to find definitive, 100 percent proof that there was no way I could possibly have contracted the virus (and in case you're wondering, there was no rational reason to be concerned, as I had not engaged in any risky behavior). But I was chasing my own tail. The more I sought reassurance, the more I fed the OCD monster.

As I pass that freeway exit for my therapist Tom's office, I recall his words when advising me to not take yet another HIV test. A kind, avuncular man, he said, "I know it feels like walking through fire to resist that compulsion. But this disorder is about your action, not your thoughts. If you resist taking action, the anxiety-provoking thoughts will eventually subside."

He was right. I got through that episode without getting another test, but my relationship with Kay did not survive. I have not seen her since the day we broke up nine years ago because of something that I did.

I pull over, shaken by all the memories, and glance at Steve Yeager's 1986 baseball card, pulling myself back to the present.

I take out my phone and text him: "Looking forward to meeting you tomorrow. Do you still own the Jersey Mike's? Do you want to meet there?"

LA is a city on steroids, a gleaming monument to excess, and, its consistently sunny weather notwithstanding, a terrible place to be poor. Reminders of what you don't have are everywhere, from the fleet of Teslas and Hummers choking the six-lane freeways (and that's just in one direction) to the nine-story billboards advertising the latest Hollywood blockbusters. In the trendy cafés and hip restaurants, people gather to *not* talk to one another, preferring to sit vigil by their smartphones for a message from someone who is anywhere but right in front of them. On my way to a "hot power fusion" yoga class last night (whose soundtrack, featuring a Jimi Hendrix "Voodoo Child" dance club remix, would make Siddhartha's mat curl), I walked by a plaza with these three stores next to each other: Just Food for Dogs (made-to-order gourmet dog food), VM Custom Upholstery, and Monica the Psychic Advisor.

It turns out Boomer does still own a Jersey Mike's sub shop, located in Granada Hills of the San Fernando Valley (or simply "the Valley"; yes, *that* valley). It also turns out that my dreams of slamming Jägermeister shots with him were short-lived. My evening text invitation to check out a cowboy bar in Chatsworth, where he lives, was met with this unexpected reply: "I'm not going to be able to make it tonight. I haven't had a drink in twenty-seven years. Call you tomorrow and try to find some time to talk and meet."

Well, shit.

The next morning I'm sitting across from him at a Starbucks near his Jersey Mike's.

"So what's this all about?" he asks, cupping a mocha with whipped cream. He's wearing khakis, brown loafers, and a blue-and-green Hawaiian-print button-down shirt splashed with plant fronds. He's slightly hunched but solidly built, like a block of ballast. Sinusoid lines cross his bronze, handsome face in parallel streams, his hazel eyes twinkle beneath a pair of glasses, and his silver hair is swept back.

I produce my props—the Wax Pack and a copy of a recent *New York Times* article that mentions my journey—and explain way too quickly why I'm buying him coffee and writing down every word he says.

He laughs at the sight of the Pack.

"They don't make those anymore, do they?" he asks, flipping through the cards, annotating with comments about his old colleagues.

When he gets to Richie Hebner, a huge grin breaks out.

"Tell Richie we need to go chase some nurses," he says of his fellow nocturnal free spirit.

He sets the cards down, and I notice his 1981 World Series ring on his left hand, bright and bold, just like Rance's.

"The thing is, if we had done this when the ball club was in town, you could have followed me for a day. I get up, go to the ballpark, mingle with the players, sit in the video room. But you follow me around today, I'm gonna get the car washed, go home, and watch the game. I'm sixty-six years old. I don't do a whole lot of anything."

I laugh. Boomer is still in the Dodgers organization as a coach for the big club's catchers. I don't care that the team is out of town, because watching him get his car washed is exactly what I want to do. I tell him this, and he shakes his head, baffled.

We make small talk about his restaurant, the thirty-eighth Jersey Mike's in the LA area. His third wife, Charlene, owned a deli when they first met and then went into real estate. When that bubble burst, she found herself at a loss for what to do next. She ate a particularly tasty sub at a Jersey Mike's, got inspired, and told her husband she wanted to open one of her own.

Hell, go for it, he told her, having learned long ago the necessity of taking action. It's been a great success, except for one little detail.

"The corporate people at Jersey Mike's won't let us put stuff on the walls," he says, explaining the lack of baseball paraphernalia. "'We don't want to take advantage of our celebrity friends,' they told me. Hey, asshole, they're not your friends, they're mine," he says.

And there, within five minutes of meeting him, is the Steve Yeager I've read about.

Brash. Cocky. Outspoken.

"I came to play. I came to beat you. That's still my attitude today. I think in order to be successful you have to walk around with a little chip on your shoulder. You've got to walk with a little swagger."

But only a few minutes later, I unexpectedly discover where that swagger came from.

"Tell me a little bit about growing up," I say.

Silence.

I follow up: "You were in Dayton through high school?"

"I was originally born in West Virginia, stayed there until I was six or seven years old." He was an only child.

"And your dad was a coal miner?"

"Yeah."

"What about your mom?"

"Mom didn't do anything. My dad passed away about 2001. Mom's still alive; she's back in Ohio. I keep trying to get her out here, but she won't come."

"Why did they move to Ohio?"

"I guess jobs. My dad got a job driving a bus for city transit."

"Was he an athlete at all?"

"I guess he was an athlete in the service. I think he boxed a bit, played baseball. Threw a hellacious knuckleball. I know that."

He drinks his mocha, the whipped cream now having dissolved away. I take a sip of my coffee, eyes locked with his. "He drank a lot," he says, adding, "I know that."

His voice is quiet. He takes his glasses off for a moment, then replaces them.

And it's here where Steve Yeager suddenly isn't so simple.

"It was a very dysfunctional family. I was close to him. When he wasn't drinking he was the greatest guy in the world. But he'd show up at a baseball game and be half in the bag, yelling and screaming. It was embarrassing."

When Boomer finally made it to the Major Leagues and had a game in Cincinnati, his dad got so drunk that he passed out in the clubhouse. They became estranged. Even if his dad came to a game, Boomer wouldn't acknowledge him.

On the playing field, Boomer's dad couldn't hurt him. All that anger was bottled up in his six feet and 190 pounds.

"He was the most aggressive kid I ever saw," his high school baseball and football coach, Ron Brookey, said.[4]

He blossomed, a three-sport star (football, basketball, and baseball) and cross-town rival of future Hall of Famer Mike Schmidt. The Dodgers took Boomer in the fourth round of the 1967 draft.

As a player he was often described as "fearless," blocking home plate like a brick wall, salivating for a collision. He had learned the cruel nature of fear at an early age and that the only way to overcome it, ironically, is to accept it. He made many mistakes off the field, but never once because he was afraid. When he found himself unsigned following the 1986 season, cast off by the Seattle Mariners and a victim of the owners' collusion scandal, he became so depressed that he couldn't watch baseball on TV. His second marriage had fallen apart a few years prior, and he still wanted to play. He had some gas left in the tank. But he found no takers, forced to retire in 1987 at age thirty-eight.

He had partied hard his whole career. Alcohol was part of his daily routine. Given those demons, most people would have sunk even deeper into the booze. But not Boomer. He poured out all his bottles in February 1987 and hasn't had a drop since. Like his failed marriages, he faced the problem, accepted it, and moved on.

"Once it's gone, it's gone," he says.

Although his playing days were numbered, Boomer could never get baseball out of his system. He didn't want to. Ever since getting on a plane scared shitless for the first time at age eighteen to fly from Dayton to Chicago to Salt Lake City to Ogden, he had been part of a sacred fraternity. And so he went to work in Hollywood, consulting on *Major League* and its sequel; he cohosted a radio show; and in the late 1990s, he got back on the Minor League bus, back where it all started, with ten-hour road trips through charmed deserts and cow country, all *for love of the game.*

We've been chatting for more than an hour without a single mention of Tommy Lasorda or the Dodgers' famous Garvey-Russell-Cey-Lopes infield, which stuck together for nine seasons, topics he still gets asked about every day but that don't offer me anything new. He's got to get his car washed, and so I ask if we can meet up again tomorrow, maybe at Jersey Mike's, to continue the conversation.

"I have to try and move some things and won't know until later tonight or tomorrow morning. My wife has me booked," he says.

"Does she run your show?" I ask, needling him.

He chuckles. "You must not be married."

A few minutes later I sit in the front seat of my Honda in the Jersey Mike's parking lot, staring at the layer of dust coating the tan plastic dashboard. That sour taste of coffee lingers in my mouth as I cradle my third cup, long past the point of diminishing caffeine returns. I stare at the dark brown liquid, some of the cream starting to separate ever so slightly on the surface, then touch the liquid to my lips and frown on lukewarm contact—I am disgusted by it and yet still want more.

Down the road about twenty-five miles is the one-bedroom apartment where I lived with Kay and waged my war against OCD, where fear beat me up before I knew that the only way to fight back was to not fight back at all. There's an important distinction between resignation and acceptance. Not fighting back doesn't mean letting fear roll over you, it just means not resisting. I wish I had met Boomer ten years ago. He knew then what I know now and what eventually allowed me to overcome my own demons: your brain can be full of shit.

The only way to beat the unwanted thoughts is to accept them, to invite the fear over to dinner rather than shutting it out. If OCD screams, "What if you left the iron on?" and you reply, "So what if I did?" without resisting the thought, then it loses all its power, creating a form of radical acceptance. OCD is simply one face of fear, and although Boomer may not be familiar with that face, he knows its other guises.

I wipe my index finger across the dashboard, creating a trail through the veil of dust.

I was right. Steve Yeager is a complex man.

═

The next morning I meet Boomer at his Jersey Mike's, located in a shopping plaza in Granada Hills next to a Fantastic Sam's and an H&R Block. He wasn't kidding: the walls are void of anything baseball related, and the interior is a brightly lit hive of young employees in their uniforms of navy blue aprons, hats, and polos with the Jersey Mike's logo. His wife, Charlene, is in charge here, while Boomer settles into the ambassador role that he has always done so well, checking up on the staff and remembering their birthdays.

"I feel like a mother hen sometimes, ya know?" he said yesterday.

He is nowhere to be found, so I wander to the back of the building, where I see him standing by his black Mercedes dragging on a cigarette. He's got a different Hawaiian shirt on, this one more orange but still splashed with fronds, along with khaki shorts and the same loafers.

"I feel like a jerk having invited you out for a drink the other day," I confess. "I had no idea you didn't drink anymore."

He puffs out a trail of smoke and answers in his gravelly voice.

"Nah, I've got twenty-seven years of sobriety. February of '87. If I could quit cigarettes, I'd quit them too. I've tried a thousand times. So now I'm on Chantix, and I picked a date to have my last cigarette. July 4."

Easy day to remember.

Other than the smoking habit, Boomer's in great health considering his Humpty Dumpty past. He had three surgeries on his left knee, broke his left leg, broke both wrists, broke both ankles, and broke several fingers during his years on the field, not to mention suffering countless concussions.

Like everything else, Boomer is nonchalant about it: "You go to bed with a toothache, you wake up with a toothache. You live with it. That's what you do."

We move inside and grab a booth in the back where Boomer can lean back against the wall. He's not a big man, but he is broad, and I can imagine him being an imposing obstacle blocking home plate. The rules surrounding home-plate collisions have changed since Boomer's days—a catcher is no longer allowed to stand in front of home when a runner is bearing down on him trying to score, and as a result, the bone-crunching home-plate collision is a thing of the past.

"I understand why they're doing it, because they have to protect the high-priced players. But the guys that did get run over and did get crushed at the plate all those years, what did we do it for?"

One of the staff, a blond girl wearing the uniform of blue polo and khakis, walks by and says hi.

"Things good?" Boomer asks her on her way to the kitchen, breaking our discussion to chitchat for a moment.

She smiles and nods.

"Do you ever go back there and cook?" I ask him.

"Do I cook?" he replies, incredulous. "I don't do shit back there," he replies.

A few minutes later, his youngest son, Evan, breezes in, fresh from summer baseball practice at Pierce College. Long and lanky, Evan, a rising sophomore, has followed in Dad's footsteps as a catcher.

"He's pretty good," Boomer tells me. "He needs to work more on the bat, but it's coming."

Like father, like son.

Boomer has three kids, all boys, one from his second marriage and two with Charlene (he didn't have any kids with his first wife, whom he met in high school). Evan is the youngest and the only one still living at home. He's got a beard that doesn't quite connect, adding some gravitas to his baby face. He grabs a pad from behind the counter.

"What are you having?" Boomer asks him. "Are you going to take something home to Mom?"

Evan scribbles down our lunch orders and disappears in the back for a while. When he returns, I ask, "Do you get a lot of good catching advice from this guy?"

"Yeah," he replies.

"You don't have to lie."

"No, I do. He's taught me a lot about the mental aspects of the game, the whole aspect of calling a game, thinking a couple pitches ahead . . ."

He goes on for a while, explaining just how helpful Boomer is. He's clearly his father's son, immediately slipping into camera-ready role as he talks with ease. While he holds court, Boomer sits to his right, face forward, ears perked.

"We'll be watching a game, and when the pitcher throws, he [Boomer] will ask, 'Why did he throw that pitch?' If there's a certain situation, what does it entail? If I really need a ground ball, what should my pitcher throw to get a ground ball?"

Boomer interjects, "And what would that be?"

"Probably an off-speed pitch low and away."

"Maybe a sinker?" Boomer suggests.

"No one has a sinker," Evan replies.

"Okay, then a slider."

A slider. It's settled then. And making me hungry—while Jersey Mike's doesn't have sliders on the menu, my sandwich arrives and I dig in.

"What do you think people get wrong about you?" I ask Boomer.

He pauses to consider.

"Uh, there might be some people that think I'm tougher than I look. Don't let the facial expression get you. I can sit there and watch a game with my glasses on and look like I'm boring a hole through you, but I might not be," he says.

"Ya know, if the kids do something good, I cry," he adds.

"Well that's for sure," Evan chimes in, ribbing his dad.

Evan is optimistic about his chances for the upcoming year. He's working hard this summer, getting the countless reps needed to master the craft of "receiving" (the word "catching" doesn't quite capture the artistry of the position, he explains to me). He started playing a lot more in the second half of last season and thinks the job is his for the taking.

Boomer taught him early on that there's a right way and a wrong way to play the game. One memory stands out for Evan, a game when he walked onto the field to start a new inning and heard a loud and familiar voice from the stands.

"Don't walk, run!" the voice boomed. The voice was unmistakable. His dad's words crossed into his mind as he broke into a trot: *It's a privilege to be on that field. You never take that for granted. Always run, never walk.*

Unlike his own father, passed out drunk in the clubhouse, Boomer is always there for his kids, heard before he's seen.

═

I open up my road atlas, the Bay Area pages so worn they fall out, and study the map of the United States. Tomorrow I'll finish the California leg by driving to San Diego to meet Garry Templeton, and then it's a long haul on I-10 to Houston, where Gary Pettis may or may not be waiting.

My hands grip the map tightly as my eyes wander off the interstate in Texas and settle on Austin, not *that* far from Houston, not *that* far out of my way. That's where Kay now lives with her husband and two kids. I haven't seen her since I walked out in 2006 after making a mistake that ended our relationship. A mistake that sent me packing to Northern California.

I haven't looked back. Until now.

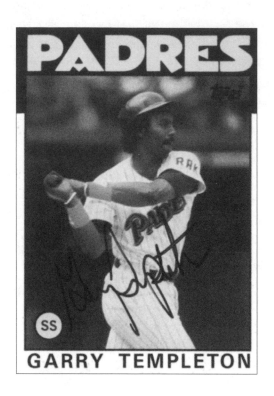

PADRES

SS

GARRY TEMPLETON

4

CAMP TEMPLETON

I wasn't that black kid that was kissing
white butt. I was an outspoken young
black man that was making hundreds of
thousands of dollars. And everybody said,
"You should be keeping your mouth shut."
—*Garry Templeton*

Days 6–7
June 24–25, 2015
Miles driven: 813
Cups of coffee: 13
Los Angeles CA to San Marcos CA

AUGUST 26, 1981

That goddamn left knee.

The ankle too. The pain, dull at times, searing at others, has robbed
Garry Templeton of the explosiveness that made him a number 1 draft
pick and two-time All-Star.

"Baseball is an eyes, feet, hands game," Tempy is fond of saying.

Eyes, feet, hands.

"There's three things you've got to do as a hitter. See the ball, get your
body in position, and let your hands fly," he says.

But how do you get through step 2 when you're playing on one leg?

Tempy's left knee has been his albatross ever since he tore cartilage
in a Minor League game in 1974, cooling his meteoric rise. His career
began on the ball fields of balmy Orange County, California, in the
city of Santa Ana, where his raw athletic gifts dazzled. When he was
five feet, nine inches tall and still growing (he'd max out two inches
later), he could already dunk a basketball, and family lore says he

could throw a football sixty yards at age fifteen. The only thing that has ever held him back was the perception that he wasn't giving his all. Even in his senior-year baseball-team photo at Santa Ana Valley High, he's smiling at three-quarters, his head tilted twenty degrees, his hands crossed behind his back. His insouciance frustrated his coaches and teachers and made his mom, Otella, and dad, Spiavia (pronounced "Spivey"), mad as hell at times; they knew all too well how tough life could be and wondered why their preternaturally talented son didn't seem to care more. Before they moved from Odessa, Texas, in 1963 (Otella left first when she grew tired of Spiavia's drinking, taking the five kids along), they worked so hard that they barely saw each other. Otella made screws and bolts on the graveyard shift for Standard Press Steel, slept two hours, and then cleaned houses all day; before he got hurt on the job, Spiavia spent most of his day hunched over or lying on his back, changing flat tires for trucks stalled on the freeway.

Otella and Spiavia had raised all their kids with a strong work ethic, but Tempy made it all look so easy. Signed in the first round by the St. Louis Cardinals in 1974 with a $44,500 bonus, he had been crowned (cursed?) as baseball royalty in the infancy of his career, compared to Willie Mays by Hall of Famer Lou Brock, and rewarded before the 1980 season with a contract that made him the highest-paid player in Cardinals history.

When he leans over to tie his cleats and gingerly flex *that goddamned left knee*, it drives him crazy to know that he is a much, much better player than his .261 batting average, as of today, indicates.

His frustration has been building, not just with his knee but also with his jealous teammates who feed manager Whitey Herzog a stream of questionable intelligence about Tempy's alleged behavior.

Tempy's hanging out with the wrong crowd, they whisper.

He's on something.

He's got no heart.

What these snitches do not know is how badly Tempy is hurting, inside and out. He had tried to talk to Whitey about his knee and ankle, asking to sit out some games. Whitey had let him rest for three games before returning him to the lineup last night, in which he got one hit in five at bats. He put Tempy back in the lineup again today but told him to take his time getting to first if he hit a routine ground ball, figuring that extra hustle wasn't worth the injury risk. Tempy understands, is grateful even, for his manager's compassion.

In the bottom of the first inning, he strides to home plate to face the Giants' Gary Lavelle in front of a sparse crowd of 7,766. Lavelle strikes him out, but the third strike bounces in the dirt in front of catcher Milt May, making it a live ball. Heeding his manager's earlier words, Tempy takes a few perfunctory steps toward first base and then trots toward the dugout, conceding defeat.

Tempy is just following orders, nursing his bad wheel, but to the die-hard Cardinals fans in attendance, he is loafing.

St. Louis takes its baseball very seriously. The franchise dates back to 1882, has won more World Series titles than any club save the Yankees, and until the Dodgers and Giants moved to California in 1958 was the westernmost team in baseball.

As Tempy walks back to the dugout, he's greeted with a salvo of ice cubes. He looks up and sees a group of seven men who have crept down to the front row, foaming at the mouth.

"Dirty n——!" they yell.

Glaring back, Tempy tenses as he reaches down and grabs his crotch.

"Suck my dick!" he roars back.

Over the next couple of innings, the hecklers become relentless. Doubling down, Tempy grabs his crotch again, smacks his right bicep with his left hand while making a fist with his right, and complains to home plate umpire Bruce Froemming. When Tempy makes more obscene gestures in the third inning, Froemming ejects him, citing a rule about "unbecoming player conduct."

As soon as he gets to the dugout, Whitey reaches for Tempy's jersey to haul him in, creating an iconic photograph that runs in the paper the next day and that shows Whitey gritting his teeth and tugging on Tempy. What the camera does not capture and what most people don't realize because of the way it is reported ("Herzog grabbed Templeton by his shirt and pulled him down the dugout steps," writes the *St. Louis*

Post-Dispatch) is that a moment later Tempy pushes Whitey back down the steps.[1] Whitey is mad, but Tempy is livid.

The next morning, the photo is splashed on the front page of the *St. Louis Post-Dispatch* with the headline "Templeton Apology Demanded." The story, by Neal Russo, never mentions the racial epithets or ice cubes hurled at Tempy. While Tempy does not comment, Whitey has plenty to say: "There's no ballplayer big enough to show up the fans and make the gestures he was making. When he grows up to be a man and publicly apologizes to our fans and to his teammates, he can come back and play. It's up to him."

Following the game, Whitey suspends Tempy indefinitely and fines him $5,000. Tempy leaves without saying a word. At season's end, he's shipped off to the San Diego Padres for another shortstop by the name of Ozzie Smith, who will one day make the Hall of Fame.

=

A large white *P* sits on Mount Mitchell overlooking the town of San Marcos, the letter built with small rocks laid out by students in 1950 to represent their school, Palomar College. It's a fitting symbol for the booming town that has quickly become the educational epicenter of northern San Diego County, home to both Palomar and California State University–San Marcos. New housing developments and twenty-two parks now dot the oak-covered hills and valleys where nineteenth-century Spanish ranchers once grazed their sheep and cattle and where a trove of gold is said to be buried in a horsehair blanket.

The *P* could also stand for Padres, as in San Diego Padres, for San Marcos is now home to Tempy, one of the most iconic Padres of all time.

As I approach San Marcos, I think back to that 1981 incident with Whitey Herzog. I know that it came to define Tempy, that even though he went on to a long and distinguished career in San Diego, he never quite recovered the form he flashed so early on. On the surface, it seems simple—he reacted to hecklers and paid the price. But did he deserve that price?

Controversy seemed to follow Tempy everywhere he went, but how much of that was Tempy, and how much of it was the bias and baggage of the culture he was surrounded by? There's a lot of misinformation out there. For example, baseball lore has it that when he was named a reserve (rather than being voted a starter by the fans) for the 1979 All-Star Game, he said, "If I ain't startin', I ain't departin'." But dig a little and you'll see that interviewer Jack Buck actually coined this phrase based on Tempy's answer to one of his questions.

For the first time on my journey, I'm about to encounter a player who reached true superstar status, albeit briefly. While Rance and Boomer were always role players, Tempy was the BMOC in St. Louis in the mid-1970s. Nothing in our brief interactions (a phone call and a few emails) indicates that he's going to "big league" me, but my expectations are guarded—he was often described in the media as "moody" and "grumpy," and when Jeff Pearlman of *Sports Illustrated* interviewed him in 2000 and asked about the Whitey Herzog incident, Tempy was tight-lipped, saying simply, "That was a long time ago. The past is the past."[2]

That past is about to be my present. I'm nervous: not only do I plan to pick that scab, I also want to ask if he had a child out of wedlock. In all of the official media guides and press accounts about his career, three kids with his wife, Glenda, are listed: Garry II, Gerome, and Genae. But buried in one 1982 article from the now-defunct *Inside Sports* there's a passing reference to another child born much earlier. When negotiating his signing bonus for the 1974 draft, Tempy said, "My parents don't have anything and I have a little baby to support."[3] From there, all references to the child vanish.

I've arranged to meet Tempy for dinner at San Marcos Brewery and Grill but have a few hours to kill. The greater San Diego area is like a Bangles music video: satisfying, attractive, and meaningless. Too laid-back for LA, too conservative for San Francisco, it's a two-and-a-half-star movie. It's not *Rocky* or *Creed*, it's *Rocky II*.

It's also always sunny, and today is no exception, topping out at seventy-nine degrees. Given that I am self-financing this quest, I am acutely aware of how much debt I am racking up, which I try to mitigate through cheap hotels and McDonald's breakfasts. I cruise the main drag, San Marcos Boulevard, past tidy, spacious homes with rust-colored

Spanish-tile roofs, past a sign for the Ramos Brothers Circus, looking for lodging. I find the Marriott and Hampton Inn way too pricey and settle on a Ramada Limited, its two stories of maroon mediocrity calling me home.

I find a frail, pasty man at the front desk, his blond hairline in retreat, his beady eyes fixed on me like two cloudy gray marbles. His grin reveals a set of top dentures with black nubs below.

We go through the paperwork ritual, and he cheerily swipes my credit card.

"Have you ever heard of Garry Templeton?" I ask, curious how far Tempy's celebrity extends. His name is Eric. He's probably in his forties.

He flashes a set of dark gums, lips spread wide.

"Baseball player for the Cardinals and Padres? No, never heard of him," he replies.

"Where are you from?" I ask.

"A small town in the Ozarks called Cabool. They just got electricity last week."

Energized by his audience, Eric's standup routine continues.

"I should be nervous. The doctor who delivered me was named Dr. Coffee," he says, handing me my room key, still beaming.

I stop in at the San Marcos Chamber of Commerce, where I chat with Tracy, a fortyish blond woman who used to work in marketing for Upper Deck, Topps's rival company, which is based in nearby Carlsbad. It turns out that not only does she know Tempy, but he was the keynote speaker for the chamber's installation luncheon last year.

"People have Garry sightings around town," her colleague Hal tells me.

Apparently, Tempy is still the BMOC.

—

"Whitey stabbed me in the fucking back," Tempy snaps, taking a sip of raspberry iced tea (just like Boomer, he quit drinking alcohol the year after his career ended). Seated across from me, the fifty-nine-year-old is dressed down in a pair of sweats and a plain black T-shirt. He slouches with purpose, still projecting that smooth swagger. His head is completely shaved, not a trace of stubble, and he has a carefully trimmed, thin goatee. He's got a Bluetooth device attached to his right ear and a pair of Prada glasses, giving him a modern, hip look that subtracts years. Even when he's agitated, the cadence of his voice is slow and almost sultry.

Like so many others throughout Tempy's life, Whitey had singled out Tempy for being too honest, too raw, too *black*. But before I press on about that fateful game in 1981, we retrace Tempy's early childhood.

Moving to Santa Ana in California's Orange County when he was in second grade was a welcome change, as he was just another part of the mix of white, black, Hispanic, Samoan, and Japanese, radically different from the town of Odessa, in West Texas, where he was born.

"You had one side of town that was black and the other side of town that was white, and you didn't cross them railroad tracks unless you had permission," he says about Odessa.

But even once he got to progressive Southern California, racism was still prevalent.

"I read somewhere, when you were in high school, did you get in trouble for being in some kind of fight?" I ask.

He nods. "Yeah, that was back when, you're probably too young to remember a lot of that, but you know there was still a lot of racist stuff going on back then in those days. We were fighting Mexicans at the school, and like an idiot I jumped in and started fighting," he replies.

"Was there a lot of tension between the Mexican kids and the black kids?"

"Nah, it was just an incident that happened and broke out. There wasn't tension. We had a bunch of those fights at our high school. And I think that was when they labeled me a militant or something." He giggles. "I used to laugh about that, because over half my friends were white or Mexican," he adds.

Our server, a tall, thin twentysomething woman, comes by offering refills.

"Do you have a straw, sweetheart?" Tempy asks her. "Let me have the crispy chicken salad," he adds.

The "militant" label stuck with him throughout his career.

"When I got to the big leagues, I heard scouts talking about it. You've got to understand, back then, in the seventies, you had a bunch of old scouts, and if you didn't do things or speak or walk the way they wanted you to, they labeled you. I wasn't a militant, I just said what was on my mind. I didn't hold back. I wasn't that black guy that just kept his mouth shut."

He giggles again, amused, maybe even proud, of his audacity as a youth.

When Tempy came into the league, African Americans were much more highly represented than they are in today's game. In his rookie year, 1976, 18 percent of players were black; now, that number has dipped to 7.2 percent. His black teammates were impressed by his willingness to speak out but weren't quick to join him.

"Back then, most black guys didn't speak up, cuz they wanted their job, and they didn't want to get labeled. So best to keep your mouth shut."

In 1974, Tempy's senior year of high school, he hit .437. A dozen scouts came to watch every game, salivating at the chance to sign him. The best athletes on a team generally play shortstop, which was Tempy's position. And baseball wasn't even his favorite sport. That was track. He was also a standout in football, playing tight end, punter, place-kicker, and safety.

"What schools offered you football scholarships?" I ask.

"Every school in the United States," he replies, completely serious.

"I don't know if that's true, Garry," I say. Athletes are prone to exaggeration.

"I mean Division I. I would say I got scholarships from just about every Division I school," he says, then proceeds to rattle off a list that ranges from the Big Ten to the Ivy League.

But baseball came so easy to him, was less dangerous, and offered the instant gratification of a sizable signing bonus. He was going to go in the first round of the draft; the only question was how high.

With one week left in the season, he made a decision with enormous consequences, one that says a lot about his priorities as a person, not just a player: he skipped his team's track meet, opting to go to his senior prom instead. At the prom, he sat at a table with six or seven of his football teammates, who were all smoking, against school rules. The quarterback passed him a cigarette, and he lit up. When he got to school the following Monday, he was called into the office and was told he was suspended.

"I asked them, 'Why didn't you guys call in anyone else?' And they said, 'We only saw you.' I said, 'How could you only see me when the guy sitting next to me was smoking?' I was singled out."

"Why do you think you got singled out?" I ask.

"I think I got singled out because I didn't go to the track meet."

Following school policy, the suspension triggered a two-week suspension from all sports, meaning Tempy was benched for the last two games of the baseball season. Disgusted by his antics, his coach, a drill sergeant named Hersh Musick, refused to nominate him for any postseason honors such as All-County, which may have cost him in the draft. Three shortstops—Bill Almon, Mike Miley, and Dennis Sherrill—were taken ahead of him in the first round; Tempy ended up being the thirteenth pick overall in the 1974 draft.

"I feel bad about that," Musick, now eighty-two, told me earlier in the day when I stopped at his house in Santa Ana. Dressed in a white short-sleeved shirt with a set of index cards and pen neatly tucked in the pocket, Musick purged his forty-one-year-old guilt as he combed through his massive archive of coaching files.

"I feel bad about it because he should have made All-County, but I pulled his name. I really wish I hadn't done that," he said.

But when I relay this to Tempy, he takes his old coach's remorse in stride, just like he does everything else. He's unfiltered yet settled, shooting off like the long, violent cast of a fisherman's rod but just as quickly reeling it back in, the line's wake converging back to stillness. He just giggles again.

Dropping lower in the draft may have cost Tempy some money, but he still did well, negotiating a $44,500 signing bonus. He went out and bought a white Cadillac and gave the rest to his parents.

"Are you married to the girl you took to the prom?" I ask.

"Yeah. Thirty-seven years, and been together forty-one," he replies proudly.

Our server brings out my Cajun pasta and Tempy's crispy chicken salad, giving me the moment of distraction I need to steel myself for what I'm about to ask next. I look up at Tempy as he stabs a big leaf of lettuce with his fork.

"I read somewhere that as you were negotiating your bonus you told the team you had a baby to support," I say, letting it fly.

"Well . . . ," he replies, his voice trailing off as he chews. "I don't know if I said that. I don't remember saying that."

"Or there was a baby there, and you told them you needed to support that baby," I suggest.

"No. I don't remember saying that. It may have just been someone writing something because that baby was there."

It's not a denial of having a baby, just a denial of what he said. I decide to give him an out.

"So you didn't have any kids at that time, right?"

Tempy may be opinionated, he may be outspoken at times. But he is no liar.

"Um . . . ," he begins. "April. April of '74 I had a daughter."

"What's her name?" I ask.

"Sharmaine."

"Was this with your wife?"

"Uh-uh. Some other girl," he says quickly, matter-of-fact.

As far as I can tell, this is the first time he's ever shared this publicly.

"So it was an accident?"

"Yup. We had been broken up for a few months, and the next thing you know, she said she was pregnant. You're the daddy," he says.

Shortly after he signed with the Cardinals, he shipped off to Sarasota, Florida, to start his Minor League career, and when he came back in the off-season, his ex had left with Sharmaine.

"She didn't tell me where she went or nothing. And then all of a sudden, three years later I get this call from the DA's office in Milwaukee. When she found out that I was playing at the Major League level, she went after me for back child support. I didn't care about paying the money, just the way she went about doing it."

He paid the child support and ended up getting full custody of Sharmaine during her high school years when she moved to San Diego and lived with the rest of the Templeton kids.

Dusk begins its descent on the brown hills of San Marcos as I pivot back toward that late August afternoon in 1981 when *Whitey stabbed him in the fucking back*. We know what was reported in the papers following the incident, how he was suspended and hospitalized, but what really happened?

"I was in the on-deck circle, and three white boys came down and started calling me all kinds of racial names, and that's when I grabbed my crotch. I told them, shit, ya know, 'Suck my dick.' And Whitey was right there on the top rail [of the dugout] listening to them. He couldn't have been no more from there to the door from them," he says, gesturing forcefully, his voice rising with frustration.

"So he knew what was being said," I say.

"He knew what was being said," he repeats, slowing his cadence by a third to emphasize each word.

"Do you remember what they were calling you?"

"Yeah, but I ain't gonna repeat it," he says firmly.

"That bad?"

"Yeah." He takes a beat and exhales, his shoulders lowering by half an inch. When he speaks again, his voice has lost its ferocity, replaced by a steady calm.

"There were some players that heard it too, but they weren't players that had my back, so they ain't never gonna say nuthin. But there are guys that saw everything that happened, ya know? Best thing that ever happened to me was coming to San Diego, except I tore my knee up.

"[After the incident] they sent me straight to the hospital," he says. "They put me in the psych ward. They gave me this plush room. All I did was go in there and play ping pong!" he says.

Whitey doubled down, burying him in the papers.

"Garry's been lackadaisical all year, playing at 60 percent like he doesn't give a damn," he told the *Washington Post* two days later.[4]

The reporting around the incident continued to be sloppy, perpetuating the narrative of Tempy as a ne'er-do-well. A careful read of well-respected papers like the *Post* reveals some of these biases: on September 23, an article by John Feinstein reported that when Tempy was growing up, his "family lived on welfare" (ignoring his mom's work in the factory and the family car-washing business) and said he was thrown off the baseball team for smoking a cigarette (he was suspended, not thrown off).[5]

According to the *New York Times*, Tempy publicly apologized for his actions at a press conference on September 14 and announced that he had been suffering from depression for three years. The article reports him saying he had met with a psychiatrist in the hospital, had been prescribed medication, and felt better than he had in years.[6] When I ask him about this, I'm shocked by his response.

"I didn't see no psychiatrist," he says. "They just had to show something for me not going cross-country to play baseball."

I push back: "Garry, they must have evaluated you. Someone must have come in and talked to you."

"I didn't talk to no one," he says, defiant.

"So what they said in the papers, it was all made up?"

He takes a moment to consider this, thinking back, realizing he doesn't want to be inaccurate.

"I talked to the Cardinals doctor," he begins thoughtfully. "I don't remember talking to any doctors in that damn hospital." Pause. "Maybe I did talk to a doctor, because they did bring me some medicine in a cup. I flushed it down the toilet. I didn't need it!"

But it was 1981. The team had to explain why its star player had acted out, and depression made for a convenient fit. Tempy bowed his head and toed the line—yes, I am depressed, yes, this medicine will help me behave, no, I won't do it again. He swallowed his tongue, because even "militants" could only protest so much in 1981. Instead, he did his talking on the field, lashing four hits in his first game back on September 16, a defiant gesture of will and skill, the militant marching to war.

=

The Santa Fe Hills neighborhood, ensconced in the gentle undulations of San Marcos, is quiet on a Thursday morning. The two-level stucco houses with Spanish-tile roofs are packed close together, a complex of wide streets and dry air that has retained its shine. Behind the garage door Tempy's 1983 Porsche awaits, with those blue old-school California plates ("Tempy" they read), waiting for its owner, who rarely takes it out anymore—it's just too hard to bend down that low with *that goddamned left knee.*

The foyer opens into a spacious, high-ceilinged living room arranged around the centerpiece, a pool table. The Templetons moved here two and a half years ago, a welcome downsize from their huge home in Poway. The desk by the door, the drop spot for keys and other knick-knacks, holds a stack of slightly yellowed Garry Templeton postcards like long-forgotten trick-or-treat candy, the photo capturing him mid-throw to first base.

I'm sitting on the plush brown leather sofa talking to Tempy's senior prom date. Glenda, fifty-five, is wearing a black-and-gray dress, her pretty brown eyes embellished by just the right amount of eye shadow, a gleaming cross dangling from her necklace. She has a classy, regal air, an instinctive emotional intelligence evident in her give-and-take, never too much. She is also a first for the Wax Pack—the first wife who has remained the only wife.

"It's kind of weird," she says. "I have a lot of friends that are divorced. When the guys leave baseball and they leave that paycheck behind, all of a sudden they start having problems. All of a sudden they're home all the time."

Or maybe the problems that were always there now have a chance to surface.

But Glenda was an exception—an athlete herself, she understood the pressures of the game, the daily, grueling test of will. And she went along for the ride at every opportunity. She was there when the upstart Padres knocked out the Cubs in the 1984 National League Championship Series and Graig Nettles, that playful bastard, dumped a bottle of Champagne on her head to get her back for pushing him into the pool at a team party. Wanda Jones, Angie Wiggins, April Wynn—the players' wives and girlfriends were *her* teammates too. She and Tempy grew together, the way any couple needs to if they want to last as long as the Templetons have. When Tempy was on the road, she filled in everywhere, the ultimate pinch hitter—*she* was Gerome's Little League coach. And through it all, when she looks across the room at her husband she still sees that playful, even shy high schooler who first approached her through a secret admirer note, asking if she'd go to a dance Friday night after the football game.

Glenda's five-year-old granddaughter, Gracelynn, walks over, cradling her Barbie doll, which has lost a limb.

"Say, 'Excuse me,'" Glenda admonishes.

"Excuse me," replies a small voice, showing her grandmother the injury.

"She'll just have to go to the hospital later," Glenda replies.

Tempy now takes his turn as head counselor of Camp Templeton with the grandkids.

"He does everything that I used to do with the kids that he missed out on," she says. Chauffeur extraordinaire, he takes them to their softball games, gymnastics classes, and horse shows. They make pretty good caddies too on the driving range—golf is now Tempy's competitive outlet, playing three to four times per week. Right now he's at the Titleist office testing their clubs.

Tempy's always been a giver—he's just not ostentatious about it. For years, in St. Louis and San Diego, he would buy an entire section of seats for local underprivileged kids, calling it "Templetown." When he finished playing after the 1991 season at age thirty-five, he sat out two years before the itch for the game overwhelmed him. From 1994 until 2013, just like Steve Yeager, he got back on the bus, coaching the next generation.

"He's a good teacher; he can deal with the kids. A lot of players still call him. He can look at a game and just dissect the fielding and the hitting," Glenda says.

The front door swings open and the head counselor walks in, wearing a navy Padres golf shirt and matching navy shorts.

"You know he's recording your ass," he says to Glenda. She laughs.

"Oh, I know. How much did you cuss yesterday when you talked to him?" she asks.

"Not too much," he says quietly.

She turns to me: "Sometimes he cusses a lot."

Tempy and I move to the other living room by the TV, which he clicks on, lowering himself into the sofa. His Padres, muddling through another tough season, are playing the Giants, fresh off their third World Series victory in five years. He keeps track of the Padres but rarely will sit and watch a whole game. It's too long, too slow—ironic, considering the decades he spent doing just that (even as a player you spend almost half the game watching from the dugout). It's also hard for a man of Tempy's pride and vision to sit and watch something over which he no longer has any control. His greatest skill—and there were plenty to choose from—was not his defense or his bat but his eyes—the first part of his *eyes, hands, feet* formula for success. While us mere mortals see a white blur when a pitcher unleashes a ninety-five-mile-per-hour fastball, Tempy can pick up the stitches on the ball, telling him its rotation and thus the type of pitch. He can tell based on the angle of the bat's contact with the ball where it's going to end up. He doesn't need a computer to tell him the launch angle; he *sees* the launch angle.

Tempy's superpowers are evident even now watching TV. It's the top of the third inning, and the Giants are already leading, 2–0. Matt Kemp, the Padres' superstar slugger who has disappointed since being traded from the Dodgers in the off-season, stands in against Chris Heston, a twenty-seven-year-old rookie. Kemp works the count full and then flails for strike 3, his bat meeting nothing but air.

"What happened there?" I ask. All I saw was a swing and a miss.

The professor begins his lecture, his voice rising in a crescendo as he talks, acting out the moves as he explains: "I don't think he starts on time. See that swing right there? He started when the pitcher's arm was right here [holding his arm out in front]. That's too late—by the time he's ready to release the ball, the ball's on top of you. He has to start a little sooner, when the pitcher's arm is back, so he can get his foot down and be ready to pull the trigger. If he's not getting his body in position on time, he damn sure isn't seeing the ball," he says. "All he has to do is come see me, and I'll tell him what's going on."

Tempy misses the game. He's still young enough to be on the road coaching, managing, doing what he does best. Golf, his current obsession, is a band-aid solution; he'd like to get back out there, drop the twenty-five extra pounds hanging around his waist, work with kids. But the phone hasn't rung since he last managed in 2013.

"Do you ever watch your old games?" I ask.

"Nah, man, I don't give a shit about that," he says. "You can't live in the past; you've got to live in the present. You want some water?" he asks, getting up and gingerly walking to the kitchen, where he pops a couple of Aleves. *That goddamned left knee*, even after eight surgeries.

"Now it's bone on bone. I need a knee replacement," he says. "I played shortstop on one leg and was still better than most of those guys."

Bored of baseball, he switches on his favorite channel, El Rey, to see if there's a kung fu movie on. If the trip has taught me anything so far, it's to be careful about expectations—watching kung fu with Garry Templeton was nowhere in my pretrip planning.

"I like to watch the fighting part because I'm intrigued with how they come up with all the fight scenes. I mean, how long do they practice all of this stuff just to make this one scene?" he wonders out loud, hands animated.

We chat about the next leg of my trip, the long haul to Houston, where I have a very tentative meet-up with the next Wax Packer, Gary Pettis. As the current third-base coach for the Astros, Pettis is the only Packer still in the Show, still riding the carousel, and so my time with him, if any, will be very limited.

"Man, you got a long way to go," Tempy says, giggling.

Just then little Gracelynn walks over with her Barbie doll, apparently looking for a second opinion.

"Looks like she has to go to the hospital," he says gently. "When I get back from the doctor, I'll fix her," he adds, bringing a smile to Gracelynn's face.

Camp Templeton is in full swing. And its head counselor is better than most, even on one leg.

While Tempy has (literal) plastic surgery to perform for his granddaughter, I have to prepare to leave the cocoon of California—I'm due in Houston in three days. But first, I have a date with my own checkered past.

5

HOUSTON, WE HAVE A PROBLEM

Maybe I don't show my anger when
things aren't going right, but that's
part of Gary Pettis. I try to appear
that nothing is bothering me.
—*Gary Pettis*

Days 8–11
June 26–29, 2015
Miles driven: 2,429
Cups of coffee: 21
San Marcos CA to Houston TX

Leaving behind my beloved California, I steer the Accord through the dusty brambles of Arizona and New Mexico, surrounded by the Southwest's stark topography and muted palette of reds, browns, and olive greens. I break up the trek over three arid days, the 689-mile haul from Phoenix to Fort Stockton, Texas, a particularly long slog made tolerable only by the compulsively addictive podcast *Serial*. Long stretches of empty freeway, save for the occasional billboard for gun shops and cheap gas (down to $2.29!), lull me into semihypnosis, the thirteen-year-old air-conditioning straining to keep up with the pounding heat. While I guzzle murky gas station coffee, history is made as the Supreme Court legalizes gay marriage in all fifty states. In less encouraging news, my mom (always being a mom!) texts me to be careful because she saw on the news that two prisoners escaped from a maximum security facility in New York. I remind her that I'm thousands of miles away from New York, and she replies (always being a mom!), "I know, but you never know!"

I also get the bad news that Gary Pettis does not, in fact, have time for me. Pettis is an enigma. While the first three Wax Packers were all relatively easy to find through public records searches (thank you, baby boomers, for keeping the land line alive), Pettis stymied me at all turns in my pretrip prep. My options exhausted, I had turned to THE LAST RESORT: public relations people. PR people have an agenda, and that's to make their client look good no matter what. It's their job to retain as much control as possible, to *stay on message*. Nothing personal—they're just doing their job—but most great stories in journalism are not born through PR.

And so I had emailed Steve Grande, the Astros' PR guy, asking if I could interview Gary when I came to Houston. We had agreed that the June 29 game against the Kansas City Royals would be a good opportunity (no promises, though!), but now the chime of a text message from Steve turns dirge: "Gary declined the interview. He wants to keep a low profile," it reads.

Low profile?? I can't imagine hordes of reporters are clamoring for time with the third-base coach, and Pettis has never been one to seek the spotlight. This, of course, is only a setback. You don't put your life on hold for two months to chase the muse of stale cardboard and then give up at the first sign of trouble.

No, no, no. Pettis may have quit me, but I've got a plan B.

=

Up to this point, I've concealed the fact that when it comes to anything remotely mechanical, I am completely, hopelessly, utterly useless. I break into hives every time I walk into a Home Depot, its cavernous aisles, wide enough for buses, taunting me with tools I don't even know how to hold, let alone use. Approaching Fort Stockton, both the Accord and I are hurting, the former gasping for oil. Having never changed a tire, let alone my own oil, I rank any type of breakdown among my biggest fears on this journey.

On the outskirts of town, I come across a cluster of buildings—a muffler shop, an RV appliance repair store, and Mingo's Burritos, along with a garage with a glint of hope. A stack of tires, three chairs lifted out of an airport lounge, and a plastic bucket of stagnant, muddy water guard the garage, whose front window reads RL Auto Service in big yellow block letters. No one is at the front desk, but a few customers stand around while two men wheel tires back and forth, calling to each other in Spanish.

"Do you do oil changes here?" I ask one of them.

He looks at his partner and says something in Spanish. They exchange several lines before the younger one returns, asking, "Do you have oil?"

Is it bring your own? I wonder to myself.

Although oil changes are clearly not part of their standard service, they study my notebook, polo shirt, and California license plates and realize this could be their good deed for the day.

I'm dispatched to pick up the oil and filter (so that's what an oil filter is!) at an O'Reilly Auto Parts down the road. Thirty-five minutes later I return, ready to apprentice. I pop the hood and watch while the younger mechanic jacks up the Accord (what a device!) and then brings over some flattened cardboard boxes to lie on. I stand in front of the car, notebook and pencil poised, slightly bent at the knees, leaning forward like a coach too nervous to stand up straight to observe the next play. From there it's all a blur of wrenches and bolts and that filter, way beyond my feeble reach. I need diagrams, YouTube videos, and lots of practice. This is not the crash course I was hoping for.

I will not be changing my own oil in the future.

—

I'm about to see Kay, my ex-girlfriend, the only girl I've ever lived with, for the first time in almost ten years.

In an alternate universe, we are married with an eight-year-old daughter. We live in Santa Barbara; she's got her own bakery, where she goes every morning at 5:00 a.m. following a run in the dark, coming in to kiss me on the forehead before leaving for work. I am a postdoc at UC Santa Barbara, its proximity to the Channel Islands providing the perfect opportunity to continue my island biogeography research. We still send each other letters through the mail even though we live together, still call each other by the same mutual pet name.

Kay was supposed to be the One, the same way I'm sure Rance and Boomer thought their first wives were their Ones. They learned to accept change and have found joy in their second (or third) chances; now it's time to accept mine.

Kay and I didn't speak for a long time after the breakup, but gradually the ice thawed—we became Facebook friends, then started texting each other on our birthdays. But I still haven't heard her voice, seen those soulful brown eyes, since the day I walked out in early 2006, ashamed but still certain that I was doing the right thing. The relationship had ended, and it was my fault.

My battle with OCD took a remarkable turn for the better in mid-2005. My therapist, Tom, introduced me to a form of cognitive-behavioral therapy called exposure and response prevention in which you overcome your fears by learning to coexist with them. How do you do this? Lots and lots of homework. In my support group, I learned of other people's suffering and their tickets out: people who had the irrational fear of stabbing their own baby had to work themselves up to holding a knife in front of their baby; those who were afraid of being gay had to watch gay porn. While these treatments may seem radical, they work because they desensitize your brain to its own bullshit. Since my compulsions were mostly mental, I had to listen for hours to a tape on a loop in which I spelled out the worst-case scenario of my irrational fears ("I contract HIV from kissing someone, give it to Kay, who leaves me, and I end up homeless and covered in sores on Skid Row dying of AIDS . . ."). That, coupled with antidepressants and a dash of metacognitive Buddhist philosophy (accept uncertainty, learn to let go) is the gold-standard treatment for the disorder. You learn that it's not your thoughts and feelings that matter, it's how you respond to them.

During the depths of my OCD, the romance in my relationship with Kay withered. We stopped having sex altogether. But her commitment never wavered, even when depression and panic attacks layered onto my OCD like an anxiety casserole. When I turned the corner, it was like stepping back into color—my humor returned, my eyes brightened, and with my wits back, I came to the horrific realization that Kay had been right all along when she had initially balked at the prospect of our relationship. *You're too young*, she had said. *We're too far apart in age.*

I had insisted that I was more mature than most, that I was different, that I *knew* that we would last where others had failed.

She was right.

Sadly, this epiphany was not one that I reached responsibly. I was in too deep a state of denial for that. Instead, I acted out, doing the one thing that I found most reprehensible: I cheated.

Growing up in a conservative, traditional family, the kind that holds hands and says grace at the dinner table, I considered cheating to be a cardinal sin. My parents set the example, taking us to church, showing their love for each other, certainly not coveting their neighbors' wives or husbands. There was no way I would ever cheat.

Yet there I was, at a conference in Chicago, absconding to the hotel room of a comely brunette from the Bahamas I would never see again. I couldn't blame it on alcohol, couldn't excuse it in any way; as it was happening I knew it was wrong, yet I wanted it anyway. And I didn't just want it, I *craved* it.

I flew home the next day, racked with guilt, not recognizing my own reflection. How could I have done that to someone who had done nothing but love me even when I was all shell and no meat, damaged and lost? But I knew the answer. She had been right. I wasn't ready.

I clung to that truth, knowing that if I stayed, the relationship would end even worse than it would now. The stakes would be higher, the damage greater. I had to go. And so I did.

—

What do you say to your ex-girlfriend after leaving her and not having seen her for nine years? What do you say to the person to whom you once promised the stars and the moon and truly meant it, only to realize too late that they're not yours to promise?

You start by letting go. You recognize that if you say anything out of a sense of obligation, it's not coming from the right place. As Tempy told me, the past is the past. Live in the present.

I exit 290 East in Austin, a detour from my I-10 path toward Gary Pettis and Houston, and pull into a park where food trucks have gathered in the late afternoon. I think about all the things one thinks about in this situation, the petty insecurities and curiosities: *How will she look? How do I look? Will she still be attracted to me? I to her? Will her husband want to kick my ass?*

And there she is, instantly recognizable, her car pulling in at the same time as mine, blowing my chance to have a few minutes to prepare. She hasn't aged a day. She still has that radiant glow, those big brown eyes alive with kindness, her short hair framing a small and beautiful face. She's wearing a purple top with an ankle-length white skirt, dangly silver earrings, and a big silver bracelet, classy as always. I walk over and give her a big hug and a tight squeeze that say I'm sorry, how are you, and thank you all in one. I turn to her husband, Dan, who it turns out is also a half Filipino ice hockey goalie, and shake his hand, introducing myself. This can't be easy for him, but he is game, just the right amount of friendly. I look away, feeling it hard to hold eye contact with Kay for too long for fear that my eyes will betray me in some way even though I no longer have anything to hide.

We small-talk, hitting all the surface notes of the past nine years. She tells me she moved back to Texas in October 2006, about ten months after we broke up, and met Dan at the school they worked at. Kay had always wanted kids, and after getting married, they adopted two, PJ and Serafina, an adorable brother and sister, following a stint with them as foster kids. Dan chases them around the park, giving Kay and me a chance to chat one-on-one.

I tell her about the beginning of the trip in Visalia, and we share a laugh about Jesse and the Kid, whom she knew well when we all lived in Santa Barbara and ate at their family restaurant every Friday night. She has continued in the food industry, putting her culinary training to good use as the chef at her kids' day care center. We talk about my road trip and this book, about the trials and tribulations I endured in grad school. She opens up about the challenges of being foster parents and adopting, as well as the ups and downs of her marriage. I'm surprised by how much she reveals so quickly until I remember that yes, this is Kay, always out in the open and willing to be vulnerable, to be *real*, which makes her one of the most beautiful people I have ever known. I feel more proud than wistful, proud of the life she has constructed and of the person she continues to be. Just like Tempy dissecting Matt Kemp's swing, in romance as in baseball, timing is everything, and ours had simply been off.

We don't delve into our own backstory or dredge up specifics. Those unspoken words pass between us in the hour-and-a-half window between spells of rain, the sticky air clinging to our skin. Our conversation is fluid and pedestrian, *easy*—catching up on life—the way people who have shared true intimacy can always do even if that intimacy is long gone.

On the way out, tears well from my eyes as the sky darkens and the late afternoon rain commences again, sapping the humidity from the air. The roots of what we had are still there and always will be there, even if we're not together. She isn't the One, but maybe there's no such thing.

Unclenching, I exhale, grateful for the present.

=

The Houston Astros are often considered a small-market team even though they play in the fourth most populous city in the country, a center of aeronautical innovation and the energy industry. They're one of those teams, like the Milwaukee Brewers and the Seattle Mariners, that rarely elicit a strong reaction. Wear a Yankees hat and prepare to be instantly judged; wear an Astros hat and witness tabula rasa firsthand. Maybe it's because the team hasn't had a ton of success in its fifty-one-year history (zero World Series titles), or maybe Houstonians are just not ones to be pushy, content to guard their home turf (albeit fiercely) but not prose-lytizing in others' backyards. The franchise has had bursts of greatness as gaudy as its 1970s rainbow uniforms: the 1980 run, squelched by the possessed Phillies; the 1986 squad, led by Mike Scott and slain by the Mets; and the Killer B's era of the 1990s and 2000s, which culminated in a World Series loss in 2005 to the White Sox. They bottomed out in 2013 with a 51-111 record, leading *Sports Illustrated* to boldly predict the following year that there was a method to the madness and that the Astros would win the World Series in 2017.[1]

Beyond their on-field performance, the Astros will always be credited with revolutionizing the sport in the 1960s, when they opened the Astrodome, then hailed, with apologies to André the Giant, as the

Eighth Wonder of the World. During the Space Race, technological advancement was prioritized above all else, aesthetics be damned. *If we can play baseball inside of a dome, we will never have to worry about the weather!* they said. *Grass can't grow inside? No problem! We'll just invent AstroTurf!*, synthetic grass laid over concrete that gave ground balls an extra charge and caused an epidemic of rug burns. By the time the 1990s rolled around, the masses had tired of these charmless comforts and were willing to brave the elements for a return to the game's roots, namely, outdoor stadiums with grass, located downtown. In 2000 the Astros flirted with disaster again, naming their new downtown stadium Enron Field; when the company collapsed two years later, the name was switched to Minute Maid Park, whose orange-flavored soda perfectly fit the garish color of the team's uniforms during its 1970s heyday. Then in 2013 an action that most teams would consider pure heresy occurred: Major League Baseball moved the Astros from the National League to the American League. *They switched leagues!* Suggest something so subversive to the Dodgers and expect to get punched. But the Astros? *Ehhhh, sure, why not.*

This season, the Astros are already exceeding expectations, soaring to a 44-34 first-place start. Gary Pettis is in his first season as third-base coach and is already under fire for being a bit too aggressive in sending runners home as they approach third base (writers joked of him tearing a rotator cuff with all of the windmill motion of his arms). I haven't heard any more from Steve, the team's PR guy, and assume that unless I resort to drastic action, I'm going to experience my first loss of the trip.

So here's the plan, hatched somewhere around Lordsburg, New Mexico, with a mouthful of McDonald's hash browns and scalding hot coffee. On game days, the team offers fifteen-dollar, behind-the-scenes tours of the stadium, including a chance to watch batting practice, where Pettis will undoubtedly be. If I can get close enough, within shouting distance, I have a chance to circumvent the official channels and try to convince him to chat. I might also get thrown out, just like one of the Astros' runners at home plate, the victim of Pettis's overzealous arm flapping.

I walk into the lobby of Minute Maid Park, located downtown just off the freeway among one of Houston's many skylines, and am instantly cooled by a blast of air-conditioning. A midday downpour has provided some relief, but the lingering humidity of this subtropical climate coats everything in a thin layer of moisture. Stadium officials have already decided to keep the 242-foot retractable roof closed for tonight's game, with the temperature expected to stay above eighty-five, the cutoff for opening it up.

The high vaulted ceilings of the lobby, connected to the old Union Station, which once spurred Houston's rail industry, hold banners of the Astros' current crop of studs—Carlos Correa, George Springer, and José Altuve. There's also a banner commemorating the upcoming Hall of Fame induction of lifetime Astro (and Killer B) Craig Biggio, a ceremony I plan to attend in several weeks in Cooperstown, New York.

I join the few dozen fans assembled for the tour, herded by a young intern named Joe with a midwestern twang that seems out of place in the Deep South. The Kansas City Royals, the Astros' opponent tonight, are well represented in the flock, with at least a dozen midwesterners clad in xxl royal blue, their pale sweaty skin slightly blushing from the deep summer heat. As we follow Joe through the lobby they don't walk so much as totter, struggling to balance their gift shop purchases.

We walk through a set of doors into the stadium itself, a cavernous greenhouse accented with local quirks and flair.

Down the lines, the foul poles are sponsored by Chick-fil-A; if an Astro hits one of the poles, you can bring in your game ticket for a free sandwich. And perhaps kitschiest of all, a train over the left-field wall (harking back to the city's rail roots) drives back and forth whenever an Astro hits a home run or the team wins the game (*driven by a real human!*).

We ride an elevator up to the suite level and shuffle into suite 28, largest and plushest and belonging to team owner Jim Crane, an energy and air freight magnate who bought the team in 2011. It's palatial, with a spread of food and drink that taunts our oversize pack.

One of the Royals' fans, his scraggly blond locks spilling onto a Straight Outta Kauffman T-shirt (the Royals play in Kauffman Stadium), says, "Maybe we can stay here for the game," and a wild idea pops into my head: given how big our tour group is and that to get back out of here and downstairs to field level we need to pass through a narrow doorway one at a time, there's a good chance I could easily get "lost" and hide out here among baseball's bourgeois. As people start filing out of the room and tour guide Joe sprints to the front, I seriously consider this half-baked idea. I may be able to remain undetected until game time, but then what? Do I hold Jim Crane hostage with my pencil until he grants me an audience with Gary Pettis? Try to charm him with the premise of the book until he can't help but do everything in his power to get Pettis to come around?

No, no, this is most definitely a very bad idea.

I head downstairs and catch up with the rest of the group. We walk through the premium seats behind home plate (the closest I'll ever get to them) and gather to watch the Astros take their hacks. Players are spread around the field, some lying down to stretch tight hips and hamstrings, others whipping balls back and forth with minimal strain, the last group gathered around the batting cage like they're having a picnic. Rookie manager A. J. Hinch leans against the cage, his body's slack perfected, watching slugger Chris Carter launch prolific bombs into the outfield, several clearing the fence with ease. Plucky José Altuve, the diminutive phenom who weathered the bad years here to become one of baseball's best, spots a group of kids out of the corner of his eye and walks over to sign autographs, greeting them with "Hey, how are you today?"

There are coaches everywhere: hitting coach Dave Hudgens joins Hinch behind the cage to scrutinize swings, first-base coach Rich Dauer plays catch with one of the players. But no Gary. Starting to panic, I scan the crowd and spot a man with a tall, lanky build several rows in front of me wearing a fuchsia button-down shirt and khakis. I have a sneaking suspicion that this is Steve Grande, Mr. Astros PR. My rogue tactics having failed, I crawl back to the PR machine.

"Steve!" I yell, hoping that I'm right about who he is.

His head turns, and he walks up toward me. I introduce myself, and we chat about Pettis. Steve is about my age, maybe even younger, relaxed but ambitious.

"At the start of the year the team decided they weren't going to have the coaches talk to the media at all," he says apologetically.

"So the manager kind of speaks for all of them?" I ask.

"Yeah."

On to plan C. Or M.

I hastily scribble a note to Pettis explaining the gist of why I am stalking him so hard and include my phone number, asking if there's any chance we can chat, even on the phone, after the game or tomorrow.

I fish out the 1986 Topps card that brought me here.

"Do you think you could pass this to Gary and see if he will sign the card?" I ask Steve.

"Sure, I can do that," he says. He asks for my cell number so he can text me when it's done, we part ways, and I find my seat in section 113 for the game.

Half an hour later, as I watch the Royals take their swings, my phone chimes, and Steve comes over to deliver the card, now autographed.

"He took the note, but he didn't open it in front of me," Steve says. He seems disappointed that he can't help me more and says, "If the guys aren't interested or if they decline, we can't push them."

I've chosen a seat behind third base so I can watch Gary flail all game and luck out with seats next to two fun people around my age—Jenna, a cute and sassy Homeland Security lawyer originally from Vermont, and Rob, a fit jock whose father, Bob, pitched in the Major Leagues for the Tigers. We watch Gary mark his territory behind third base, stomping around, flashing signs to runners, and spitting out sunflower seeds. He's only sixty yards away, so close, but I'm all out of ideas on how to get to him, resigned to the hope that he will read my note and give me a call.

The Astros triumph, 6–1, the train in left field with the real human blowing its horn to celebrate. But my phone never rings. Perhaps for Pettis, the past is the past, and he just wants to focus on the present.

=

Although I never heard from Pettis and don't know if he ever read my note, here's what I would have said if I had had the chance:

Dear Gary,

Please don't call the police.

I know that even if you wanted to participate, you couldn't, that the team has a gag order this season on coaches talking to the media. I get it. I also think it's funny to think of myself as "the media." I'm just an eight-year-old stuck in a thirty-four-year-old's body.

I know a lot about you. We have a lot in common—I teach at Laney College, where you played baseball. In fact, before I left for this trip I visited your old coach, Tom Pearse. He's doing well, living up in Winters with his wife, Justine. He thinks so highly of you, he's so proud. When I asked him what you were like as a person, he said in that aw-shucks way that only the old-timers can, "He wouldn't talk shit if he had a mouthful." He wanted me to give you his card if I saw you. Call him—it would make his day.

I know it couldn't have been easy growing up in East Oakland—a lot of my students went to your alma mater, Castlemont High School. I see the struggle every day written on their faces. One of my students recently missed an exam, and when she came in the next day she explained that her brother had been shot and was in the hospital. I'm sad to report that this wasn't the first time this happened to one of my students.

I know how strong your family was, especially your mother after your dad passed away. I know how seriously you took that responsibility to be the man of the house. I know because I had a long conversation with your younger brother Stacey at a mall in Concord. He told me about how the whole family would go to church on Sundays and then straight to a Giants game at Candlestick before your dad passed (but honestly, Gary, you were an Oakland kid; *the Giants??*). He told me about what a tight ship your mom ran, how she instilled that preternatural work ethic that got you to the Major Leagues, the same work ethic that Stacey wishes he had had (he told me he had more talent, but you had the *drive*). He loves you so much, is so proud of what you have accomplished. When I asked him for an anecdote, he told me about how you guys used to run the 3.5-mile loop around Lake Merritt and how for the last hundred yards or so he would be right there behind you, saying, "C'mon Stacey, you can do it," willing you forward. Tears filled his eyes when he told me that. I saw your brother, the king jock of Castlemont, reduced to tears because he loves you so *goddamned much.*

I also know how much adversity you have faced in your life, how you are the quintessential underdog, not scouted during high school, cast off by two community colleges before Laney finally gave you a chance. How you signed in 1979 for a measly $5,000 with the Angels, already older than most Minor Leaguers, and then proceeded to prove them all wrong by marching right up the Minor League ladder to break into the Majors in late 1982 and hit a home run (your first hit!) on the last game of the season in front of 62,020 fans in Anaheim (right after Reggie Jackson, on deck, told you, "Win this game, rook").

I know how close you came to the World Series in 1986, literally one strike away, before Dave Henderson ruined everything. How the next season the team wouldn't believe how hurt your hand was and made you play through it, leading to the humiliation of being sent down to the Minors. And I know how lightning somehow struck you twice, how you got all the way back to the Show as a coach, this time to the World Series itself, and were again one strike away from winning the World Series in 2011. You have faced a lot of adversity and not always emerged victorious.

What I don't know is how you dealt with the failure, how you coaxed yourself through those excruciating lows. I don't want to know what it felt like, the way so many reporters ask (we all know that it felt like shit); rather, I want to know what Gary Pettis did about it. What action, thought process, behavior propelled you forward, because you never did give up. You're still there all these years later, waving your arms and rah-rahhing the next generation forward, just like your little brother all those years ago at Lake Merritt.

Sincerely,

Brad

P.S. Call your old coach. Really.

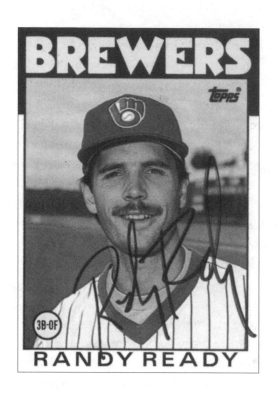

6

RANDY IS READY

You don't want to come in too hot.
—*Randy Ready*

Days 12–13
June 30–July 1, 2015
Miles driven: 2,914
Cups of coffee: 26
Houston TX to Dallas TX

JUNE 14, 1986

One day after being traded from the Milwaukee Brewers, the only professional baseball organization he has ever known, Randy Ready is on the bench watching his new team, the San Diego Padres, destroy their Southern California rivals, the Los Angeles Dodgers, 12–0 in front of forty thousand fans.

Back in the clubhouse after the game, he unbuttons his uniform, still clean, and removes his brown hat with the rust-colored intersecting *S* and *D*, running his hand through his spiky blond hair. Veteran Graig Nettles, who was bashing home runs for the Yankees when Randy was still getting ready for his high school prom, just had a monster day at Randy's usual position, third base, hitting a home run and letting Randy know that he isn't going to let the new guy come in and take his job.

But Randy is always up for a challenge. Nothing has ever come easy to him—at five feet ten and 175 pounds, he has always been the little guy. While many boys have to fight to break free of their older brothers' shadows, Randy had to follow in his *sister's* footsteps, she of eleven varsity letters in high school. One day when he was fourteen and taking batting practice, coaches stood around the cage and said, "Gee, Randy, don't you wish you were as good as your sister?"

Every day at JFK High School in Fremont, California, he would go to baseball practice, come home, eat a box of macaroni, go to bed, and get up five hours later to make his graveyard shift at Winchell's donut shop on Fremont Boulevard. He got to keep some loose change for himself, and then he turned the rest over to his parents to help with the rent—his mother, Jeanne, was a waitress, and his father, Max, worked on the Alaskan oil pipeline, spending much of the year away from home. During the summers Randy went up to work in Alaska himself, starting when he was only thirteen (illegally, of course). He started off on the docks cleaning fish and driving a forklift, and before long he had a union card saying he was eighteen and had joined Max on the pipeline. He worked fourteen-hour days, seven days a week, and with union wages pocketed $500 a week, good money in the mid-1970s. If that kind of schedule didn't test his resolve, the tragedy that soon struck certainly did. At 4:00 a.m. on the day Randy and his family were scheduled to fly to Alaska to start a three-city vacation with Max, they received a phone call at the house: Max had dropped dead of a heart attack. Randy was sixteen.

"I didn't want to grieve, so I played baseball, played all the time, and eventually it got better," he told the *Los Angeles Times* back in 1988.[1]

He was a solid player in high school but not a great one, and it took a couple of years at Cal State Hayward and a standout season at Mesa State College in Colorado for Randy to catch the attention of big-league scouts. The Milwaukee Brewers signed him in the sixth round of the 1980 draft, and three years later, he made his Major League debut. The Brewers liked his bat, liked his play, liked *him*—newspaper accounts invariably referred to him as "friendly" and "fun"—but there was always someone a little bit better ahead of him on the depth charts.

The 1986 season started well enough, with Randy making the team out of spring training and doing what he always did best: living up to his last name, whether starting a game or coming off the bench to pinch-hit. But his playing time shrank, his bat went cold, and by early June he had been sent back down to the Brewers' Minor League team in Vancouver, British Columbia.

But before Randy could board the plane, word came in: he had been traded to San Diego. He called home and told his wife, Dorene, who screamed, "We're going to San Diego!" when she heard the news.

And now, sitting in his locker, having just been upstaged by a guy fifteen years his senior, he sighs and packs his bag for the hotel. They have one more game against the Dodgers in the series, and who knows, maybe manager Steve Boros will give him a chance at redemption. He thinks of Dorene and immediately feels better—she will be flying to San Diego from their home in Tucson in the morning. Dorene makes everything okay.

Back at the hotel, he calls her like he always does when he's on the road, and they talk about her trip in the morning. He asks about their kids—Andrew, age three, and twins Jarrod and Collin, only ten months. They discuss looking for a house in San Diego during her visit. Within minutes, Graig Nettles couldn't be further away from Randy's mind.

And then a couple hours later, the phone rings again.

But it isn't Dorene.

It's her cousin, who has just discovered Dorene on the floor, completely unconscious. The message is clear: we have no idea what happened, just get here as fast as you possibly can.

Randy dashes to the San Diego airport, even though there aren't any flights until the morning. He calls a friend, prays so hard his hands ache, and waits and waits and waits. He has often described Dorene, a ballet dancer, as the family rock. He met her during spring training in Phoenix in 1981 when the team bus pulled up to their motel and he spotted a group of young women by the pool. Randy had gotten off the bus and gone straight to a burger shack nearby to grab some food when he saw her come by in a bathing suit, still dripping wet.

"Didn't I see you by the pool?" he asked.

"What was your first clue?" she shot back.

A little more than a year later, they got married in El Paso, Texas, where Randy played Minor League ball. Their congregation consisted of two people, and the foursome celebrated by ripping down the highway in Randy's 1968 Chevy Nova blasting Frank Sinatra. They were young, poor, and unimaginably happy.

And when Randy walks into Dorene's room at El Dorado Hospital at 10:30 a.m. later that morning and sees all the machines and the wires, hears all the beeps and hums, for the first time in his life, he realizes he might not be ready.

====

I grab one of the high-top wood tables by the window of a Dallas restaurant / brewery / bowling alley named Bowl and Barrel, located in one of the ubiquitous suburban plazas. Earlier this morning I spoke with Randy on the phone as I drove in on I-45N past the most bizarre storefront I've seen yet: "Condoms to Go" (imagine the alternative).

"Do we have a plan today?" he said, his voice peppy and younger than his fifty-five years.

I told him no real plan, just meet and chat. Keep it casual.

"Just toolin' around and shootin' the bull," he affirmed. I like him already.

My server, Rose, is a Latina with a comely combination of light skin, dark hair, and high cheekbones. She brings me a mimosa, and I tell her I'm working on a book about baseball.

"Yeah, I don't really follow that at all," she replies, already bored.

I show her Randy's baseball card with his slight grin and thin mustache.

"It's from thirty years ago," I say.

"Yeah, I wasn't even born then," she replies, spinning and walking to the next table.

A black Chevy Silverado whips into the parking lot, and I watch Randy dismount. He comes in cool, his dirty blond hair slicked straight back, looking trim in a blue-and-white golf shirt neatly tucked into a pair of navy shorts with a belt and complemented by a pair of sandals and wraparound shades. A fringe of facial hair borders his bottom lip, a kind of inverse mustache, and his skin is bronzed from the Texas sun. He's half an inch shorter than me, handsome and lean. There's a lot I want to ask him, but nothing more so than the epilogue to Dorene's story. Newspaper accounts tell of her vegetative state stemming from the heart attack and the $24.7 million award Randy received from a lawsuit alleging that a doctor's diet pills had caused the attack, but after that, the trail runs cold. I don't even know if she's still alive; I do know from my research that Randy got married again, in 1994, to a woman named Tracy. Along with Garry Templeton's illegitimate child and Doc Gooden's drug addiction, it is one of the hardest things that I plan on asking about on my journey. The fan in me is at odds with the journalist—I want these players to like me, to confide in me, and so I don't want to risk upsetting them. But I know that my responsibility is first and foremost to the story, even if that means alienating my heroes.

I also want to kick his ass in bowling, which is why I've chosen to meet here.

"What's up, kid?" Randy says, gripping my hand firmly, cologne wafting off his quik-dry golf shirt.

I show him the Pack, always a good ice breaker. He laughs as I recap my visit with Tempy, one of his old friends from their Padres days, and he stops when he gets to Jaime Cocanower, by far the most obscure of the Wax Packers.

"Jaime!" he says with genuine delight. "I hid out from a tornado with him in Milwaukee in a cellar one time. That thing bounced right past the house we were living in and tore up a barn like five hundred yards away. It was eerie. You've got to say hi for me."

I tell him that Carlton Fisk, the only Hall of Famer among the Pack, refuses to talk to me.

"He's one of those old-school guys. Some of them just kind of shut down with the media. Something probably left a bad taste in his mouth, or he had a bad experience at some point. I think we all have at some point. But it goes with the territory, you know?" His hands are crossed, sitting straight up, his words full of vim. He says everything with an easy grin and a wink.

Rose comes by to take his order (a Miller Lite and a water), and as she walks away Randy's eyes light up.

"She's cute," he says conspiratorially, and I nod in agreement. Baseball players are known for their wandering eyes, but as I'm about to find out, Randy's got every reason to wander.

"What are you up to nowadays?" I ask. His playful demeanor has me completely at ease.

"I've got some downtime now. I came out of the game and decided to start drawing my Major League pension." Beginning in 2002, Randy followed the typical postplaying career path of coaching and managing, working his way up the Minor League ladder and landing a gig as hitting coach with the Padres in 2009.

"I've got one son in med school, one in law school, one runs a recording studio, one's in college in Kansas City, one went into the Air Force Academy last week, and I've got the last guy, he's a rising junior at Jesuit College Prep School," he says, ticking off the list of children (six sons: three with Dorene and three with Tracy). "And Mrs. Ready decided to go her separate way, so I'm dealing with her too," he adds.

I do a double take, not sure I heard him correctly.

"Wait, what?" I ask.

"She decided to go, time for her life. She wants a divorce," he replies, matter-of-fact.

"You're getting divorced right now?" I ask, still incredulous.

"Yes."

"I thought you were making a joke."

"It's been painful. It's been going on eight, ten months now. She decided she wanted her life. She was tired of being Randy Ready's wife and the kids' mom," he says.

"Did that blindside you?"

"Yup. I didn't see it coming."

He asks me to turn the recorder off so he can discuss details off the record, and I comply; the last thing I want is to somehow hurt his position legally.

"Okay, we're back on the record now?" I ask a few minutes later.

He nods.

"How are your kids taking it?"

"It's tough. They're having a tough time," he admits.

I can relate. I tell him about my childhood, how I was the typical firstborn, ever dutiful. My parents told me not to swear, and I listened, chastising myself on the rare occasion when a swear word slipped out. They told me to stay away from drinking and drugs, and I did, always straightedge. I imprinted on their example of the ideal marriage, wishing the same for myself, convinced that I had found it at twenty-two when I met Kay. And then a few years later, when I was still reeling from having left Kay, my mom called. I knew from the way she said "Hi, Brad" that something was amiss.

"Your dad and I are getting divorced," she said, knocking the wind out of me.

It was unthinkable. Not only that, they had both met other people. The castle of stability and certainty that had been my foundation was obliterated. And I was mad, mad at them for not practicing what they had preached. I felt like they were hypocrites.

Most of Randy's kids are now grown, just as I was when my parents split, but I know that doesn't necessarily make it any easier. I wonder if they are feeling what I felt, especially the oldest.

"The best line I heard is this," Randy begins. "I was in Guatemala doing this mission work, and I just got home like ten days ago. This guy that was bunking next to me, this dentist, Mike, was sixty-nine, and we're talking a bit, and he asked me if I was married, and I said, 'Yeah, I'm going through a divorce right now,' and he goes, 'Well, I've successfully completed two marriages.' I said, 'Mike, can I use that?'"

Randy is down but far from out. He radiates positive vibes, practically glows, chirping with strangers nearby, ribbing me at every turn, bouncing around like a caffeinated beagle, his greenish eyes dancing. He tells me about enjoying his newfound independence, living on his own once again. Today he got up at six, went to yoga class, paid the bills, cleaned up "the pad," made himself something to eat, and then hung a picture that one of his sons sent him for Father's Day. He takes out his phone and shows me a photo of him with all six of his boys; every single one is taller than him.

"You're short, Randy," I tease.

"Dynamite comes in small packages too," he replies. "This guy, he's six feet, three inches and 235. Never played baseball. He's a frickin' animal, dude," Randy says.

"Six boys, what are the odds of that?" I ask.

"Just shots in the dark," he says with a smile. "I don't know, you're the scientist."

A new server arrives, bearded and in his midtwenties, and Randy orders a refill.

"Where did Rose go?" he asks. "Send Rose over here, dude."

"I know, she's way cuter than me, but she had to go home," he replies.

"Would you ever get married again?" I ask him.

"I haven't got that far yet, kid," he replies. He thinks for a second. "Shit, I've got to get out there again!"

I glance down at my phone and see the orange-and-white flame icon.

"Have you ever heard of Tinder?" I ask. His eyes brighten even further, eyebrows arched.

"That's the dating site, right?"

"It's an app, it uses the GPS on your phone. I can set a radius for how many miles around me I want to cast a net. And I can specify an age range," I say, opening it up to show him my settings.

"Wow, Brad, an age range of twenty-one to fifty-five?" he says. I feel my cheeks darken.

"I've set the radius to twenty miles," I say, changing the subject.

"No, change it to four. Let's see if there's anyone around," he replies, getting excited.

He's holding the phone now, his index finger hovering an inch above the image of Erica, a thirty-one-year-old self-described skeptical vegetarian.

"I'm gonna say no," he says politely.

"Okay, so you swipe left."

I'm on Tinder with Randy Ready. Jesus Christ.

"There's got to be some crazies out there, too, though, right?" he asks.

"The last girl I dated I met on there. She wasn't crazy, just too restless."

"I've got to stay off of all that because of the divorce," he says, coming back to reality and handing my phone back. "My first wife, it was kind of weird dealing with her having the injury and everything, but my second wife, we liked to do all the same stuff. We liked to boat, water ski, I taught her how to shoot guns, how to hunt, fish, and we had great vacations and stuff. But we sold the house we built just four years ago, with the divorce."

Dorene. It's the first mention of her, just in passing, with no elaboration. I consider asking him what happened, how things ended up, if she's even still alive. But it's not the right time, not yet.

Instead, I go back to our anchor: baseball. Like Gary Pettis, Randy was not heavily scouted in high school and had to prove himself during three years of college ball. I ask him why he thinks he made it to the Show when so many others failed.

"Well, there's no such thing as a bad Major Leaguer. Even if you just get a cup of coffee, you were there," he says. "I was never a gifted defensive player. I was adequate. But the old school has a saying: if you shake a tree, ninety-nine gloves fall out and only one bat. And I could hit."

But the real separator, even beyond his bat, was above the shoulders. Don't be fooled by his carefree spirit at the surface.

"You keep telling me no, just keep telling me no," he says, reflecting on the struggle. "You're telling me I'm not fast enough? I'm gonna work on my speed. I can't hit? I'm gonna be a better hitter. I don't hit any homers? I'm gonna understand some things to slug a little more."

Randy's not just a doer, he's a thinker, which is why he has always been in demand as a coach since he quit playing in 1997. That year, after a season overseas in Japan, he went to spring training with the Anaheim Angels. He was thirty-seven years old. Before one of the exhibition games, he was messing around in the outfield catching fly balls over the fence and landed funny on his knee, his first injury in seventeen years. He was placed on the disabled list and then joined the Minor League team in Lake Elsinore for rehab. The general manager, Bill Bavasi, told him they were about to make some roster moves on the big club and to sit tight.

"'Tell you what,'" Randy told him. "'I'm going to make a move for you,' I said, 'I'm going home to my family to figure out everyone's name. This is the end of the road.'"

His phone immediately rang with offers to start coaching, but Randy knew better. He knew he had to ease himself back in when the time was ready.

"You don't want to come in too hot," he says. "There's that transition where you've got to get the player out of you."

He enjoyed retirement, taking the family on vacation to the California redwoods, hanging out by the pool, just being a dad. He joined a softball team, perhaps the most stacked softball team in the history of beer leagues: Randy, Kevin Mitchell, John Kruk, Kevin Towers. They called themselves Spike and the Fatboys. When the time felt right, he came in cool, starting as a manager for the Single-A Oneonta Tigers.

Having been out of professional baseball for the past year and a half, he lets me in on a secret: he wants back in.

"I plan to go back to the game next year," he says. In order to begin collecting your Major League pension you can't be employed by a Major League organization, but now that he's started receiving the money, he can go back and continue to collect. One day he would love to have the privilege of managing at the Major League level; he reached the interview stage twice before, with the Mariners and Astros, but never landed the job. I wouldn't bet against him.

Randy finishes off his third Miller Lite, and I decide it's time to issue a challenge. "Let's bowl, Randy. I'll smoke you," I say, brimming with false confidence. The last time I bowled (sober) was at a birthday party in fourth grade, when Randy was playing left field for the Philadelphia Phillies.

He laughs and says he doesn't have any socks. But I pressure him, telling him that as a professional athlete he'd better be able to beat me in anything, socks or no socks.

"Alright, I'll beat your ass, but only one game. None of this best out of three," he says.

We change into our bowling shoes and grab lane 3 next to a group of girls in their early twenties. Randy is having fun, stretching out, swiveling his hips, getting ready to roll.

"Man, I've got to get back out there. Right after the divorce, I was going out a lot, took hip hop lessons," he says, his eyes scanning the bar.

"Why did your ex want to move to Dallas?" I ask.

"I guess to divorce me?" he shoots back. "Good question, why would I come here? Have you seen San Diego?" he asks, referencing his former home.

I keep my feelings about San Diego to myself.

He cradles one of the bowling balls, sizing up the string of pins. He takes three steps, swinging back his right arm and rolling the ball forward with good velocity. It tails left, knocking down only four pins. I needle him, putting my hands around my throat.

"You pulled it," I chirp.

"Yeah, I did," he replies, hanging his head. "Let's see what you got, kid."

I proceed to do the exact same thing, hooking the ball left despite my every effort to roll it as straight as possible without any spin. Why is this sport so hard? He laughs.

"Didn't we just talk about this?" he says. "C'mon, use your Ivy League education to figure this out."

One of the girls in the neighboring lane squats low, her feet in a wide stance facing the pins, and rolls the ball at a glacial pace from between her legs, using both hands. The ball inches down the lane, hitting the first pin softly but triggering a slow-motion cascade that eventually topples all ten for a strike.

Randy gives her a high five, saying, "Wow, you had a nice throw on that!" It's not hard to imagine him in a baseball clubhouse, pin-balling around the room with boundless enthusiasm, calling everyone "kid." I feel like I'm out with an old college buddy.

We chat while we roll about his hot yoga class (not Bikram, but still heated) and his love of hunting and fishing. He's a Renaissance man, shattering stereotypes of the ex-jock. I look up at the TV screen and realize how close I am to actually beating him, only a few points behind. But when the last frame is done, the cream has risen to the top: Randy 130, Brad 129. I snap a photo.

"Put that on Twitter," he says with a wide grin.

―――

"Are you here yet?" I text Randy.

Today is the day I ask him about Dorene.

I spread my feet in a wide stance, sucking in my stomach and keeping my back as straight as possible as I lean over to the right, grabbing behind my right knee with both hands. My hamstring screams as my head drops with gravity, trying to pull it closer to my knee, feeling the accumulated knots of thousands of miles on the road. I've only managed to squeeze a few workouts in so far, and I can already feel my muscles tightening from disuse.

From this bent-over position I glance up and see Randy bound into the gym, his hair flopping to one side, earbuds wrapped around his neck.

He walks by, gives me a "morning, kid," and chitchats with the trainers and staff gathered behind the desk. He's got an appointment with his therapist at 11:15, and since I'm in bad need of a workout, I asked if I could join his morning routine at Gold's Gym.

"What time did I tell you to meet me here? Nine a.m.?" he says to me, exaggerating every word, pretending to be annoyed. "And what time is it now?" he asks, craning his head toward the clock on the wall. "Ten of. *Ten of!* And you're already texting me. You're so high maintenance," he says, cracking up the entire staff, then adding, "Give this kid my guest pass."

I follow him toward the free weights, and he says, "I'm not working out with you, I'll tell you that right now. You do your own thing." An impish grin spreads across his face as he talks out of the side of his mouth. I convince him to spot me on the bench press and add a 45-pound plate on each side, for a total weight of 135 pounds.

"What do we got, kid?" he asks, and I tell him I'm shooting for six reps.

"Can I get help on the liftoff?" I ask.

"Man, you're high maintenance," he replies with that grin.

I push the bar up (with his help) and do my best to control its descent toward my chest, feeling the microfibers in my pecs tear with each inch.

"Straight up, you got it, no problem," he coaches as I grimace with each rep, breathing hard through my nose. I stand up panting and tell him that when he was traded from the Padres to the Phillies in 1989, my dad told me after he read it in the morning paper and how excited I was that Randy was now on my favorite team. That year in fourth-grade art class, each student had to design a plastic dinner plate. Most students drew pictures of their favorite animal or a scene from a family vacation; I used the space to write out the name of every single player on the Phillies. Not a single drawing or picture, just letters, including R-a-n-d-y R-e-a-d-y. I still eat off that plate in my room back in Oakland.

Following our workout (true to his word, he ditches me for his own series of exercises while I huff on the elliptical), we walk across the street to Southpaw's Grill for some breakfast. Randy orders the Major Malcolm, a sandwich with two eggs, Swiss cheese, bacon, sliced turkey, jalapeños, and tomatoes, and shows me pictures from the medical mission he just completed in Guatemala. Always giving back, Randy joined 120 doctors to provide relief and assistance to the village of Chimaltenango. He was on the stove team, assembling seventy-six stoves in ten days. He beams as he shows me photos of the families he worked with, multiple generations crammed into single-room huts with mats on the floor for beds.

"It was crazy, dude. It's way out in the middle of nowhere. It was nuts. It was so rewarding."

I want to know more about his childhood—he's a Bay Area boy at heart, having been born in San Mateo and then moving to Fremont at age six. I'm also curious about his father—my experience with Rance (fantastic father) and Boomer (alcoholic father) has me thinking a lot about the vital role that dads play in these elite athletes' lives.

"What was your dad like?" I ask, taking a swig of the Muscle Milk he bought me at the gym. ("Don't say I never bought you anything," he said as he tossed it to me.)

"Super tennis player, Oklahoma State wrestling champion," Randy replies. "Moved to California when he was eighteen. I tried to find out if he graduated high school, but I'm not sure that he did. He loved the horses, loved betting on the horses. He used to take me out of school to go to the horse races," he says. He talks over the whir of blenders as people file in and out of the bustling café.

"Were you guys close growing up?" I ask.

"Well, you know, he was busy working. We went camping as a family, we fished a lot together, but he wasn't at a lot of sports events because he was working all the time," he says evenly.

Not exactly a yes.

He tells me that one day when he was about ten, he came home from school and found his dad in their backyard. "Look what I did for you," his dad told him. "I built you a pitcher's mound." Randy was ecstatic. He grabbed his glove as his dad positioned himself behind home plate, a Pall Mall hanging out of the side of his mouth. Randy prayed that he would throw a strike.

"I threw him one pitch," he tells me, his voice void of any emotion. "He said good job and figured that was good enough. Satisfied the requirement." His dad walked back inside and never played catch with him again.

Six years later, Randy's dad dropped dead of a heart attack while working in Alaska, the night before the family was set to fly to Juneau to meet him for a vacation.

"I remember the last time I saw him was one of those moments where he wanted to give me a hug, and I said, 'Hey, we're in public. We should probably just shake hands.' It wasn't cool hugging your dad in public at that time. So I backed off and shook his hand, and I never forgot that. Later I said if I have children, I'm gonna do it different."

He hugs his six boys every chance he gets.

I glance at my watch and realize it's already 10:30. Randy has to leave soon for his shrink, and I haven't yet worked up the nerve to ask him the question I've come all this way to ask.

I glance down, then back up to meet his eyes.

"So yesterday you mentioned your first wife," I say.

"Y-y-essss," he replies slowly and cautiously, clearly nervous about what comes next. But the horse is out of the barn.

"So what ended up happening?"

"She had a heart attack."

"I know the story from the press, but what ended up happening in the long run?"

"Um, she's still alive," he replies. I hadn't realized until this moment that I had expected her to have passed.

"She's fifty-two, fifty-three years old. She lives in Tucson, she's set up in a nice house, her brother takes good care of her, her parents are since deceased." He talks like he's reading off a checklist.

"Did she recover anymore?" I ask.

"No. Still the same. The boys go and visit her. They spent Christmas with her this year. I was there on Christmas Day; it was a lot of fun." He shows me pictures to lighten the mood.

"Is she able to talk?"

"Eh, about the same. Like I said, she's well provided for, and . . ." He pauses. "The kids over the years have learned to have a relationship with her."

"Even though she can't speak, she knows who people are?"

"Ah, ya know, it's hard to tell. Seven to ten minutes without oxygen is a long time."

I can sense the burden of these questions growing heavy on him.

"Anyway, she's doing good. She'll probably outlive us all. Next question." He giggles, then adds, "See how I got out of that?"

I smile but decide not to drop it. Not yet. I now know the facts, but I want to know what's underneath them. I push on.

"Can I ask you a little more about it? Are you okay talking about it?"

"Right. What do you want to know?" he replies, not defensive, willing to continue.

"What got you through it?"

It's not a great question. It's cliché and one he's clearly been asked a thousand times before, but in this tense moment I can't think of any other way to ask how you possibly keep moving forward when life has just delivered you a knockout blow.

Randy recognizes the banality of my question and replies, "Everything that's been put down on paper, the support, friends, faith, all those things."

I ask him to elaborate on the faith part.

"I think everyone has to have a belief, some type of foundation. You have to have something."

"Did you ever think about retiring when all that went down?" I ask.

"No, not at all. I figured if I can pull this off somehow, some way, it's just going to make me stronger."

And it did. Because Randy is not afraid. All his life he's been dealt a five of clubs, but he doesn't discard it, doesn't tear it up and leave the table; he adds it to his deck, ready to play the next hand.

A few minutes from now, I will get back on the road, driving backward (west) to Oklahoma to do some research, and Randy will drive to see his psychologist to talk more about his feelings. It's not easy—back in 1985 a writer for the *Milwaukee Journal* commented that Randy tends to bury his feelings deep inside. That may have been true then, but it isn't now.

Randy is ready.

7

CARMAN'S CRADLE

Farm. Work in the oil fields.
Crystal meth.
—*Resident of Camargo, Oklahoma,*
when asked what people do there

Days 14–15
July 2–3, 2015
Miles driven: 3,401
Cups of coffee: 33
Dallas TX to Camargo OK

None of the Wax Packers live in Oklahoma. At least not anymore.

My favorite baseball team growing up was the Philadelphia Phillies, which in the late 1980s was a bit like saying your favorite *Star Wars* character is Aunt Beru. By geography (growing up in Rhode Island), I should have been a Boston Red Sox fan, but two things conspired against that outcome: I never followed the crowd, and my favorite letter was *F*. Apparently, I also couldn't spell.

Scrawny, industrious, and shy, I was picked on a lot as a kid—throw in a debilitating stutter, and I had season tickets to the nerd table in the lunchroom. I attributed my academic success more to a diligent work ethic than any innate intelligence—I got straight As because I worked hard, I figured, not because I was naturally smart.

My parents provided the most idyllic childhood one could hope for— long days spent playing by the backyard lake, limitless support for all my quirky hobbies, unconditional love—but also made it clear that I was expected to excel in school. "Your education is what will get you ahead," they told me. My brain became my best friend. It wasn't until many years later with the onset of OCD that I saw my best friend's ugly side.

I followed my parents' marching orders, churning out All-Star numbers on my report cards year after year. As early as the third grade I was creating spreadsheets on my grandfather's medical pads in order to track my school assignments.

I spent my free time poring over everything I could find related to the Phillies and my favorite player, pitcher Don Carman. I felt an intrinsic kinship with Don, a cerebral type in a world of alpha jocks, possessed of limited ability but tireless work ethic. His career statistics don't jump off the page, they crawl: fifty-three wins and fifty-four losses with a 4.11 earned run average (ERA) compiled over ten Major League seasons. I met him briefly in 1994, when he was trying to make a comeback with the Phillies and my family took a vacation to spring training in Florida. My dad and I caught Don for a few seconds during practice, just long enough for me to get his autograph and take a picture, my thirteen-year-old head coming just to the letters of his jersey. I was so smitten by the experience that I wrote a letter to the editor of *Phillies Report*, the team newspaper, which got printed, my first-ever publication.

Carman grew up here in the Sooner State, which I cross into a couple hours after leaving Randy Ready behind in Dallas. Although this is a complete detour, I only have one favorite player of all time, and so spending a little extra effort telling his story seems perfectly reasonable to me. A week from now I'll meet Carman himself in Florida.

Oklahoma is as opposite California as you can get. Born late to the Union (the forty-sixth state), it was constructed out of land discarded by neighboring states or set aside in perpetuity for Native Americans, who now number more than a quarter million here. Overwhelmingly white and conservative (Mitt Romney won two-thirds of the popular vote in 2012), the urban areas lean liberal. My goal is to visit Camargo, the tiny outpost where Carman grew up, but I decide to rest for a night in the capital, Oklahoma City (OKC), smack in the middle of the state.

Like many other cities, OKC experienced an urban revival in the 1990s following decades of nearby suburban development. The rebirth brought baseball, shopping, and a canal bustling with water taxis and nightlife to a downtown dominated by the fifty-floor Devon Energy

Center skyscraper. Having saved some money by staying in an Airbnb in Dallas, I splurge, knowing my dollar will go a lot farther here than it will on the East Coast, where I'm soon headed.

I park at the Sheraton Downtown and in the short walk to the lobby am reminded of why this part of the country is nicknamed tornado alley, a blast of wind tousling my gelled hair and sending strands in all directions.

Another city, another hotel front desk, I think, the same kind of routine the Wax Packers endured for six months at a time while living out of a suitcase season after season.

At the front desk, Colin, not a day over twenty-one, greets me behind a bowl of Red Delicious apples, his hair slicked straight back in clumpy wet tendrils.

"Since we're low occupancy, we're going to upgrade you to our deluxe California room," he says, handing me a key. (To the rest of the country, California is still exotic enough to inspire the names of special rooms.)

"I actually have the room right next to you," he adds. "Last night I had people on both sides of me having, shall we say, intimate moments, and I couldn't sleep. I figure I'll get some quiet with you next to me."

I'm insulted.

I head out, hoping to prove Colin wrong, and end up at the R&J Lounge and Supper Club in the midtown neighborhood, northwest of downtown. An homage to the supper clubs and cocktail bars of the 1950s, the lounge occupies a one-level beige brick building that used to house a printing company. I walk into a den of red and gold, the lighting low, with multiple retro accents (record player, pin-up-girl posters). I take a seat on the patio, covered in plastic grass, where a large man named Maurice is onstage strumming an electric guitar. He finishes a song, and someone calls out "Happy birthday!"

"Fifty-six," he says softly, winking to everyone.

It's a decent crowd for a Wednesday night, locals slurping grasshoppers and whiskey sours to fight off the humidity. I order a Cuba libre (only $4.30!) and turn to the two women at my table, one an older brunette and the other a redhead named Lacey. The brunette is a nurse and bartender with some miles; "I don't drink," she tells me, "but most of my friends who work in bars are alcoholics." She excuses herself (early shift at the hospital in the morning), leaving me alone with Lacey, whose green saucer-eyes are devastating. She sits with her legs crossed, her seafoam purse positioned perfectly straight in her lap.

"Mickey Mantle!" she exclaims when I explain the baseball theme of my journey.

"Well . . . not exactly," I reply. "More like Don Carman."

I get crickets in response.

I offer to buy her a drink, but she says she's already had a couple and wants to be responsible. She was born in Buffalo and is studying to be a traveling nurse.

"What's dating like here?" I ask, hoping to learn if she's single.

"I've been in a relationship for about a year," she replies, friendly but not flirtatious.

"How did you guys meet?"

"We worked together. He really liked me, found out when my shifts were, and asked me out like five times before I said yes."

The expression on my face betrays my thoughts, because she quickly adds, "But I really liked him when we finally went out."

She goes on: "I thought it was kind of tacky that we worked together, so I resigned and found a new job." The sleeves of her billowy peach-colored top spill past her elbows.

"How old are you?" I ask. I've always felt that the taboo against asking a woman this question is silly.

"Twenty-five. Getting up there."

Ha.

"I want to make sure before I get engaged and married that he has a plan. More than anything else, I need security," she says. "He's studying for the MCAT right now. I haven't seen him in a week. He failed the first time but didn't really show any initiative."

"Are you actually into this guy?" I ask, now fully skeptical that her relationship has any future. In the five minutes we've been talking, her boyfriend's sole redemptive quality seems to be that he was nice after having stalked her.

She giggles nervously and replies, "Well, he doesn't really listen to me." She holds her drink with both hands, tracing the brim with her index finger.

"You don't seem too happy to me," I reply. "I don't think it's going to work."

"What should I do?" she asks.

"Well, obviously, I'm not objective here, since I'm attracted to you, but I think you know the answer. Better to end it sooner than later. Don't drag it out."

Damn, that was blunt, I think to myself.

She is not thrilled to hear this, but a glint of agreement flashes in her eyes, and for the first time, a hint of seduction spreads across her face.

"Well, if I do, I'll come find you," she says, finishing her drink and wishing me a good night.

I settle in to listen to Maurice's solo scat, his encore now having stretched to forty minutes because the crowd is eating it up. I wish Jesse and the Kid were here to raise a glass with me, to recap the interaction with Lacey. I know she will probably not take my advice, that even though she may complain to her friends about her boyfriend and spaces out in the shower wondering what life could be like, she will probably wake up ten years from now with two young kids and a distant husband and will see a picture of Mickey Mantle and remember this night and smile wearily.

She will have the security she wanted. But will she be happy?

===

In western Oklahoma, diversity consists of blond, strawberry blond, and dirty blond. The moment I walk into a restaurant, all heads turn toward my pastel shirt, tar-black hair, and swarthy complexion, which add up to *definitely not from western Oklahoma.*

"Would you like white gravy or brown?" the server at Home Cookin' Café asks me the next night. Back in Oakland, gravy is a novelty that hipster restaurants serve with an ironic sneer, but here it comes in multiple colors.

I pick at the iceberg lettuce on my plate, its translucent tissues drenched in Italian dressing, washing it down with coffee I sip out of a thick white ceramic mug. Coffee has become my emotional crutch, appropriate at any time of day. Home Cookin' is attached to the Econo Lodge, which for only forty-six dollars is my quarters here in Elk City (population: 11,997), a cosmopolitan hub compared to where I'm heading. The police log in the local paper is dominated by entries such as "cattle standing in road."

The motel is located in a cavernous three-story hangar with the rooms facing an indoor pool and a courtyard festooned with potted plants on a concrete floor. I look around at my company in the café—there's a pair of women in their fifties or sixties sitting at the table next to me, one with short dyed brown hair and a floral print button-down shirt, the other with the fiercest mullet I've seen since walking by a mirror in fourth grade. I eavesdrop for a moment on their conversation. "I haven't been with anyone for eighteen years!" the mulleted one says. They giggle. My server brings some brown gravy.

My phone chimes with a text from Wax Packer Jaime Cocanower, whom I'll be seeing in a couple days in Arkansas: "Brad, Gini [his wife] and I would like to invite you to celebrate the Fourth with us. We live on Beaver Lake and our neighborhood puts together a fireworks display. You and anyone traveling with you are invited. How many should we count on?"

As usual, no plus-one is necessary. Unless Lacey is free . . .

I've been pleasantly surprised by how accommodating the Wax Packers have been, but this raises the bar to another level. I remember sitting on the floor of my bedroom as a kid, organizing and then reorganizing my baseball cards and always liking Cocanower's in particular. I'm not sure if it was his unique name or the pensive expression on his face, but it's surreal to now think that the dude with the bushy eyebrows just invited me to a Fourth of July barbecue at his house.

I finish up my steak dinner, picking through the gristle, and walk the forty yards to my room. The discordant odor of dirty socks mixed with lemon-scented air freshener blasts my face as the door swings open, and I collapse onto the bed, glancing down at a maroon carpet showing the scars of many beer binges and highway trysts. I open up the drawer of the bed stand to see if shitty motels in middle America still have Yellow Pages (no) and Bibles (yes) and then crumple back into the clammy sheets.

I read over my notes. Earlier in the day I drove from OKC to Weatherford, a midsize college town where Don Carman's mother, Betty Walker, now lives. It's the kind of community where people other than UPS workers still ring doorbells. Eighty years old, Betty is a throwback, a deceptively tough woman who is proud of all eight of her kids. Although only one was a professional athlete, she speaks of each of them with equal reverence. When I ask about Don, she makes sure to also mention the others, such as Charles, who she tells me worked for a security company in Iraq and wrote for his college newspaper. ("Isn't that a cute picture?" she says, showing me the clipping.)

Betty lives in a modest ranch-style house with an excitable dog that hurls itself against the screen door on my approach, and she has an assortment of scrapbooks ready for my arrival. Wearing a pink-and-white floral top, her gray hair falling to her shoulders, she brews a fresh pot of coffee while I scan the walls of the living room, decorated with the famous "Footprints" poem, a framed copy of the Ten Commandments, and yellowed pictures of the kids, including a clock with a photo of Don in his Phillies uniform. Betty met Don's father, Marion, at a grocery store in San Jose, California, when she was only eighteen; they married a year later and moved to Camargo in September 1954 to be close to Marion's family. Marion died of a heart attack at age forty-six, and her second husband also passed young. But Betty keeps on. For years she cooked in the elementary school cafeteria, then came home and played catch with Don and the other boys. She was an athlete in her day, competing in basketball, softball, swimming, even ping pong, filling the dad niche for Marion, even when he was still alive.

"He was always working in the oil fields, sometimes double shifts," she says.

Three of Don's brothers who live nearby join us to share their memories, each of them very different, but all of them sharing a western reticence when we veer from facts to feelings.

"What was Don like as a kid?" I ask.

"He was kind of shy," Betty replies in a slight drawl.

"Yeah, shy," one of the brothers says.

Back in bed in the Econo Lodge, I curl up under the sheets with my phone, feeling the urge to connect with someone, listening to a midsummer thunderstorm pelt the pavement outside. My brain, always trying to think one step ahead, hasn't shut off in two weeks. I wonder what Kay is doing right now, think about Tempy and whether or not he fixed his granddaughter's Barbie doll, worry about whether I'll get to the more challenging Wax Packers like Carlton Fisk and Vince Coleman. I take a deep breath and clear my head, opening my text messages and writing to a few women back home whom I have casually dated.

"Hey," I type to each of them.

I stare at the artificial glow of the screen, waiting, hoping for a response.

I fall asleep to the sight of my own messages, unrequited, the phone dropping out of my hand and onto the stained floor.

＝

This is truly the middle of nowhere.

I'm standing next to the Accord on the outskirts of Camargo, if Camargo can even be said to have outskirts. Sky and land meet halfway at the horizon, the gently rolling Great Plains blanketed with grasses covering sandstone and shale dating back hundreds of millions of years. These lands are the closest our world gets to permanence, but they change too, slowly but inexorably.

Founded in 1911, four years later Camargo already had four general stores, two hotels, two lumberyards, and two grain elevators. The population peaked at 315 in 1950, but at the last census in 2010, it had dropped to 178. At one time, the Carman family almost had a quorum (the town was nicknamed "Carmango"): Don's father, Marion, was one of ten children who settled here, and now only one, Tom, is left. A railroad leading to the town of Leedey, eleven miles to the south, acted as the town's main artery from 1912 to 1972, sustaining local commerce as a shipping route for livestock, wheat, and bentonite. But like so many other small towns across the country, once infrastructure and transportation routes changed, so too did the town's fortunes.

A 1984 clipping from the *Daily Oklahoman* shows Don and his child-hood coach, Bob Ward, standing in front of an enormous road sign that said "Welcome to Camargo" in cursive on top and "Home of 'Don Carman' of the Philadelpia [*sic*] Phillies" in even larger lettering below. I chuckle at the incorrect usage of quotes around Carman's name, as if he was an idea and not a person, and the omission of the second *h* in Philadelphia. Carman and the sign are now long gone, but Bob remains, perhaps the most famous resident in the town's hundred-year-plus history. He's best known for his contributions to baseball, founding an American Legion team, the Travelers, in nearby Woodward and turn-ing it into a factory of corn-fed professional ballplayers. Don's mom and brothers told me yesterday that it was Bob and Bob alone who saw potential in the scrawny, sniffly kid who got picked on in school. What did he see that no one else could?

When I called Bob from Elk City earlier this morning to get his address, he scoffed.

"We-ell," he began, his drawl adding syllables, "you don't need no address. Just drive straight to the north edge of town, and my house will be the last one on the right. There are three cars in the driveway. Two of them are white."

I follow those directions up Route 34, and sure enough, there on the edge of town, is the Ward homestead, one block away from the now-vacant lot where the Carman family home once stood. A lawn sign with big black letters spelling WARD marks the house. Planted next to the sign is a large American flag. When Don comes back to visit, this is where he stays.

Bob, seventy-nine, is waiting for me on his porch with a firm grip. He's wearing a Woodward Travelers hat and T-shirt, the American Legion team he coached for thirty-seven years. His rough skin is splotched with sun damage, his faded green eyes are slightly sunken behind a pair of thin-rimmed glasses.

We walk into the air-conditioned comfort of his living room, where his wife, Sharrie, offers me a cup of coffee (number 33 of the trip) and sits in an adjacent room to knit. A photo of their ten grandkids sits on the mantle, and on top of a coffee table is a lit candle and an open Bible.

It takes a bit for the old man to warm up to me, but once we get into baseball, his eyes come alive.

"I played at the University of Oklahoma," he tells me proudly. "And I had a chance to sign with Boston when I was a junior. This was before the draft and everything. Then I broke my leg sliding into home plate in Nebraska. That took care of that."

Like so many other men who devote their lives to coaching, Bob was a player first, one who had exceptional talent and promise but who never made it. His own dreams dashed, he's lived vicariously through the feats of his pupils.

"My grandfather established Camargo in 1911. He started First Bank here," he says.

"Is Camargo incorporated?" I ask.

"Oh yeah, but it's still just a town. My granddad was mayor, then my dad was mayor, then I was mayor for thirty-seven years, and my youngest son, Mark's the mayor now."

"Is it an elected position?" I ask, curious how a hundred-year political dynasty came to be.

"No, I don't think it's ever been voted on," he replies.

Wait, what?? I think.

"It's sort of unofficial?" I wonder aloud.

"Yeah."

"There's no government in a formal way?" I'm trying to clarify, so confused.

"You've got a mayor and two to three council members and that's it. They run the whole thing."

I give up trying to figure this out, and Bob doesn't offer any further elaboration.

"You pretty much know every person who lives in Camargo, right?" I ask.

"We-ell," he begins, "I did for a long time, but there's been some migrants who have moved in who I don't particularly know. At one time I could have told you everybody in town."

Everything changes, no matter how slowly.

"How did you discover Don?" I ask.

"I went to a Little League game over in Leedey. He was maybe thirteen. He knew nothing about pitching, but he had a tremendously free arm. He could throw. So I told him to come over to the house."

Bob started at the very beginning, lesson after lesson, hour after hour, starting with a tennis ball and working up to a baseball. While Don's real dad, Marion, was always off in the oil fields, Bob picked up the slack.

Don was a quick study but was slow to develop physically. Some of Bob's players asked why he kept trotting the lefty out there when he couldn't throw that hard, and Bob would just stick to his instincts. Don's arm was just so *loose*. When Don went off to Seminole Junior College he was five feet, eleven inches tall; when he came back a year later he had shot up to six feet, three inches and had gained thirty pounds of power.

"His fastball went from about seventy-five to ninety-three in that one year," Bob says.

"What gave you such faith in this kid?" I ask.

"We'd have practices up in Woodward in the afternoon. We'd go up there at four, work out for two hours, and then come back here. Within thirty minutes he was over behind the gym throwing. Two more hours of throwing after practice."

Don knew his destiny. He would tell anyone who would listen that he was going to be a professional ballplayer when he grew up. They would laugh, and he would grab a ball and keep throwing.

Bob leads me outside to his car for a driving tour. Even creeping along at five miles per hour, we cover the entire town in eight minutes. I ride shotgun, trying to avoid the various splatters of tobacco juice on the upholstery while he grabs his flip phone and an empty cup, stuffing a wad of tobacco below his lip.

"You can't be a good baseball man if you don't have some chew," he says.

The tour consists of pointing out where things *used* to be—that's the old abandoned elementary school over there (closed in the mideighties); there's the old café, the old theater, the old grocery store. All that's left is Jack's Backhoe Service, the bank, and a Blackhawk Quik Stop. And the grain elevator, the main attraction to Bob's grandkids.

I thank him for the tour and his time.

"When you see Don, tell him that his bed is waiting for him," Bob says, turning me loose on Camargo.

I park by the old elementary school to take some pictures and start wandering, fully aware that word has probably spread of a stranger carrying a notebook and driving a car with California plates. *Is he a cop?* is probably the rumor.

I walk over to a house where two men and a woman are hanging out on the porch watching me, with four kids running around playing. They're sitting on an aluminum bench, the ground a simple slab of concrete. It's a Friday morning at 11:00 a.m.

"Hi, I'm Brad Balukjian. I'm writing a book about Don Carman," I say, putting their law enforcement fears to rest and then explaining the premise of the book. They instantly relax and invite me to sit.

"One of Don's cousins lives over there," the woman says, pointing down the street.

She's youngish, with freckles and green eyes. She takes a drag of her cigarette and says, "I saw those California tags and said, 'Please let it be someone I know.'" She grew up in Vacaville, an hour north of Oakland, but moved to Camargo to get away from all the people. One of the men, with a narrow face and a "Born to Hunt, Forced to Work" T-shirt, tells me about how great the town's Fourth of July celebration will be tomorrow.

"You have to work pretty hard to get a DUI in Camargo," he says. "But I did," cracking everyone up.

"What do people do here?" I ask.

"Farm, work in the oil fields, crystal meth," the woman replies. "I like to just sit on the porch here and watch all the drug deals go down."

The other man, pot-bellied and unshaven, tells me he's originally from Tulsa and shares his law enforcement story with me.

"I was driving through town looking to see if I could spot some deer. Usually I'll have a beer in my hand, but this time I had water. I was driving with my son in the back, and he was throwing poppers out of the window, and one of them hit a cop car," he says, eliciting another chorus of laughs.

I excuse myself ("got to get back on the road!") and drive back toward Bob's house to see the old Carman homestead. All that remains is a small knoll overgrown with weeds and some dead branches. I wade into the brush, a thicket of locusts suddenly emerging and hopping about, powerful hind legs vaulting them onto my body. There's no trace of the two-bedroom home in which Marion and Betty crammed eight kids, six boys in one room and two girls in the other. No sign of the Carman boys' endless days spent throwing rocks at coffee cans, too poor to get proper equipment. Buried deep in the soil beneath my feet are the roots of a Major Leaguer's life, sealed off, an unspoken mix of hope and anguish. Standing here, I feel a deep sense of melancholy; I sense there is more to the Carman story than I have heard, but what that is I don't exactly know.

In a few days, after I get to Naples, I have a feeling I will find out.

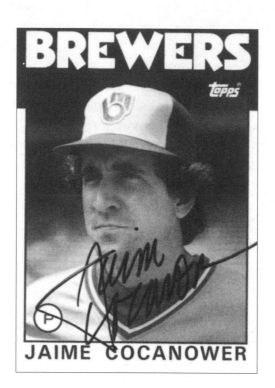

BREWERS

JAIME COCANOWER

8

THE BATTERY

You know it's just a game, right?
—*Gini Cocanower*

Days 16–17
July 4–5, 2015
Miles driven: 3,721
Cups of coffee: 35
Camargo OK to Lowell AR

"Dear Abby, I'm having some trouble with _____ and would like your advice," reads the prompt in the next round of Cards Against Humanity.

My teammate, Dale, and I glance at our hand of cards, considering our options to best fill in the blank and prove our comic chops: "growing a pair," "a hot mess," "riding off into the sunset," "giving 100 percent," "eugenics," "the token minority," "the Big Bang," "Barack Obama," "Mecha-Hitler," and "pixelated bukkake." This round is winner takes all, and my chest is already wheezy from laughing so hard. I pull at the corner of the bukkake card and raise my eyebrows at Dale, a polite man in his sixties, who lets out a laugh. I am 97 percent sure he has no idea what bukkake is. I am not about to explain it.

Across the kitchen table sits a former Major Leaguer whose own card brought me here to the northwestern corner of Arkansas. He is the most physically imposing of the players I've met so far, six feet four, with a barrel chest, but his soft tone belies his physicality, like a bear who never learned to growl. His once-raven-black hair has turned grayish white and is cut back above his ears; his soft, Smurf-blue eyes are close-set and crested by bushy eyebrows like two fuzzy caterpillars. He's dressed for the occasion, wearing a short-sleeved USA shirt, sandals, and red-white-and-blue shorts, ready for the Fourth of July fireworks that will follow shortly. He has the most unique yet least recognizable name in the Wax Pack: Jaime (pronounced "Hi-Me") Cocanower.

His wife, Gini, a blond spark plug from Little Rock, is also at the table but paired with someone else for the game. Her laugh, which manages to be both commanding and soothing, ricochets around the room with every new card she reads.

I throw our bukkake card facedown into the pile, and the host reads each group's submission out loud one by one, filling in the blank and bringing tears to our eyes with laughter.

"Dear Abby, I'm having trouble with *when you fart and a little bit comes out* and would like your advice" is the winner, crowning Gini's team as champions. She raises both fists in the air and laughs again, rubbing it in Jaime's face. He smiles quietly, a sheepish grin that manages to express both deep love and abiding pride in his wife of thirty-five years.

We encore to the spacious wood-paneled deck high above the water, looking out on Beaver Lake in the heart of Ozark country. I lean back in my chair and breathe in the sweet scent of damp earth whisking off the lake's surface. A shower of green, purple, and red fireworks blast into the air, raining down with staccato explosions.

I'm having the time of my life, surrounded by complete strangers. Lifting weights with Randy Ready, watching kung fu with Garry Templeton, and now playing Cards Against Humanity with Jaime Cocanower—these are the unexpected thrills that have made this trip such a pleasant surprise. But like I'm discovering with so many of these men, there's more to Jaime's story than meets the eye.

=

Of the nine positions on a baseball team, one stands apart: the starting pitcher. While everyone else plays every day, the starter trots out every five, meaning he may only play thirty to thirty-five times all season. Baseball is already a game about the spaces in between, and for the starting pitcher, those spaces are even longer. If a hitter goes 0-4 with four strikeouts, he can come back the next day to avenge them; if a starting pitcher gets roughed up, he's got four days to stew. And stewing is not good for Jaime Cocanower.

"Baseball was very frustrating," he tells me, standing in front of a wall-paper display of row after row of pink cows on a yellow background. "I don't look back on it as my fondest memories of life. I did have quite a bit of talent, but I was just not able to put it all together." He speaks slowly and haltingly, ending his sentences with an allergy-induced sniffle.

We're visiting the *Warhol's Nature* exhibit at the Crystal Bridges Museum of American Art, a beautifully landscaped series of glass-and-wood pavilions in Bentonville, Arkansas. The brainchild of Walmart heiress Alice Walton, the museum opened in 2011 with free admission for all. It turns out Andy Warhol not only had an interest in consumerism and popular culture but also took on the natural world, from his early days as a commercial artist to his later years painting plants and animals. I have no idea what pink cows on a yellow background symbolize, but they have all of Warhol's customary panache.

"I kind of have admiration for those guys that get their heads beat in one day, and the next day they're talking on TV like they've never given up a hit," Jaime says.

This is a first. Every other Wax Packer so far excelled at processing that daily failure, taking it head-on and moving forward. And while they all had low moments, none would sum up their overall baseball experience with a word like "frustrating." They are still connected to the game in some way, and those who are out (Tempy, Ready) are chomping to get back in. But not Jaime.

Then again, Jaime's origins story is anything but typical. He was born in Puerto Rico, the son of missionaries who moved the family often throughout his childhood—Costa Rica, then Peru, a year in Indianapolis, and finally Panama when Jaime was twelve. Jaime inherited his father's size and athleticism, and in baseball-crazed Panama, he thrived.

"What is the background of the name Cocanower?" I ask quietly, hoping to not disturb the other patrons as we move along to Warhol's *Flowers* series from the 1960s. We stand side by side, a comfortable viewing distance away from the paintings, talking in parallel.

"It's German. My dad's German, my mom's family is Swiss. My dad grew up Mennonite in northern Indiana," he replies. "I was one of five kids, and I was always trying to please my parents."

Jaime is a pleaser. While the rest of the Wax Packers took a "see you when I see you" attitude toward my visit, Jaime bent over backward preparing for my arrival, with multiple texts and emails, confirmations, and invitations. He even had done research on *me*.

"I've been reading your blog," he said when he first picked me up at my Super 8 motel. "And your Rate My Professors page. Pretty good."

He attended Balboa High School, located in the Panama Canal Zone, an American-run school for kids of parents who worked on the canal or for the military. It was demanding—in his senior year, three of his teachers had PhDs. He began pitching in the ninth grade, and his potential was obvious as a big, strong kid with a live arm. But then the injury bug (which would plague his entire career) struck, and surgery to remove bone chips from his elbow ended his high school pitching career.

Jaime's parents took great pride in their kids' education—all five graduated from college—and when the time came Jaime moved to the States to attend Baylor University in Waco, Texas. In his freshman year he walked onto the baseball team, and by his sophomore campaign he was throwing gas in the College World Series and catching the attention of Major League scouts. By the end of his junior year he was a hot commodity, with thirteen Major League teams showing interest.

We stroll the gallery, occasionally pausing to examine a painting in more detail. Although he's only a few inches taller, I feel like Jaime towers over me in his black button-down dress shirt, his hands stuffed into his pockets.

"How did you end up getting signed?" I ask, pretending to pay attention to a purple-and-orange butterfly.

"Major League Baseball sent an off-duty FBI agent to my apartment to do reconnaissance. He had this questionnaire and said, 'We're trying to figure out if you have to go through the draft.' Turns out Puerto Ricans don't go through the draft. They're free agents."

It all checked out: because Jaime was born abroad, he was allowed to sign with any team whenever he chose. The Toronto Blue Jays, a recent expansion team hungry for talent, were the highest bidder, offering him $50,000 to sign. The Milwaukee Brewers, on the other hand, came in at $35,000 but promised to take their time in grooming him, making sure that he was healthy before he started pitching. Most players would go to the highest bidder, but Jaime was not most players.

He signed with the Brewers.

He got his shoulder fixed (turned out he had a torn rotator cuff and bone spurs from overuse at Baylor) and went back to school for the fall of his senior year, majoring in accounting. Playing with spreadsheets may have been boring, but it was safe and secure—he could control the numbers, knowing that they wouldn't suddenly change on him, the perfect antidote to his struggles on the mound, where he could not harness his own power. He was an unbroken stallion, a wild fastball pitcher without a second gear. Most pitchers can throw a fastball straight on command; Jaime would try to will the ball straight, and still it would hook.

"Control was something that I could never master," he says.

He had flashes of greatness: in his second season in the Minor Leagues, he was named California League MVP, going 17-5 with a 2.18 ERA. When he got called up to the Majors for the first time in 1983 along with Randy Ready ("I do remember that!" he tells me when I mention Randy's story of hiding out together during a tornado), he impressed the brass with some quality starts, so much so that he made the starting rotation in 1984. But he was always treading water.

For most of his four years with the Brewers he rode the yo-yo, shipping back and forth between Milwaukee and the Minor Leagues. Injuries and wildness were his undoing; at one point in 1986 manager George Bamberger even arranged for him to see a hypnotist.

"He tried to get me to wear headphones in the dugout and listen to that stuff during the game. I was like, I can't be doing that," Jaime says.

By 1987 he was out of the game, having compiled a forgettable 16-25 record, the shortest career of any of the Wax Packers. He enjoyed the sport itself but not the culture around it. He never got comfortable. Jaime Cocanower was too smart, too timid, too *nice* for baseball.

But where he slumped in baseball, he starred in life. Done at age thirty, he had two things going for him: a college degree and Gini.

===

The relationship between pitcher and catcher is a sacred one. They are symbiotic organisms, so reliant on each other that in baseball parlance they are collectively referred to as "the battery." The catcher has the more thankless job, squatting down and getting up hundreds of times over the course of the game, but he is also the brains of the operation. It is the catcher who calls for each pitch, indicating his choice through an elaborate series of hand gestures directly in front of his crotch as he squats out of view of the batter. For the uninitiated, the twenty to thirty seconds between each pitch are a dreadful lull in the action, but for baseball's devout, this abeyance holds the true beauty of the game, the chess match between the battery and the batter. For example, if the count is two balls and one strike, the pitch called will be very different from what it would be if the count is one ball and two strikes; if there are runners on base, things get even more complicated. While the pitcher has veto power (which he indicates by shaking his head vigorously), his main job is to simply execute. If the battery consists of dance partners, the catcher is leading.

Gini's been catching Jaime for thirty-five years. They met at Baylor on a blind date, a pledge task for Jaime's Sig Ep fraternity. He was a sophomore and she was a freshman from Little Rock, and he was told to meet her in the lobby of her dorm when she came home from class. Their recollections of that first meeting differ: "When I saw her, I said, 'I'm going to marry her,'" Jaime says; according to Gini: "I had just taken a test, and I was dating all these preministry students at the time. I wasn't gonna date just one person until I was engaged. You have to also understand, I wasn't sleeping with any of them. So we didn't go out for a while." This is vintage Gini—honesty for days, a completely open book, unapologetic. When I was having trouble finding Jaime in the lead-up to the trip, I Googled around and found a reference to Gini on the website for Bentonville High School, where she is an AP computer science teacher. I wrote her an email explaining the project and received the following response, written to Jaime with me cc'd:

Jaime,

This is what comes of answering fan mail. ;). I opened and read Dr. Balukjian's email in the hopes that he was a computer science Professor and I could parlay your cooperation into future admissions to Berkeley for my students. It turns out he is interested in bugs of the biological variety not the digital variety.

In any case, he sounds nice (with stalker tendencies) and you should reply to him.

Gini

Being a ballplayer's wife was hard, especially when you're as independent and smart as Gini. She never loved the game, but she deeply respected her husband's commitment to it, so much so that she signed on for the gypsy life (albeit with reservations) when they got married in December 1979. Following her graduation from Baylor, they uprooted themselves to Stockton, California, a cow town over an hour inland from the coast, more like Visalia than San Francisco. From Stockton to Vancouver to Puerto Rico to El Paso back to Vancouver to Milwaukee back again to Vancouver back to Milwaukee to Beloit to Little Rock to Albuquerque, Gini hung in there, holding down the fort. When the kids got older, she went back to school for her master's in education. And unlike most wives, she educated herself on the business side of the game, understanding contracts and labor law and the tension between union and management. While Jaime tended to be laid-back about such things, Gini was wife/lawyer/advocate all rolled into one.

"You have to remember that we wanted them all to die," Gini says, seated next to Jaime on a plush brown sofa in the tastefully decorated living room of their home on Beaver Lake ("our retirement home," Jaime says, even though they're two years out from retirement).

"That's a little extreme," I reply, sitting across from them.

"Okay, let me clarify: die slowly and painfully," she says.

The "them" is the Brewers' management, and Gini excoriates them as only she can, with humorous hyperbole.

"They just treated people so poorly," she adds. It's a refrain I'll hear from several of the Wax Packers: management's tendency to make false promises. *We're going to call you back up to the Majors! This is just temporary. We've got a place for you.* But the reality is that everyone is expendable, and everyone's time is short. Players are chess pieces on a board, statistical amalgamations. Gini, who has devoted her career to building people up through teaching, can't stand the ruthless nature of professional sports.

"Ray Poitevint [the Brewers' director of player procurement], what a jerk. The first time I met him, shortly after Jaime signed, was in Phoenix. He saw my engagement ring and said something like 'Who paid for your trip to come here?' or something incredibly rude. And I thought, 'You don't even know me.'"

The Cocanowers moved here to Lowell from Conway (outside Little Rock) nine years ago and can't wait to enjoy the spoils of lakefront retirement—the eighteen-foot speedboat is already in the water, and a pontoon party boat isn't far off. Their kids are grown and successful: their daughter, Blair, is a CPA and recently got married, and their son, Whit, is about to start as a clerk for a judge at the U.S. Tax Court in Washington DC. The house is huge and immaculate, nestled into the hillside shore of the lake. Early in their marriage, Gini reminded Jaime to keep his long game in mind: "She would always say there's a lot more CPAs living in the nice neighborhood in Little Rock than former baseball players," Jaime says.

While he dreamed of making it to the big leagues, Jaime was always strategic about his plan. He had twenty-eight units left at Baylor when he signed with the Brewers, went back to school that fall to finish most of them, and then graduated via correspondence course. When he was still in the Minors, he began working at KPMG in the winters as a tax accountant; behind a desk, nose buried in ledgers, Jaime could be in control.

In 1987, while toiling for the Dodgers' Triple-A team in Albuquerque, he knew it was time to wind down.

"I called the managing partner at KPMG and said, 'You told me when I wanted to get out of baseball you would have a spot for me. Well, I'm ready,'" Jaime says.

After Albuquerque ended up winning the championship, Jaime flew home and traded his cleats for a pair of dress shoes.

"I threw my stuff in my Brewers bag and still haven't unpacked it."

Gini was thrilled—she had her husband back full-time. His years in the game had put a strain on the marriage. I share what I've learned from Rance, Boomer, and Randy about divorce and ask, "What kept you guys together?"

"Poverty. Mainly we couldn't afford to get a divorce," Gini says, making Jaime laugh. Then she turns more serious: "Some of the people you're gonna meet today, we've been friends with since we very first got married. Those were our friends from church who have b en with us through thick and thin," she says, touching Jaime lightly on the shoulder.

"It was tough. We had our times when you would have thought we could easily have gotten divorced. But we ultimately found our commitment to each other was stronger than anything else," Jaime says, his voice growing soft.

"Did you see the strain on other couples?" I ask.

"Yeah, because the guys were all sleeping around," Gini replies. Baseball players, more than athletes in any other sport, are known to be dogs. I think back to Rance describing his teammates as "kids in a candy store" and his ex-wife's suspicions that he had had an affair.

"Between that and being away, the celebrity must go to their heads," I offer.

"Yeah, well, that was never a problem for us," Gini cracks, smiling at Jaime. They form the perfect battery, finishing each other's sentences, laughing and then laughing harder. She leans over and whispers in his ear, reminding me of a meeting on the mound where the pitcher and catcher discuss strategy while covering their mouths with their gloves, stymying potential lip readers from the opposition.

The company is arriving soon to ring in America's 239th birthday, and there's pork shoulder to smoke and dips to put out and beer to chill. Gini gets up to start putting out the spread. "If you're at my house and you're hungry or sober, it's your own fault," she tells me.

⸗

"Where's Jaime?" I ask Dale, one of the guests and my Cards Against Humanity teammate, when I get back from running an errand. Short on booze, the gang had sent me out for reinforcements, during which I came across my first *drive-thru liquor store*. Yes, in Arkansas this is a thing.

"Check downstairs," he says.

I walk downstairs to Jaime's man cave past the framed lineup cards and ball from his first Major League win (September 24, 1983, versus the Orioles) and find him sitting on the couch in a giant home theater, an entire wall taken up by a screen.

"I just struck out Eddie Murray!" he yelps as I sit down. A few years back Gini had several old VHS recordings of his games transferred to DVD, and today, for the first time, Jaime has popped one in. Fifty-eight-year-old Jaime watches twenty-seven-year-old Jaime stalk the mound in his powder-blue Brewers jersey, his ritual of nervous tics and compulsions on display between pitches: tug hat, wipe nose, wipe hand on sleeve, rub ball, etc. It's from June 1984, one of his better games, one of the days when he was locked in and could quiet the voice of self-doubt in his head. I watch his catcher, Jim Sundberg, come to the mound for a visit, and I ask Jaime something I've always been curious about: "What is the catcher saying to you?" Does he reveal an elaborate strategy for the next hitter, a sequence of pitches based on voluminous scouting reports designed to exploit a weakness? I've spent many games trying to read lips, burning with curiosity over the wisdom that must be imparted in these sacred time-outs.

"Usually he said, 'C'mon!'" Jaime replies.

I am devastated.

We watch a few more innings of Jaime's prime in relative silence, enjoying the respite from being social. We both enjoy the company of others but prize our solitude as well. Being on grill duty gives him an easy excuse to duck out whenever he tires of the conversation—*got to check on the meat!* Watching baseball on the Fourth of July in the middle of the country with an ex–Major League baseball player feels like living the childhood fantasy of every boy who has ever collected baseball cards.

And then the unexpected. This quiet, borderline-shy elite former athlete turns to me and says over the whir of air-conditioning, "This December will be thirty-six years I've been married to Gini. Four and a half years ago she was diagnosed with inflammatory breast cancer."

He twirls his wedding ring while he talks, his voice steady and earnest. "Only 2 percent of breast cancer is inflammatory. It's the worst. Ten years ago, 40 percent would die in five years. But we've made a lot of progress."

My stomach tightens, and I look away toward the floor. No, no. That's just not right, not fair. Not with these people, not this couple that lives so fully and honestly.

I find my voice: "Did she have surgery?"

"Yeah, she had a mastectomy. After she was diagnosed one of the things they figured out is that the order of the treatments is a big deal. She had chemo, and then a drug called Herceptin, then a third drug. She did that for eight months and then the surgery and the radiation down in Houston. She's clean. Every six months she has a checkup. Next year she starts going once a year."

I'm sure he has said all this a thousand times to dozens of people in the same matter-of-fact tone. But then he continues in a different vein: "It metastasizes in the brain. We're just . . ." He pauses. "It was really tough, and at the same time it gave me an opportunity to show her how I felt about her. I'd say that's probably my main drive today is keeping her . . ." His voice trails off again.

He takes a moment, resets. "She's awesome, she's smart, she teaches, she loves to teach and is a really good teacher. I read some of the stuff on your teaching website. Anyway, she teaches programming and AP computer science. All electives, and she has probably 85 percent boys, and they all have Asperger's."

He catches his breath.

Finally, finally Jaime is allowed to be out of control.

The words and the love spill out, his emotions wild and running ahead of his brain, and it's all good, it's great, actually. He may be a pitcher, but he knows a pitcher is only as good as his battery mate, and with apologies to Jim Sundberg, there's none better than Gini.

"Got to check on the meat!" he announces, springing to his feet and out of the room.

I sit alone in the darkness of the theater, holding on to the emotion, smiling faintly. I've never been a big fan of the Fourth of July—like New Year's Eve, there's too much hype, too many expectations—but I know this is one I will never forget. I get up and walk upstairs, ready to rejoin the party.

═

The next morning when I say good-bye to Jaime and Gini, I feel like I'm leaving family. But no sooner am I back on the road than dread creeps in. I know what's coming next, and I don't like it. I'm going to have to do something that I hate and that I'm not particularly good at: I'm going to have to lie.

9

CHASING CARLTON

Carlton Fisk never won any nice guy awards.
—*Doug Wilson, author of* Pudge:
The Biography of Carlton Fisk

Days 18–20
July 6–8, 2015
Miles driven: 5,013
Cups of coffee: 46
Lowell AR to Sarasota FL

OCTOBER 21, 1975

Carlton is used to this.

As he saunters to home plate with his distinctly erect posture, shoulders square and chin out, he knows he can win this game. Nearly forty thousand hoarse Fenway Park faithful pray his bat will end their agony and let them once again exhale. It's the bottom of the twelfth inning of Game Six of the World Series between the Boston Red Sox and the Cincinnati Reds, tie score. All of the gut checks, the forks in the road where Carlton kept on the path of *most* resistance, refusing to quit—dropping out of the University of New Hampshire after his freshman year; four years in the Minors working off-seasons as a clerk in a clothing store and reporting for duty once a month in the Army Reserve; the shredded knee last season when doctors questioned whether he'd ever be limp-free again, let alone play baseball—were necessary to arrive here, with 75.9 million people (out of a possible 216 million) around the country watching on television, studying every cloud of breath snorted into the crisp autumn air.

Long before he was the star catcher of the Boston Red Sox, he was one of only forty-two in his graduating class at Charlestown High School, a tiny outpost in New Hampshire along the Connecticut River. The second oldest of six kids, Carlton learned the value of hard work from a young age under the strict and demanding eyes of his parents, Cecil and Leona. If the house and yard work didn't get done, down came the switch that was kept above the back door.

With the frigid weather keeping the season so short, baseball was a mere diversion from Carlton's true passion, basketball, in which he excelled, leading his high school to the semifinals of the state championship in 1965, his senior year. Despite a heroic effort in which he scored forty points and pulled down thirty-six rebounds, Charlestown High lost by two points to rival Hopkington. Following the game, the first thing that Cecil said to him was, "You missed four free throws."

It was typical Cecil. Whatever Carlton did, it was never enough.

"I never got a pat on the back," Carlton would say years later.[1]

But now as he stands in the batter's box in the wee hours of the morning (12:33 a.m. to be exact) and peers out at Reds pitcher Pat Darcy, his back doesn't need any pats—it's been carrying the Red Sox since his return in late June. Weighing twelve pounds at birth, he had been nicknamed "Pudge" from an early age, but he is anything but soft. He thrives on the responsibility, relishes the individualistic nature of baseball, a pseudo–team sport really, with its one-on-one duels between pitcher and batter. Carlton enjoys being alone because he can control the outcome, not having to worry about anyone else doing their part.

He begins his ritual, patting the dirt with his cleats, reaching up to tug his jersey above his right shoulder with his left hand, jerking both arms back twice in a violent stretch, opening up that back as wide as an aircraft carrier. Now he reaches the bat completely over and behind his head, a yogic salutation to the baseball gods. He shakes his head violently for just a second, his cherubic cheeks rattling at spasm speed, fighting the bite of October. He taps the plate once with the bat, then cocks it behind his head, locked and loaded. Wasting no time, Darcy rocks and throws a fastball over the plate but eye-level, for ball 1. Carlton steps out briefly and takes a deep breath, his chest visibly rising and falling.

Darcy delivers the second pitch, an inside sinker, and Carlton strides forward, planting his right foot forward, his left knee bent low, jerking the ball high with an uppercut swing. It's clearly got the distance, but will it stay fair? He takes a step toward first base, watching the ball sail, then takes another lateral hop, and then, in what will become one of the most iconic images in sports television history, he waves both arms to the right once, twice, three times, willing the ball to stay fair, and when he sees it collide with the top of the foul pole to signify a home run, he jumps straight up, both arms extended toward the sky. He jogs around the bases, fans pouring onto the field like a spilled drink, disappearing into a mass of humanity by the Red Sox dugout. While the Red Sox will go on to lose Game Seven and the World Series (the Curse of the Bambino remaining intact), this moment delivers Carlton into baseball providence.

But it isn't *just* Game Six or *just* extra innings of the World Series—this game will age so well (considered by many to be the Greatest of All Time) because of its historical context and the accidental shot of Fisk waving the ball fair. The last several World Series were snoozers, football is growing in popularity and threatening baseball's grip on being the National Pastime, and there is widespread acrimony between the owners and players that has fans calling them all greedy. But the 1975 World Series brings the joy back, delivering close, suspenseful games between two franchises with passionate fan bases. The image of Fisk's reaction is pure luck. Cameraman Louis Gerard is stationed behind the Green Monster (Fenway Park's iconic left-field wall) shooting through a hole in the scoreboard and has been told to follow the ball if Fisk hits it, as is the custom. But right before Fisk launches the bomb, a rat scurries onto Gerard's leg, forcing him to keep the camera trained on home plate and landing the footage of Fisk. The clip forever changes the presentation of sports on TV (it will earn Gerard an Emmy) as editors and executives realize the gold they have in following the players' expressions and reactions, not just the action itself.

Carlton's life will never be the same.

—

For the next 1,216 miles, I sweat. Not just tingles-at-the-edge-of-my-hairline sweat, but rivulets running down my sideburns and dripping onto my lap, sweat that works like gel each time I reach up with both hands to slick my hair back. I unstick one butt cheek and then the other from the seat of the Accord, then reach down to separate my boxers from the skin of my butt cheeks themselves, the damp fabric suddenly cool when I sit back down again.

I'm not just sweating because I'm driving through oppressive heat in the heart of July. I am also nervous that I'm about to fail. When I missed Gary Pettis back in Houston, he had a reasonable alibi—it's midseason, he's with a Major League club, and his boss had issued a gag order. But with Carlton Fisk I'm the nerd in high school asking the head cheerleader to the prom and getting flat-out rejected.

Passing through the Deep South exposes the tortured id of America. While I ruminate on Carlton, playing out wildly fantastic scenarios that end with me getting arrested for trespassing or stalking, a gallery of billboards streams by, alternating salvation and sex: *He's coming*, then *New Fleshlights!*, followed by *Evolution is a Lie* and *Exit Now! Spa!*, a tug of war between our chaste and depraved selves. I suddenly long for the banal roadside of San Diego with its ads for George Lopez shows and Kansas concerts.

From the moment I unsheathed his half snarl from the Wax Pack, I knew Fisk would be a problem. The bigger the player, the bigger the ego. One of the greatest catchers of all time and a bona fide Red Sox hero, Fisk reached a level of celebrity that has kept him always in demand. While Jaime Cocanower and Randy Ready are now just two guys on the street, Carlton Fisk never stopped being *Carlton Fisk*. My initial approach to contacting him before the trip was the same as it was for everyone else: I snail-mailed a letter of introduction to his two addresses on file, one in New Lenox, Illinois, the other in Bradenton, Florida. When that led to radio silence, I went through the proper channel of finding his agent, Kim (Fisk is the only Wax Packer to still need one), to whom I dashed off an email asking for Fisk's cooperation. Her initial response was encouraging, asking how much time I would need and even suggesting some possible dates in late July when we would both be in the New England area. She said she would be with him in person soon and would approach him with the idea.

A week later, her tone had changed: "Thank you for your interest in Carlton. Unfortunately he is going to pass at this time," she wrote. I closed my email, swore so loudly that my landlord asked if everything was okay, and knew at that moment that I was going to have to go rogue.

I didn't take it personally. When the MLB Network recently shot an entire documentary on Game Six of the 1975 World Series, hosted by Bob Costas, Carlton declined to participate. (Who rejects Bob Costas?) In a rare interview at the end of his career, he told writer Pat Jordan, "Why the fuck should I tell them?" when Jordan asked how he felt about the media wanting to know more about his life. When journalist Doug Wilson decided to write an entire book about Carlton, *the* definitive biography, Carlton once again passed even when his brother Calvin, sister Janet, and ninety-seven-year-old mother, Leona, were happy to cooperate. "Carlton Fisk never won any nice guy awards," Wilson wrote in the concluding chapter of his book, adding, "As far as anyone knows, he never tried out for one."[2]

He was known as private, prideful, and reclusive, his personality matching the salty New Hampshire woods he had emerged from. Players respected him for his intensity and old-school defense of the game's traditions (he memorably yelled at Deion Sanders when he didn't run out a pop-up) but kept at a distance.

"Stoic and in control, he spoke what he believed, said what needed to be said and little else. He was Calvin Coolidge in John Wayne's body," wrote Wilson.[3] While never the social chair in the clubhouse, he was immensely popular with fans in blue-collar Boston; in his rookie season, he was already receiving more fan mail than any of his teammates, including legends like Carl Yastrzemski.

But throughout his career, and it was a *long* career—twenty-seven years in pro ball, twenty-four of those in the Major Leagues, the story of Carlton is one of longing for acceptance and of pride. He did things that no other catcher in history had ever done, things that enshrined him in the Hall of Fame in 2000. He caught more games, hit more home runs, probably got in more shouting matches with opponents and teammates who didn't play the game "the right way." He could talk the talk and walk the walk (shoulders square and chin out). But no matter how many games he caught, how many home runs he hit, it was never enough. He never felt appreciated enough, never respected enough. He did have legitimate gripes: every time his contract expired with the Red Sox and later the Chicago White Sox, management seemed to lowball him. In his later years, it became an absurd recurring dance, with the White Sox thinking he was through and Carlton defying time, doubling his effort in the gym and tripling his discipline to extend his career. The very end says it all. In 1993, at age forty-five, everyone but Carlton knew it was time. The White Sox kept him on the team long enough to break Bob Boone's record for most games caught, 2,225, even holding a special ceremony to commemorate the night, and then a week later delivered the call that every athlete fears most—we're letting you go. Carlton was sad and furious—*how can they treat people like this?* But reality bites: he was hitting .189 and could no longer throw out base stealers.

Unlike Rance Mulliniks and Randy Ready, who knew when their time was up and graciously volunteered to step down, Carlton didn't want to go. In a rare moment of vulnerability during that final season, he told *Men's Journal,* "I'm afraid to leave the game because I'm afraid there's nothing out there for me. I have no burning desire to do anything else. Baseball has been so much of my life. Will anything else be that rewarding?"[4]

He was forty-five, but in many ways he was still that twelve-year-old back in Charlestown, he and his five siblings always fighting for the love and respect of his father, Cecil, and never getting it. In his Hall of Fame speech in 2000, the pain surfaced. He first thanked his mom, Leona, saying, "She was the warmth in our family. She was the warmth and the comfort and the love. And we wouldn't have made it without her." Then he paused, pivoting to his father, thirty-two minutes into a thirty-seven-minute speech. He kept his eyes low, moving his arm and leg back and forth, gripping the podium and trying to stay in control. He exhaled, making a shallow sound, then said, "You know, sometimes good didn't seem to be good enough." Long pause. The crowd of twenty-five thousand assembled on a grassy knoll in Cooperstown, New York, waited silently. "But . . ." Another long pause as he folded his handkerchief, another shallow breath, then a small sniffle. "I always wanted you to be proud of me, Dad. Sometimes, just because you could have done better doesn't mean you've done badly. Through the years you always made sure that people knew that I was your son and I'm proud of that. But this weekend, guess what, you're Carlton's dad."

In his twenty-two years of retirement, Carlton has largely remained a recluse. Unlike every other Wax Packer I've met so far besides Jaime, he never went back to the game despite many opportunities (other than a stint as a goodwill ambassador for the White Sox and Red Sox). Now sixty-seven, he will show up now and again for a paid autograph appearance and is active in charity work with his wife, Linda, but the only recent news item I find in my research is a story from 2012 that states that he was charged with DUI after police found him asleep in his truck in a cornfield in New Lenox, Illinois, with an open bottle of vodka on the floor. Never one to shirk responsibility, he pleaded guilty to the misdemeanor charge and accepted his consequences, retreating back into seclusion.

So where are you, Carlton, and what are you so afraid of?

═

What do you do when someone you're writing about doesn't want to talk to you?

I've hunkered down for a couple nights in the West Florida city of Tampa, within striking distance of Carlton's home in Bradenton. While many write off Florida as a converted swamp that's home to Disney World, it's a remarkably complex state, a mash-up of old South, northeastern snowbirds, and Latinx immigrants. Following a visit to the Tampa Bay History Center, I sip on a strawberry lemonade at Ruby Tuesday and look at a map, spotting Bradenton sixty miles to the south. I have an address for Carlton's house from public records searches but imagine I won't get anywhere close to the front door. But I have another lead: I'm texting with a source, a sports agent whom we'll call Gene who's familiar with many of the athletes who frequent the area. Tampa's warm climate is ideal for grooming ballplayers, and it's no coincidence that Wade Boggs, Gary Sheffield, Wax Packer Doc Gooden (who now lives in

New York), and many others grew up here. Gene is familiar with these various celebrity personalities and is sympathetic to my conundrum.

"Carlton golfs almost every day at this private course called the Founders Club in Sarasota. He likes to drink after he plays; you can probably find him at the clubhouse bar," he types.

"Can I get onto the property?" I reply.

"You can ask for a tour of the club. You tell them that you are interested in buying a home there and would like to check out the golf course first," he says.

So that's it—to catch Carlton, I'm going to have to ambush him. But before that, I need to somehow convince the staff of one of West Florida's poshest real estate developments that I belong there to begin with.

Let me remind you that I'm currently eating my dinner at a Ruby Tuesday.

This could go very, very badly.

═

While I drive down the West Florida coast to Sarasota, my mind swirls. For the first time on the trip, I am truly scared. One of my long-standing OCD compulsions is being way too honest (my therapist Tom termed this "hyperscrupulosity," a fairly common type of OCD), and so lying to get to Carlton has my heart racing. One incident from childhood stands out. One day after school, I walked into our kitchen to find a glass broken on the floor and reported it to my mom. When she asked me if I knew what had happened, I told her that maybe I had broken it, potentially confessing to something I knew I hadn't done. The OCD brain can be a sinister thing.

Even if my ruse succeeds and I get to Carlton in the clubhouse bar, I have no clue what I'm going to say. *Thanks for blowing me off? Nice home run? Can you pass me a coaster?*

A bloom of bright pink flowers on the side of the freeway streaks by my window, and it hits me—orchids! In my research on Carlton, I stumbled across a surprising and odd fun fact: the Hall of Fame catcher also happens to be a devoted orchid collector. The more I think about it, the more it makes sense that he would find a passion for orchids.

They are among the most finicky of all cultivated plants, demanding constant attention from growers to keep environmental conditions just so. Only the most dedicated, disciplined horticulturists dare to enter the orchid trade. But Carlton is up to the challenge, having expanded his collection to more than forty varieties and three hundred plants during his retirement.

Orchids, I decide, will be my entry point. A taxonomist myself (although of insects, not plants), I can bond with him over a common language—Latin—as I inquire about his favorite genera and species, talk shop about our favorite pollination techniques. I won't even bring up baseball.

I exit onto Fruitville Road, a wide, two-lane street lined with drive-in churches and the occasional strip club (more sin and salvation!), scanning for signs of the Founders Club. It's way too hot for coffee, yet I can't stop drinking it, somehow believing that the caffeine is going to make lying easier. I've got bullet points for my story—I'm a biology professor at UC Berkeley who's obsessed with golf and just really want a second home on the East Coast where I can get away and play. About 25 percent of that is true, which will hopefully make it slightly easier to pull off. The club's website has a page dedicated entirely to its dress code, which reads in that perfectly passive-aggressive tone, "It is expected that members and their guests will choose to dress in a fashion befitting the surroundings and atmosphere provided in the setting of The Founders Club." I've brought out the only semidressy attire I have on the trip, a seafoam green polo shirt and khakis, which I desperately hope are "befitting the surroundings." I look in my trunk, and beneath a pile of old towels I find a pair of golf shoes I had bought for a round of golf at my sister's wedding five years ago, the last time I saw them. The Founders Club features not just an eighteen-hole, Robert Trent Jones Jr. golf course; it also has custom-built London Bay homes scattered about its premises.

I see a sign for the club, turn in, and am immediately stopped at a gate.

"Welcome to the Founders Club!" says the immaculate attendant, his white-glove service perfected.

Here we go.

"Hi!" I say too excitedly. "I'm interested in seeing some of the homes at the club. Big golfer!"

I feel the sweat start to run down my back, which stirs up anxiety and makes me sweat more, my follicles tingling.

But he waves me in, telling me to park outside reception. I ease the Accord down the private road lined with palms and bright flourishes of ornamental plants, waving to groundskeepers. There is a single spot outside the reception building marked "Future Residents," which I pull into. I kill the ignition, check my face in the rearview mirror, swig the last drops of my coffee, and then catch a glimpse of my own backseat. I've become so used to spending time alone in the car, lost in my own thoughts, that I've forgotten what it looks like to an outsider: yesterday's McDonald's wrappers are strewn on the front seat, an empty coffee cup lies on the floor, the backseat is full of open Staples file boxes overflowing with printouts and old newspaper articles, and all of this is inside a thirteen-year-old Honda Accord with peeling paint on the driver's-side door.

Future resident? Not a chance.

I scramble to clean up the scene, stuffing the wrappers and coffee cups in the glove compartment, putting lids on boxes that have never been closed, generally doing the exact opposite of what someone who does not want to draw attention should do. By the time I get out of the car and approach the front door, an older woman elegantly dressed in an ankle-length dress has come out to greet me.

"Hi! Sorry, we don't normally come out and stare at people, but we were wondering if something was wrong," she says, shaking my hand.

I laugh a little too hard. "No, no, just getting some stuff in order," I reply. "I've heard a lot about your club and am interested in buying a home here."

"Of course!" she says, snapping back into professional mode. "Come inside, and I'll get you a sales associate."

Another of the office staff, a matronly woman with curly hair, brings me a bottle of water as I avail myself of the free chocolates sitting in a decorative dish on a coffee table.

A few minutes later I'm in one of the showrooms with Janelle, a shapely sales associate around my age who is trying to get a read on me.

"So you're a big golfer?" she asks as I try to avoid looking her square in the eyes, not wanting to reveal my lies. I settle my gaze somewhere on her forehead. It is a very nice forehead.

"Yeah, I love Florida. Come here all the time for the golf," I say with as big a smile as I can muster. "When I'm not teaching at UC Berkeley, that is."

God I'm bad at this.

"People out in California complain about the humidity back east, but I actually like it. That's why I want to have a place back here where I can come during the summers and relax," I add, unprompted.

I glance at the fees for a golf club membership here at "Sarasota's premier golf and country club community": a $25,000 one-time contribution, $11,950 in annual dues, and a $75 "capital fee."

The one-time contribution is about what I make in an entire year.

"What kind of square footage are you thinking about for the house?" Janelle asks, her soft brown eyes tugging me back from her forehead.

Fuck, how much square footage do homes even have?? I've been renting rooms my whole life.

Trying not to panic, I steal a glance at the display mounted behind her, looking for an approximate figure.

"I'm thinking three thousand, thirty-five hundred," I finally say, hoping my face looks less guilty than it feels.

She nods. "I think you really might like our Clara model," she says, directing me to a poster with details.

I scrutinize the floor plan, scrunching my eyebrows for effect, trying my best to look picky and elitist. The Clara appears to be one of the more modest styles of custom London Bay Homes built on this seven-hundred-acre forced imitation of Eden—only three bedrooms to go with the private pool and spa.

"Do you know what kind of granite you want for your kitchen countertops?" she asks.

Is there more than one kind? I want to reply.

While we chat, I think about how I am going to slip away to look for Carlton. It's about 11:00 a.m., and I figure he should be done with his round of golf (assuming he's here today) and at the clubhouse bar in an hour or so. My only chance is to somehow get away from Janelle for a bit, to be left on my own in this palace.

"So you want to buy here because you have a lot of friends in the area?" she asks, still digging.

"Yeah, I have some buddies in Tampa. Came down here to golf a few years ago and fell in love with the area."

"If you want to try out the course, I might be able to set up a tee time for this afternoon," she offers, catching my eyes, which makes me feel naked.

Shit. If she or anyone sees me hit a golf ball, the jig is up.

"Aw, I'd love to, but I have to be back in Tampa by three for a meeting," I lie. "But thank you."

She drives me around the grounds of the club, shows me all the sites where custom homes are slated to be built, and, taking a cue from my biology profession, adds bits of color to entice me. ("We have one woman here who is president of a birdwatching group who's making a list of all the species spotted on the property. I think she's up to sixty.")

I find my opening: "Hey, do you think you might be able to drop me off in the clubhouse for a bit so I can try the food? I'm kind of a foodie and would really like to see what the menu is like."

I'm relieved when she says yes, going so far as to drop me off at the clubhouse while giving the chef instructions to give me whatever I want, on the house.

"Here's my number. Text me when you need me to pick you up," she says.

Maybe I'm a better liar than I thought.

I have about forty-five minutes on my own, plenty of time to find Carlton. I wander the halls, trying not to look like I'm snooping, reading the WASPY names of all the past tournament champions on various plaques and trophies, ducking my head into the pro shop. No Carlton.

I walk back into the restaurant, where Wimbledon is playing on the TVs, and grab a seat at the bar near two guys in their fifties, fresh from their morning round. The dining room is stately and somber, empty save for a table of six ladies. I nosh on a gourmet fried chicken sandwich and chips, looking up suddenly every time someone walks by the doorway, hoping to see that distinctive gait, shoulders up and chin out.

But no Carlton.

I consider asking the bartender in that I-know-I-shouldn't-ask-about-your-celebrity-members-but-c'mon kind of way but don't want to draw any more attention to myself than I already have.

I stretch my allotted forty-five minutes to the max and then give up, texting Janelle. She comes back within five minutes.

"How was your lunch?" she asks.

"Outstanding. Amazing how good a fried chicken sandwich can be."

When she drops me off back at my car, she sees the license plates and turns back to me, her tone suddenly curious.

"You drove here from California?" she says, her eyebrows raised slightly.

What kind of millionaire drives a beat-up Honda Accord from California to Florida just to look at houses?

"Uh, yeah. It's summer, so I'm off. I figured, why not make a road trip out of it?"

I thank her for her time and generosity and get back on the road. Once I'm safely away, I pull over and take out my phone to text Gene: "I managed to sneak my way all the way to the clubhouse bar, but Carlton was not there," I type.

"Sorry. Everything is timing and luck!" he replies. Then a minute later, "He'll probably be in Cooperstown for the Hall of Fame in a couple weeks."

Yes! A second chance. It's the bottom of the ninth, but I'm not out yet.

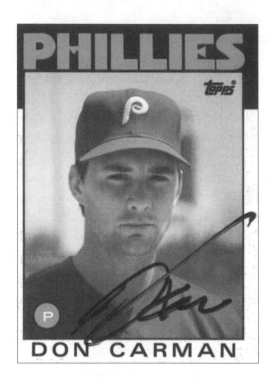

PHILLIES

DON CARMAN

10

LEADER OF THE PACK

I don't get to write the script. Whatever
it is, I just get to respond.
—*Don Carman*

Days 21–23
July 9–11, 2015
Miles driven: 5,129
Cups of coffee: 49
Sarasota FL to Naples FL

AUGUST 15, 1989

Don Carman can't sleep.

Tired of tossing and turning and disturbing his wife, Sharon, he finally gets up and faces the wall, turning his head ninety degrees to examine his posture in the bedroom mirror. He imagines his fingertips rubbing against the coarse red stitches of a baseball as he feels for his fastball grip, his index and middle fingers extending over the seams in four places. His heart thumps as his mind races through each of the nine Dodgers hitters he will face the next day and how he will approach each one.

Attack, attack.

Before throwing a single pitch, Don maps out the entire game in his head, drawing on input from the voluminous scouting reports collected by the front office and his past encounters facing a particular opponent. The battle plan for each individual hitter is specific and exact, a finely tuned conspiracy between him and his catcher—pound Alfredo Griffin with fastballs down, jam Willie Randolph inside, keep the ball away from Mike Marshall and make him hit to the opposite field—but the overall strategy is simple: be aggressive, no matter what. Stick to the game plan even if you give up a hit or a home run.

And if there is one emotion Don Carman has perfected from a young age, it is aggression.

Growing up in Camargo, Oklahoma, the middlest of middle children (he was fourth of eight), all Don knew and was ever told was that he was too slow, too small, too stupid to amount to anything. Kids at school picked on him, his brothers picked on him, even his own father picked on him. In front of the whole class, Mr. Moore, one of his seventh-grade teachers, told him: "How can you be so stupid? I can't even believe you're in here. You can't be this stupid."

It was fight or flight. And every time, Don put up his fists.

He needs a big game tomorrow. He started spring training as the default ace of the pitching staff but faltered badly. Since rejoining the Philadelphia Phillies' starting rotation in late July, he has pitched well, his only really bad start coming four days ago in Chicago when he walked seven Cubs and was in the showers by the fourth inning. He knows he's on a short leash with manager Nick Leyva, who has already exiled him to the bullpen once this season and who has the maddening habit of throwing his players under the bus after a bad performance. Following the Cubs game, Leyva told the *Philadelphia Inquirer*: "That was terrible pitching. I mean, you can't expect to be behind every hitter and try to win. That was awful."[1]

Leyva thought he was being refreshing, feeding the media raw honesty and hoping it would kick his players in the ass, but to Don it was just stupid, a public betrayal of what should remain in the temple of the clubhouse. So in what is otherwise a meaningless game in a meaningless season, his next start against the Dodgers (who are scuffling in the hangover of a World Series victory), Don has a chance at redemption: a strong outing would make the Cubs fiasco look like an anomaly, and perhaps Leyva would start to rebuild his faith in him.

Closing his eyes and raising his clasped hands over his head, he practices his windup in slow motion, feeling his weight shift from his back foot to his front as his arm whips forward to release the imaginary ball. The night before he pitches is always like this, an anxious dress rehearsal in his underwear.

Attack. Attack.

Resetting his arms and legs for another practice pitch in the mirror, Don looks down at his left hand, examining the quarter-inch bulge of bone at the base of his left thumb. He flexes his hand, thinking back to the car accident more than two and a half years ago that forced him to relearn how to pitch. The physical strength had returned, but it had felt like one step forward, one step back ever since. He had come back too soon, reporting to spring training and telling the team he was fine, great actually, even though his hand felt like it was being smashed by a hammer every time he gripped the ball to throw. To say anything else was unthinkable—you always felt "fine."

Attack. Attack.

Later that evening, under an overcast evening sky, Don walks out to the mound at Veterans Stadium to begin warming up. The Phillies had trained him well, teaching him from the beginning of his Minor League journey to grab the opposition by the throat and squeeze. The adrenaline pumps through his veins, his breath quickening, his heart loud in his chest. The Dodgers are Mr. Moore, his brothers, and his father all rolled into one blue-and-gray monster that he now needs to slay. His catcher and buddy, Darren Daulton, who has been with him since the low Minor Leagues, crouches behind home plate, ready to receive.

The first inning is always a struggle, quieting the butterflies enough to get locked into a groove. He never could understand the advice of "just relax out there." This is war.

Come out hard. Fastballs down. Pound it down.

Alfredo Griffin, the Dodgers' free-swinging leadoff hitter, begins his strut to home plate.

Be aggressive.

The thought floats in front of Don. He sees it and scowls, catching himself. He knows that the moment he has to tell himself to be aggressive, he is no longer capable of doing so. That voice is passive, meek.

Only one person is going to throw this pitch, he reminds himself.

Either that pussy—

Or this fucking guy here.

He peers into Daulton's squat for the sign, tugs on the brim of his hat, slams the ball into his glove.

So who's gonna throw it?

As he rocks back and extends his arms overhead, the crowd roars to life. And up in the nosebleed seats of that sea of maroon-and-powder-blue-clad Phillies fans, I sit watching with my father, an eight-year-old with a squeaky voice and buck teeth whose biggest dream is to meet the man on the mound.

Twenty-six years later in a zoo over a thousand miles away, that dream will come true.

=

Expectations are dangerous, I remind myself as I drive down I-75 between Sarasota and Naples.

For the first five thousand miles of the journey, I've managed to maintain professional distance, working my way into the lives and psyches of the Wax Packers while remaining objective. But with Don Carman, my idol of idols, the eight-year-old inside is winning. I have always wondered why Don stood out so much from the rest of the underdog players I liked. His name didn't have any *F*s in it, and other than playing for the Phillies, there was nothing else obvious to distinguish him. But my feelings were involuntary—I just liked him.

I'm sweating even with the air-conditioning blasting my face. The parched mountains and brown plateaus of the western United States, all I saw for days at a time just a week ago, are now a distant memory. The pancake-flat landscape of southern Florida stretches around me, row after row of tropical pines and palms flanked by mangroves at the shore, their tentacle-like roots breaking the surface of the water. This state is predictable and green and sticky.[2]

One of my goals as a kid was to collect all of Don's baseball cards, which I displayed at the front of my baseball card album. In the pre-internet age, this meant scouring lists of cards published in hobby books and then pleading with my mom to drive me to dealers' shops in their parents' garages or basements to spend my allowance. Too sweet to say no, my mom would stand by while she watched her squeaky-voiced son haggle with man-children wearing tank tops. But again, having Don's cards still wasn't enough. For my hero, I wanted to do something truly special: send him a birthday card.

My mom drove me to the Greenville Pharmacy, where I selected a Hallmark card with the image of a sailboat basking in a magnificent sunset and the following message inside: "Wishing you smooth sailing all year long." Dissatisfied, I grabbed a blue pen, crossed out the word "sailing," replaced it with "pitching," and then sat back beaming, admiring my own cleverness. I enclosed one of his baseball cards to sign, composed a personal message explaining exactly why I considered him THE GREATEST PITCHER IN THE WORLD, and took out my copy of *Sport Americana Baseball Address List, No. 5*, a listing of the home addresses of every player to ever play Major League baseball (yes, this exists). I copied Don's home address onto the envelope, slapped a twenty-five-cent stamp in the corner, and tried to time the mail so the card would arrive exactly on his birthday. And then I waited.

I'm still waiting.

Puberty ensued, my baseball cards got boxed up, and I returned from college one summer to find my bedroom converted into a guest room painted yellow (*yellow!*).

Snapping myself back to the present, I rearrange the vents of the Accord, hoping to somehow channel the air even more directly in my face. A few minutes later, I reach the outskirts of Naples, now home to Don Carman.

This is not the Naples that I expected.

During the Florida land grab of the late 1880s, Walter Haldeman, founder of the *Louisville Courier-Journal*, led a group of Kentucky businessmen to establish the town of Naples, naming it for its similar climate to the famous Italian city. A six-hundred-foot pier, hotel, and general store were constructed for the town of 80, but more than forty years later, the population had only grown to 390. While the posh Naples Hotel was a retreat for such celebrities as Greta Garbo and Gary Cooper, the town didn't flourish until the army arrived during World War II and spurred development. Today the population hovers around twenty-one thousand.

Modern-day Naples is a symbol of the nouveau riche, a carefully manufactured paradise of high-rise condos and beachside excess inhabited by one of the most homogeneous populations I've ever seen—not just white, but white and old. Other than the similarity in complexion, you couldn't find a place more different from the sparse prairie of Don's hometown of Camargo.

Right now, though, all I see are strip malls and swampland. I exit the interstate and pull into a worn motel called the Fairways Inn. The sky is already dark and heavy overhead, foreshadowing the daily late afternoon downpour in southern Florida, when the humidity finally snaps and the heavens open. The lobby is stuffed with colorful brochures for the kitschiest of activities—airboat tours and go-karts—and the guest rooms are arranged on a single level amid gardens of exotic plants. A shriveled woman with dyed blond hair and corrugated skin checks me in, and I walk past a group of guys in their early twenties in the courtyard, the scent of fresh cannabis wafting by.

Once in my white-tile-floor room, I grab the remote control and turn on the air-conditioning unit mounted in the wall. I hear the rain arriving in force just outside the door, a quick crescendo of drops pummeling the lush vegetation, the kind of sudden onslaught that never happens back in Oakland. I rub my feet together like a cricket under the dry cover of my bedsheets and open my Tinder account, craving a distraction. I swipe right to several profiles and a minute later match with Sophia, thirty-one, a brunette with close-set eyes and light freckles wearing an expression of soft determination in her profile picture. We begin texting.

Brad: "Yes!"

Sophia: "You stole my line." Cookie emoji.

Brad: "Haha. I got a cookie! This is my first time in Naples."

Sophia: "Ugh! A tourist?! I need my cookie back."

Brad: "Not quite. I am here to research a book I'm writing. It's about tracking down all the players in a single pack of 1986 baseball cards. One of them lives here."

Sophia: "Oh my god. I'm in love with you."

We go on speaking Millennial for the next hour, discussing her career as a trainer for executive assistants, our shared affection for the movie *Love, Actually*, and our mutual interest in yoga. We make tentative plans to go to her favorite yoga studio tomorrow afternoon after I'm finished meeting with Don at the Naples Zoo. He's my childhood hero, and what place better evokes childhood than the zoo?

I lie on the bed in my underwear and stare at the wall in the dark, wondering if I'm hungry enough to get dressed and go out for a late bite to eat, then turn on my side and start imagining how the meeting with Don will go. How do I possibly prioritize what to ask? I toss and turn, mentally annotating my checklist of questions, then finally get so frustrated that I spring out of bed and hit the light switch, grabbing my spiral notebook and writing out a series of questions that I know I need to ask.

At the top of the list: *Did you ever get my birthday card?*

Don Carman is very earnestly trying to explain his job as a sports psychologist to me. And I'm very earnestly failing to understand.

The giraffe a few yards behind him wraps its eighteen-inch purple tongue around a leaf of romaine lettuce offered by a little boy, who squeals and looks back to his parents for approval. The zoo's website points out that the lettuce comes from a local fine foods vendor named Wynn's Market.

In Naples, even the giraffes eat well.

Tilting its triangular head in our direction, the giraffe beams with that slightly amused expression that giraffes seem to have permanently stuck on their faces. His ears rotate toward us.

"Almost every team has a sports psychologist now. But players never want to talk to them," Don says.

He's wearing a white T-shirt that says "Escape Travel Live" and a pair of brown striped shorts. The Florida sun has left his face and neck permanently flushed, and his hairline, already visibly receding in baseball cards from twenty-five years ago, seems to have miraculously stopped its retreat, frozen in a peninsular shape. He sports a neatly trimmed gray goatee and at fifty-five is handsome, with small wrinkles around his eyes.

I scribble furiously into my notebook, trying desperately to ignore the safari enveloping us.

He goes on: "And that's because the psychologists have to report to the general manager and the owners. If a player is about to go into free agency or arbitration and there are millions of dollars on the line, the team wants to know if you're vulnerable, if you've got a drug problem, something else going on. And do you think a player is going to volunteer that?"

He pauses, then answers his own question: "I don't think so."

Baseball has always been the most mental game simply because there's so much time to think. Each pitch is followed by a twenty- to thirty-second gap in which the brain can betray the body in dozens of different ways, while sports with more continuous action, like basketball and hockey, rely more on pure instinct. Until fairly recently, mental troubles were treated with a simple dismissive prescription: "Get over it." But as baseball's wealth grew from big to obscene, executives began seeing the importance of players' psyches and their direct correlation with performance.

Nineteen years after he threw his last pitch, Don now has one of the most fascinating and unusual jobs in all of baseball. He is one of two psychologists on staff for Scott Boras, the agent to the stars, the same Scott Boras who helped Alex Rodriguez sign a ten-year, $252 million contract back in 2000, at the time the biggest contract in the history of sports. Boras runs his own secretive miniempire out of an office in Newport Beach, California, employing not only psychologists but also an MIT-trained economist and a former NASA engineer. Decades ago, before he was accused by owners and fans alike of being Satan's money-hoarding spawn, Boras was a hungry young sports agent looking to build a client base. He liked what he saw in Don and offered his services. Now they've switched places, with Boras as the boss.

Players will talk to Don because he works for their agent, not for their employer. During the baseball season, Don is always on call. When one of Boras's clients goes into a slump, Don bolts to the airport and catches a flight to whatever Major League city the player is in for some in situ treatment.

"Is a lot of what you talk about with players baseball specific? Or is a lot of it more general psychology?" I ask.

"I would say it's only 20 percent baseball."

His eyes shift to a point behind me.

"Trying to get that last tidbit," he says, motioning toward the giraffe extending its tongue for the last scrap of lettuce.

Don has perfected the art of watching and listening. Like the giraffe, he tilts his head but keeps his blue eyes rapt and intent, releasing an occasional lopsided grin that seems slightly bashful. His long, trim frame is athletic, the product of years of intense martial arts training and discipline. He and Hall of Fame pitcher Steve Carlton were among the few Phillies players willing to endure conditioning guru Gus Hoe-fling's Northern Sil Lum kung fu program. Every morning at nine, he drove to the back room of the clubhouse at Veterans Stadium to work with Gus, Steve, and an occasional curious teammate. Most wanted nothing to do with it.

"[John] Kruk would come back with a drink, sit down, and make fun of us," he says, referring to the Phillies' rotund prankster. Although almost all players now have rigorous training regimens, in the 1980s it was exceptional.

"Kent Tekulve would smoke cigarettes in the bullpen while warming up. He would actually take a puff of a cigarette, put it down on the corner of the rubber, throw a pitch, pick it up, and take another drag," Don says.

A typical workout with Gus included twenty-five fingertip push-ups followed by twenty-five sit-ups, then twenty push-ups and twenty sit-ups, dropping by sets of five at a time and finishing with a set of one-armed push-ups. Don would then sit with his legs elevated and outstretched and do sit-ups while a partner (often Carlton) used his legs to try and push Don's knees together, forcing him to resist. He spent the next fifteen minutes in a constant squat as he shuffled across the room, practicing punches and other techniques while Gus coached and kicked his legs out if his form got sloppy. And that was just the warm-up.

Don loved every second of the three-hour torture sessions. He thrived on that intensity, the chance to focus every cell on whatever was right in front of him. He attributes making the big leagues to that capacity to be entirely present; although many others had more talent, they didn't have his drive. Even now, he works the same way.

"When I'm meeting with someone, often it will go for two hours, and it will feel like ten minutes. And if we happen to be in a restaurant, I'll have to tip double for not opening up the table."

We leave behind the giraffes and head toward the open-air tables outside the gift shop. Grabbing some bottled waters and prepackaged sandwiches, we sit down across from each other next to the macaws and the live animal theater stage.

Although I had read about Don being a bit different, I'm beginning to see what an original thinker he is.

As a player, he grew so weary of hearing himself recite the same old clichés to sportswriters that one day he simply posted a list of thirty-seven canned responses to their questions in his locker and asked them to pick their favorite for that day's sound bite.

I'm just glad to be here. I just want to help the club any way I can.
If we stay healthy, we should be right there.
And my favorite: *I don't get paid to hit.*

(Don was an abysmal hitter, even by pitcher standards. He hit .057 in 209 career at bats.)

"What is it like to now be on the other side, working with players?" I ask.

"Players are impatient, like children," he explains, two multicolored bracelets sliding around his right wrist. "They need a hit today. Not tomorrow or in three weeks. They need a quick fix. And I know that. They'll call me and just say, 'Tell me something good.' I know what that means. It means I'm confused, I'm not sure about my approach, and I have anxiety."

For most of his life, Don used aggression to fight anxiety. So when today's superstars (Bryce Harper and Stephen Strasburg are among Boras's clients) come calling with insecurities of their own, he knows how to help them fight.

"Growing up, I was on high alert at all times, as if something was about to go wrong. It was a terrible way to live."

The sun is in full force, beating down on the crowns of our heads, the muggy air clinging to our bare arms and legs. I wipe the sweat from my forehead. I want to know more about what made his childhood so difficult but don't want to press him just yet.

"My intensity came out of fear, fear of not making it, fear of having to go back to Oklahoma, which was the biggest fear of my life," he says.

He goes on: "Baseball was just all I could do. I didn't hate it, but if I had grown up in a place where there was ice hockey, I would have been a hockey player. When I played I would stand on the top step of the dugout and see thirty-five thousand people there and just shake my head. I didn't get it."

I tell him about my visit to Camargo, sure to mention that I had met with his coach, Bob Ward.

"It's interesting, right?" he says with a chuckle. "It's a whole different world. You can see why, when the scout from the Phillies came, I didn't even know what city they played in. That's how little I knew about Major League baseball," he says. "I'm from Oklahoma. To me, a filly was a female horse."

Every year from age fourteen to eighteen he grew at least an inch, many years several inches, topping out at six feet three. He played first base for Leedey High (Camargo was too small to have its own high school), where he was a slow runner and a mediocre hitter. But the one thing he could do, maybe the only thing he could do, was pitch. Although his high school coach didn't give him a second glance, Bob Ward made Don the ace of his American Legion team staff. Don seized the opportunity, once striking out twenty-four of twenty-seven batters in a single game. Despite that success, he remained off the radar of Major League scouts because of his marginal role on the Leedey team.

As usual, Don took charge of his own destiny.

Following graduation, he sought out the meanest coach in the entire state of Oklahoma, someone who would push him the way he knew he needed to be pushed. That man was Lloyd Simmons of Seminole State College, a community college three hours southeast of Camargo.

"I knew how much the players hated him. Three guys quit on the first day," he says. "I went into his office and said, 'Listen, I want to play here for a year and see if I can make it to pro ball, and if not, I'm going to the

University of Oklahoma.' The last thing I wanted was a friend. I wanted someone who was going to pound me into the ground."

Simmons pounded him. Don blossomed.

"I went 7-2 and got into the starting rotation. I didn't see him smile all season. I go in the last day of the season and made sure the door was open so I could run. I said, 'I want to thank you. It's been great here for me, but I'm not going to be coming back,'" Don says. "Apparently, he didn't think I would follow through on my promise to leave after one season. He said, 'You'll never step on another field, you piece of shit.'"

Don got his big break on August 25, 1978, when the Phillies held an open tryout in nearby Oklahoma City. Scouts Doug Gassaway and Don Williams watched him throw, then took him out to an Oklahoma 89ers (a Minor League team) game, where they offered to sign him.

"I kind of feel like I was manipulated by the scout, because he said, 'Look, you might never get this opportunity. You need to decide by the end of the game or it's off the table.' They offered me a Minor League contract and $7,500, plus $7,500 in education expenses, which I never got." He adds, "I had nobody to talk to. It's just me sitting there. I pretty much made all my decisions from the time I was eleven or twelve. When to go to bed, when to get up, when to do whatever I wanted to do. My mom was busy and hardly ever saw me play. I think she saw me play once in American Legion ball when I was eighteen, but she hadn't seen me play since Little League. It was just impossible with that many kids." I think back to Camargo, where I stood on the site of the Carman homestead, imagining how hard it must have been to squeeze ten people into the two-bedroom house.

His voice grows soft.

At three in the morning, having just turned nineteen, Don signed the contract that would forever change his life.

"I was kind of like Mayo, 'I've got nowhere else to go.' I got in my car and drove away. I said, 'I'm not going back to Camargo.' Even when I was a kid I knew it wasn't for me."

I do a mental double take, thrown by his dated reference to *An Officer and a Gentleman*.

"Did that have more to do with the place or your family dynamics?" I ask.

"That's a tricky question, because I'm sure the family dynamics had a major impact on the way I viewed the town," he says. "It's difficult to separate them. But I hated farming. I hated working cattle, I hated pigs. I hated them all. I swore I'd never make my kids grow up there and do those things, even though they might have loved it."

His one escape lay in the endless fields of the Oklahoma prairie, where he and his best friend, Bobby Sumpter, would hike, ride motorcycles, and dream. They learned to swim by pushing an inner tube to the middle of a pond outside of town and willing themselves to not drown trying to reach it. They both left Camargo at the first chance, Don through baseball and Bobby through books—he went on to get his doctorate in chemistry from Cornell.

"When I talked to your mom and your brothers, they said you were really quiet and shy as a kid," I say.

He considers this, turns it over in his head a few times the way you study a shell you just picked up on the beach.

"I was crazy quiet. I used to just watch people. I would make assessments when I was a little kid. I would take little pieces of everybody I ran into and try to build the kind of person I wanted to be," he replies. "I was afraid of everybody. I was that kid in school at the end of class who would take his books, put them in the desk, and then wait until everyone else was gone so I wouldn't bump into anybody. I thought I was sick all the time, but I had allergies. I always had a runny nose. I thought I was ugly, I was stupid, because I had been told that so many times."

It's surreal to realize that my hero could just as easily be talking about me. I think back to being bullied in junior high, ostracized to the nerd table in the lunch room wearing headgear and praying my allergies wouldn't flare up.

"But I also felt like I had something else, something that made me really special. I was especially weird, especially quiet, especially geeky, and I felt especially stupid, but I did feel special in a way, and I didn't know what exactly it was. But I knew I was different," he says, his voice even.

Up until now I've been reluctant to ask him about his father.

I know the basics—his name was Marion, he worked in the oil busi-ness, and he died of a heart attack when Don was only fifteen. But when I interviewed his mom and brothers in Camargo, they seemed suddenly vague and evasive when the topic of Marion came up. Clearly there was more to this story.

"How old were you when your dad passed away?" I ask, even though I already know the answer.

His voice gets quieter. "Fifteen."

"How did that affect you? Were you close with your dad?"

He leads with a deep breath, then a heavy sigh, and looks around the zoo. He's processing, feeling for a grip on his own thoughts and emo-tions. I watch, trying to appear neutral, waiting.

"My wife asked me earlier today if I was going to talk about that," he finally says, almost to himself.

"I don't know. I don't know."

Then a third time: "I don't know if I am."

He's straddling the picnic-table bench, hands on his knees, shoul-ders taut.

"The only reason I say that is, just to give you an idea . . ."

Another deep breath. A long pause. The humidity is unbearable.

"Let's say this: I never spoke directly to my father his whole life. And he spoke to me directly maybe twice, other than for, let's say . . ."

His voice trails off.

"Let's just say 'disciplinary reasons.' We'll use that."

I hold eye contact, but it's more difficult, watching the pain increase in his eyes with each word. Moving even slightly feels intrusive.

"He never talked to me. Not 'hey, how was the game?' He never saw me play, not one game, not basketball, baseball, nothing. The dad thing was, umm . . ."

There's not a trace of anger in Don's voice. But the sadness finally overwhelms him, chokes his next syllable, and he stops, his eyes fill-ing. I don't know what to do, how to react. My eyes start filling as well, and now I break off eye contact, overwhelmed by his raw vulnerability. I want to hug him, to give voice to his emotion, but instead I just sit with him and wait.

He collects himself, takes another deep breath, then continues in a tone just above a whisper: "I will just say this: he died in our front yard. He had gone to find my sister, who was late from a date, and we were all afraid of when he was going to come home. He had a heart attack and crashed into a tree in the front yard at two miles per hour. We were all home. Everybody, Mom, Arthur, Glenn, ran outside.

"But I didn't," he adds. "And I justified that by huddling the little ones and telling them that everything was going to be fine. But . . ."

Long pause.

"I'm debating whether or not I should talk," he says, his blue eyes, full of tears, looking greenish in the light.

He lets go.

"I felt bad because I was hoping he would die."

He gives a little nod and looks away. Several moments of silence pass, several long breaths. I picture that kid in the cramped two-bedroom house in Camargo, scared and angry and confused.

A few minutes later, we get up to resume our walk of the zoo. The grayish gravel crunches under our sandals as we walk past families and tourists with fanny packs, peering into the striped hyenas cage, the Florida panther exhibit, the South African lions.

Wanting to ease the tension and curious about his thoughts on "the baseball code" (the tendency for pitchers to throw at hitters when pitchers felt they were being shown up), I ask, "Did you ever catch guys peeking?" (Peeking is when a hitter steals a glimpse of the catcher's hand signals, which indicate the next pitch.)

"Yeah, but I was considered a little bit crazy. They knew I would dump them [hit them on purpose]," he says. "I had times when they would bring me in just to hit people because they knew nobody would charge the mound."

It's hard for me to believe that this same man, this kind, deep thinker, could have once been a headhunter.

"How do you square that?" I ask.

"I think a lot was left over from childhood," he says. "I fought all the time in grade school. I never lost. I didn't care if I got hit or got hurt.

I just kept coming. I never understood that, but it's what I did. And I think that carried over."

When he found his second career of sports psychology, he started to understand his own trauma, and the anger dissipated.

"When you're that angry, what you're really doing is feeling sorry for yourself. Anger and fear are not my motivators any longer." He pauses. "A big part of my philosophy is, I don't get to write the script. Whatever it is, I just get to respond. I quote Viktor Frankl a lot to players, where he said, 'The only true freedom we have is the freedom to choose how we respond to a given situation.'"

We've literally come full circle, back at the giraffe pen. One of the zoo docents standing nearby is eavesdropping on our conversation. Like almost everyone who works here, she is at least sixty, probably one of the herd of retirees who migrated from the Northeast.

"If you have any questions, I might know the answers," she offers.

Beyond the fence, half a dozen giraffes mill about in a vast pen, browsing the tops of palm trees when there are no tourists to offer them organic greens.

"Do the giraffes have names?" I ask.

"They do, but we're not allowed to give them out. Only the keepers can use them," she says.

"Do they respond to them?" Don asks.

"Um, they do," she replies cautiously.

"Okay," Don says, grinning. "Kevin! Bill!"

"This could take awhile," I say, laughing.

The attendant does not seem amused.

"Do they have friendships, like Bill prefers Kevin?" Don asks.

"Actually, they're all males. This is a bachelor herd, and there's constantly fighting going on and different power struggles," she says. "The one just coming out of the gate there is the current leader of the pack, but he was not the original leader. He had to fight his way to that position. We think there must be a power struggle going on now. So there may be a new leader soon. In fact, I'm putting my money on this one," she adds, pointing to the giraffe closest to us.

"You mean the one here trying to eat the pole?" Don asks dryly.

Unamused, the docent continues with her narration of the herd: "He used to be the smallest. He got picked on all the time. But he's getting bigger and starting to assert himself. I always said, someday he's going to say, 'I've had enough,' and *bam!*, watch out," she says.

=

I walk into the Green Monkey Yoga Studio and spot Sophia in a pair of tight yoga pants and a snug top that features her ample cleavage. We exchange an awkward half-hug greeting, the way it's always awkward when you meet someone for the first time after having had a deeply personal conversation online, and she leads me into an airy space with full-length windows and wood floors where she has kindly set out a mat, foam blocks, straps, a towel, and some water.

"I thought I'd set you up," she says, a bit embarrassed by her own thoughtfulness.

With the adrenaline still pumping from my meeting with Don, I want to get out of my head and into my body.

I sit on the mat and extend my legs straight out in front of me, reaching for my toes while using my core muscles to push my stomach forward, taking the hunch out of my back. My hamstrings burn as I strain to barely reach the tips of my toes, then force myself to reach farther, going over the top of my feet and pulling. The burn intensifies, blotting out all thought other than how horribly stiff my body is after being scrunched in a driver's seat for three weeks.

Sophia goes through her own warm-up, cracking with each contortion of her strong but limber body, her breath in perfect sync with her movement. She's graceful and attractive, and I can't help but be drawn to her. I have done my fair share of yoga, but this is clearly a fixture in her life.

By the end of the hour, I feel restored and loose. My brain is calmer, less frayed, the distance between thoughts longer. It's several seconds before I notice I'm staring at the bare studio wall.

"Thanks, that was just what I needed," I tell her as she walks by, her mascara smeared a bit below her eyes, making her cute face look even cuter.

"So we'll shower up, and then I'll come by and pick you up at 8:15?" I ask as we walk out, greeted by the daily late afternoon downpour.

We race to our cars through sheets of rain, drenching us.

===

"Pull over here," Sophia says as I swerve the Accord over to the curb.

"If we're quick we won't have to feed the meter."

Sophia moved back to Naples five months ago from Washington DC, where she worked as an executive assistant. I'm grateful to have a local show me all the spots, including the best place to watch the sun set. I haven't taken much time on this trip to appreciate the beauty of the places I'm visiting. I've already traveled through eleven states in twenty-one days, but whatever down time I've had has been spent in hotel rooms flailing away on my computer or scribbling in my notebook, trying to record every morsel of information before I forget it.

We run to the beach, where a large crowd of tourists and locals is lined up along the edge of the water, their phones extended to the sky, a magnificent blend of purple, blue, and yellow. I fumble with my phone and Instagram filters, trying to capture the moment.

"Let me see," Sophia says, grabbing my phone as we dash back to the car.

She laughs.

"That's terrible. Clearly not a social media guy," she says, handing me her phone to show off her skills.

It feels so good to have this banter, this connection with someone other than a former baseball player. I have rarely felt lonely since I left Oakland three weeks ago, but Sophia's presence, her playful teasing, makes me feel physically lighter.

"What was it like being an assistant for all these powerful people?" I ask.

"It was awesome. I'd exhaust my type A self all over someone else's life, leaving me free to be laid back in my own," she says.

"The yoga must help."

"Yes sir."

I want to kiss her. Right here in the middle of the wide Naples street.

"I could never do it," I tell her, opening the Accord's passenger-side door before going around to open my own.

"Do what?"

"I could never be someone's assistant for a living. Doesn't it drive you crazy having to be at their whim? Some of those people must have enormous egos."

I am suddenly aware of how haughty I sound.

"Yeah, but it's funny, I get so much satisfaction out of organizing their lives for them," she says. "It's like I know how lost they would be without me," she adds.

She navigates us to a restaurant downtown where there's a three-person band playing rock and jazz covers.

"I dated the harmonica player. He drank too much," she says.

I'm having one of the most romantic dates of my life in Naples, Florida, with a girl I met on Tinder—yoga, sunset, and dinner in a tropical paradise. It's certainly more romantic than any date I've had recently back in Oakland. It's kind of sad, I think to myself while we drive the brightly lit city streets back to her apartment, that I'm only willing to make the time when I know there is no chance of commitment, just a fly-by-night rendezvous with a stranger in a strange place.

Unable to resist any longer and wanting to end this most romantic of dates, well, romantically, I put the Accord in park in the driveway and lean in. Her body responds, shifting to meet mine, our lips open and pressed together.

She pulls away a moment later, looking flushed and guilty.

"I'm sorry, I'm not good at casual sex," she says.

"It's okay," I say with a smile. "We're not having sex. I don't want to."

I'm full of shit, of course. Sophia knows this.

"Yeah right," she says, rolling her eyes.

But first base is, in fact, as far as this date goes. We sit and chat for a while longer.

"Why are you single?" she asks me.

It's one of my least favorite questions. I launch into a meandering explanation that she also rolls her eyes at.

The truth is that I'm single because I don't want to end up getting divorced like my parents did. I'm scared that I will mess up again like I did with Kay. And I'm scared of making a commitment I'm not sure I can keep.

I don't say any of this. Instead, I talk about being independent and liking my space and being picky, things that are also true but don't tell the whole story.

I say good night and watch Sophia walk up the driveway. I watch in the rearview mirror as she shuts the door behind her.

I turn the ignition, feeling content. Don's words float back to me: *We don't get to write the script in life. Whatever it is, we just get to respond.*

=

The next morning, Don leads me into his study, his private sanctum, where he remotely massages some of the biggest and most fragile egos in all of baseball. I wanted to see him in his home environment so I can fulfill a twenty-six-year wish: to play catch with my hero.

At the center of the room is a brown leather chair in front of a desk with a small lamp and a MacBook, its lid closed. I spy a yellow legal pad on the desk with the handwritten names of several clients—Addison Russell, Mike Moustakas—with little notes in the margins and a hand-drawn check box next to each name. But they're not actually check boxes, they're check cubes, drawn in three dimensions.

On a second yellow legal pad is his daily to-do list, with such entries as "set up phone e-mail," "expense report," and "homework." I'm there too, noted simply as "Brad" with my own check cube. He's taking classes toward a doctorate in psychology after having recently completed his master's.

The study is full of mementos from his career, baseballs piled high on a shelf, framed newspaper clippings, plaques and awards. There's the ball from his near-perfect game against the Giants in 1986 and an autographed, inscribed ball from teammate Mike Schmidt, one of the greatest players of all time. If I ask about any of them, he provides an explanation, but all of the items he points out have little to do with him.

He points to an oil painting on the wall of a wolf staring directly ahead with a whimsical expression on its lips. It's good.

"Jackson painted that," he says, referring to his youngest son, who's now a junior in high school. "There something different about Jackson in an unbelievably wonderful way."

He tells me a story about when Jackson was in the sixth grade and forgot a paper at home. Don drove to the school to drop it off, and as he turned to go, a teacher stopped him and said, "Are you Jackson's father?"

"Yes," Don said.

"I have to meet the father of Jackson Carman. I've been teaching for eighteen years, and I've never met a child like him," she said.

For every conversation Don never had with his father, he has ten with Jackson and his other two sons, Jared and Aaron.

"I was a stay-at-home-dad. We played catch a lot, worked the yard, went to the beach, rode bikes. My oldest [Jared] loves to talk about philosophical things, about my work. And Aaron was really shy, a lot like me. Watching him grow up, I could see what it would have been like [for me] without the other pain. It was fun to watch."

On one of the bookshelves, in front of *Socrates to Sartre, Cultural Literacy*, and Philip Roth's *Everyman*, stands a row of four bobbleheads: Don Carman and three characters from *Napoleon Dynamite*, Kip, Pedro, and Napoleon.

"I've seen it at least fifteen times. I can quote the whole movie pretty much."

He leads me back into the kitchen, where I take a seat on a stool at the island in the middle. He stands up at the counter, cradling a mug of coffee. The house is big and comfortable but not ostentatious. There's a screened-in swimming pool in the backyard and Trivial Pursuit laid out on the coffee table in the living room.

I want to know what happened at the end of his career, how he transformed from a head-hunting pitcher for the Phillies into a psychologist working on his doctorate. I knew from my research that the end of his career had been much different from that of players like Rance Mulliniks, who rode off into the sunset with a World Series title.

His last full season in the Majors was 1990 with the Phillies. For the next five years, he was a baseball gypsy, fighting for a job every spring training, bouncing from the Astros to the Reds to the Tigers to the Royals to the Rangers to the Mariners back to the Phillies to the Twins organizations, with a stop in the Mexican League mixed in. He finished his professional career in 1995, seventeen years after it began, pitching for the Gaston King Cougars, an independent team based in Gaston, North Carolina. Finally, a year older than I am now, he was done.

"For two years after I stopped playing, I went right into depression. I couldn't even breathe," he says.

I mention the other players I've met and how they also struggled with the transition—Steve Yeager too depressed to watch his beloved Dodgers on TV, Carlton Fisk's self-induced exile—and how surprised I am that none of them seem particularly nostalgic about their careers.

"I think it's self-preservation," he says. "Because it's your dream, and then it's gone. It's like, okay, I woke up, and I don't get to go back to sleep and dream again."

Don, as always, was different. Never a fan, he didn't mind letting go of the game itself, but leaving behind the lifestyle was harder.

"What was missing from my life was structure. I had spent my whole life under structure. I knew where I was supposed to be, when to go to camp, when to show up, when to get up, everything was structured," he says. "I started drinking. I drank quite a bit, and I didn't even think about it. But then I realized I was doing it five days a week. It became my activity."

His second wife, Kathy, whom he married in 1995, was the one to get him up off the floor. Literally.

"We had chatted about me going back to school, and I kept going 'yeah, yeah.' I was scared. It seemed like such a daunting thing," he says. "One day I was sitting on the floor, leaning against the door of the garage. I just sat there. And Kathy came over and said, 'What's going on?' I said, 'I don't know.' She said, 'I know it's scary out there, I know it's scary to go back to school, but you've got to get off the floor. Just take one class and go from there.'"

He got up.

Toward the end of his playing career, when he was struggling with the end of his first marriage, his then agent and now boss Scott Boras recommended he talk to Harvey Dorfman, a pioneer in baseball psychology and the author of the landmark textbook *The Mental Game of Baseball*. Don flew out to Dorfman's Arizona compound for a weekend and met the man who would become his second dad, neither of whom was his father. In Don, Dorfman saw the same untapped potential that Bob Ward had seen in his backyard in Camargo, except this time it was the talent Don possessed above the shoulder rather than the skill of the arm attached to it.

Dorfman became Don's mentor. He was the one who encouraged Don to continue his education after Kathy picked him up off the floor. He got his bachelor's in psychology, then his master's in sports psychology, and now he is working on his doctorate, although Dorfman won't be there to see him receive it. He died four years ago at the age of seventy-five.

"I miss him every day," Don tells me.

Don walks over to the microwave to heat up his coffee.

"What impact has your marriage to Kathy had on you?" I ask.

And here, for the first time since our conversation began at the zoo yesterday, Don's tongue gets tied. Not because he's got nothing to say, but because he has *so much* to say that he constantly edits to get it just right.

"I'd say the broadest, the biggest—besides know that—a couple things that I would say, without thinking too much—one is that people can be what they present themselves as."

He pauses, resets, then starts again.

"It took years for me to realize that she is everything that she appears to be. And I don't know anyone else like that, not one person, who is truly a great friend, who is truly truthful, I don't know anybody, not one person."

His voice trails off, his eyes well up. He sniffles, says "mmm-hmmm" with a slight nod. For the second time in two days, I'm watching my childhood hero cry.

I never get to meet Kathy, but I feel like I already have.

"Do you want to throw a bit?" Don asks me, suddenly aware of the time and leading me into the garage. I remember reading that he found an old shoebox full of fan mail in this same garage, letters he never replied to. He turned writing responses into a project with his son Jackson. I ask if he remembered getting a birthday card with a sailboat on it, but he doesn't.

He plucks a couple of gloves and a ball out of a box, leading me out to the driveway. The hot sun, already high in the sky, beats down on us as we stand fifteen yards apart and start tossing. He demonstrates the same windup he used for all those years for the Phillies, the same series of movements that I watched from the nosebleed seats on that August day in 1989. The high leg kick, his hands held just below his bent right knee, and then the arc of his left arm as it comes whipping over the top, releasing the ball, which snaps into my glove an instant later with a loud pop, stinging my palm inside. Even in a simple catch, decades removed from his playing days, Don's arm is still free like it was in Bob Ward's backyard forty years ago.

The ball feels smooth and cool in my sweaty palm, a five-ounce core of rubber wrapped in yarn and covered by cowhide. I grip it tightly, moving my fingers over the relief of the red stitching, feeling its coarse surface. I toss it back.

We start out chatting about how to grip different pitches, about his fielding position after completing a pitch.

Then we just stop talking and throw in silence, the ball's white parabola soaring against a bright summer sky.

'85 RECORD BREAKER

VINCE COLEMAN, ST. LOUIS CARDINALS
Most Stolen Bases, Season, Rookie

11

VINCENT VAN GONE

When I get on, nobody's
going to throw me out.
—*Vince Coleman*

Days 24–27
July 12–15, 2015
Miles driven: 5,546
Cups of coffee: 66
Naples FL to Jacksonville FL

Ever since he was a little boy, Vince Coleman has been running. Growing up an only child raised by his mother, Willie Pearl (he never knew his father), in a rough part of northwestern Jacksonville, he once told a reporter, "I had to survive as best I could and a lot of times, I got out of trouble with my feet." His need to escape was so deep-seated that it seeped into his sleep. "Even now my dreams are just running, running, running. I think that just carried over to sports, so that stealing bases was a natural."[1]

He's so good at running, in fact, that I have no idea where he is. While I had strong leads on every other Wax Packer before I hit the road, the man once nicknamed Vincent van Go for his base-stealing prowess has gone completely AWOL. He is a base-running instructor with the Chicago White Sox, but the team's PR rep said that Coleman had not been with the team in weeks, and the rep had no idea when or if Coleman would return.

I have my work cut out for me, but after the Carlton ordeal and the emotionally exhausting couple of days with Don, I'm spent.

I lie under the covers in my Jacksonville hotel room, splayed out on my stomach with my head turned sideways. The smell of the coffee I put on five minutes ago percolates through the air, but I have no will to get up and taste it. I peek out from under the covers and see the bright red light of the coffeemaker, the same shade of red as the uniforms of Van Go's old team, the St. Louis Cardinals. On the floor next to the bed lies a stack of notebooks and newspaper articles where I dropped them last night, too tired to set them on the desk a few paces away.

I'm at the All-Star Break of the trip, halfway through. I've driven almost six thousand miles in less than a month through eight different states. Outside the womb of my air-conditioned room lies another Florida Groundhog Day, more unrelenting humidity and clear blue sky. But right now I want nothing more than to turn off my brain and lie completely still, to be swallowed whole by this soft mattress. For twenty-four days I have followed a strict writer's regimen of late nights, early mornings, and too much coffee; I've blogged daily when the last thing I wanted to do was to be creative, let alone entertaining, when all I wanted to do was watch old reruns of *Wings* on my shitty hotel TV. I've eaten food whose grease soaked through the wrappers and watched the whites of my eyes turn more and more the color of rosé with each passing day. I haven't done laundry or gone to the gym in a week and have reached the low point of recycling underwear.

Somewhere out there is the fifty-three-year-old Vincent van Go, even more intractable and difficult than Carlton, not wanting to be found. I should be in detective mode, working the phones, looking for leads as big as the ones Van Go used to take off first base with his eye on stealing second. Instead I want nothing more than to turn off the radio in my brain and disappear into the sheets.

=

Several hours later, a text message wakes me up. I squint at the screen, disoriented from a deep sleep, the coffeemaker light still burning red across the room.

The message is from Dwight Gooden Jr., better known as Little Doc, who is the youngest of Dwight "Doc" Gooden's seven children and who serves as his dad's agent. We have been negotiating back and forth about setting up a meeting when I'm in New York in a few days, and the answer at last arrives: "We will be here."

I bolt up like a piece of toast, suddenly invigorated by landing the second most famous Wax Packer (and some might argue that his fame rivaled that of Carlton's). I pour myself a cup of still-warm coffee and fire off a text reply. The only way the Goodens would agree to talk to me was for me to pay them, which I'm not thrilled about (the practice of paying sources is frowned upon in journalism) and which I would only do as a last resort and with full disclosure to readers. I consent to pay Little Doc $200 and Doc $500 for an interview.

"He is doing a documentary with [Darryl] Strawberry and maybe when they start shooting you can come follow and make it happen. I know they will be shooting some day in July. If not, there's plenty of signings or public appearances coming up," Little Doc texts.

This is big. So big that I jump right into the shower, washing away the road grime and weariness, turning my sights back on Vincent van Go. He is the reason why I've come to Jacksonville, the largest city (by land area) in the United States, consisting of a maze of bridges and buildings centered around the St. John's River on Florida's northeastern coast. The city's numerous pockets and neighborhoods include a major naval station and university, but despite its immense size, it lacks any defining character. When I ask the bartender downstairs what Jacksonville is known for, he simply shrugs and offers, almost apologetically, "The Jaguars?" (the football team, not the animal). Still, Jacksonville has more character than San Diego.

Van Go grew up in the blue-collar Moncrief Park neighborhood in the northwestern part of the city, spending as much time as he could in Scott Park playing sports with his older cousin Greg and other local athletes. Without a father in his life, he found male role models in Greg and his uncle Carter, a deacon at Abyssinia Baptist Church who made the best sweet potato pies around. Van Go followed in Greg's footsteps to Florida A&M University in Tallahassee, where he excelled as a punter and kicker on the football team and as a center fielder in baseball, once stealing seven bases in a single game. He dreamed of following Greg to the NFL, refusing to sign with the Phillies when they drafted him after his junior year. The following spring, in 1982, he got a tryout with the Washington Redskins but was put at wide receiver, a position where he had no experience and faltered.

"He could have made it. But you see so few blacks kicking in the NFL. . . . I think there's really a bias there that kept Vince from getting a fair opportunity," his college coach Rudy Hubbard told *Sports Illustrated* in 1985.[2]

When the baseball draft rolled around again a month later, he was quick to sign with the St. Louis Cardinals in the tenth round for $5,000. Possessed of otherworldly speed, he shot through the Minor Leagues, swiping 145 bases in only 113 games for the 1983 Macon Redbirds, a pro baseball record that would stand for twenty-nine years. By 1985 he was the St. Louis Cardinals' starting left fielder and the National League Rookie of the Year, and by the time the playoffs started that fall against the Los Angeles Dodgers, he was a bona fide celebrity, hanging out at the Playboy mansion. Young, single, and on top of the world, Van Go was the personification of the American Dream.

But he never grew into his fame, never matured enough to know how to handle the success. He was cocky by his own admission, frequently referring to his "egotistical" attitude like it was a good thing. On the rare times he got caught stealing, he attributed it to something he had messed up, refusing to honor the opposition. "If I get thrown out, I always think I did something wrong. I don't give credit to the catcher," he said.[3] The sportswriters who covered Van Go said he dripped with entitlement, outraged when umpires would call strikes on him and overly sensitive to any negative press even when it was justified. "Some of the time, if the play is close, shouldn't it go in my favor?" he said when asked about his frustration with umpires.[4] It didn't help that he was woefully ignorant of history; when he was asked about Jackie Robinson during the 1985 World Series (after Robinson's widow threw out the first pitch), he infamously replied, "I don't know nuthin about him. Why are you asking me about Jackie Robinson?"[5]

Pride goeth before the fall. The man known best for stealing bases took his larceny a bit too far at Florida A&M, the first of a series of run-ins with the law. In 1981 he and his roommate were arrested for stealing one hundred dollars' worth of wood from a lumberyard in the middle of the night. They said they were going to use the wood for bookshelves, and after they pleaded no contest, the judge dropped the charges and put them on probation with community service. During his six seasons with the Cardinals, Van Go stayed clear of legal trouble, but as soon as he chased the money to New York, signing a four-year, $11.95 million contract with the Mets after the 1990 season, his problems resumed. The small-town kid from the Florida back waters who had been nurtured by midwestern kindness was now eaten alive by the Big Apple. Overrated to begin with, injuries and age slowed him down, turning Mets fans against him. (Other than stealing bases, he was a pretty mediocre player, subpar defensively and striking out way too much for a leadoff hitter—his career WAR was only 12.5.)[6] He didn't do himself any favors with an increasingly cantankerous attitude and immaturity in the clubhouse. "Coleman had also long since alienated reporters with his surliness, and he had a piercing laugh that seemed to echo throughout the clubhouse, sometimes even during the quiet brought on by a tough loss," wrote beat reporters Bob Klapisch and John Harper in their book on the 1992 Mets. His round, cherubic face and pencil-thin mustache became stuck in a permanent frown. Through it all, Van Go became more and more delusional; rather than listening and learning, he doubled down on his own greatness and victimhood. "What this field is doing is keeping me out of the Hall of Fame," he said, claiming that the playing surface of Shea Stadium was the only thing keeping him from immortality (a truly preposterous remark; even in his prime, Van Go was nowhere near Hall of Fame status).[7]

Off to a bad start in New York, things got even worse. During spring training in 1992, a thirty-one-year-old Manhattan woman accused Van Go and his teammates Doc Gooden and Daryl Boston of having raped her the previous March 30 in Port St. Lucie, where the Mets spent spring training. As Gooden wrote in his autobiography, *Doc*, "At night, we'd go out drinking and looking for women, and women would go out drinking and looking for Mets. The hookups were never hard to come by." He went on to recount how he met the accuser at a nightclub and brought her back to the house he was renting, where they found Van Go and Boston playing the Nintendo game *R.B.I. Baseball.* Doc says he and the woman had sex, and when they emerged from the bedroom, Van Go allegedly asked her, "You ever been with three guys in a night?"[8] She allegedly said no, that she had only been with two guys in a night. Van Go then asked her if she'd like to go to the bedroom with him. She ended up sleeping consensually with all three players, Doc says, and a year later came out of the woodwork to accuse them of having raped her.

The Port St. Lucie police conducted an investigation, with the state attorney general ultimately dropping the charges as the accuser's story of coercion fell apart. But the damage was done—Van Go was once again in the headlines for the wrong reason, and his wife, Lynette, back in their Arizona home, was not happy.

A little more than a year later, the Mets visited Los Angeles for a three-game series. At 32-65, the Mets were buried in last place, and the team had started to go a little stir-crazy. Pitcher Bret Saberhagen threw an M-100 firecracker near a group of reporters in early July and then a few weeks later smashed a hamper with a baseball bat in the locker room *before* a game. Following an afternoon game on July 24 in front of 43,301 fans that was won by the Dodgers, Van Go and teammate Bobby Bonilla met up with their buddy Eric Davis (who played for the Dodgers) in the players' parking lot, climbing into Davis's Jeep. Van Go, always looking for a prank, dropped a firecracker out of the car window only thirty feet from a crowd of fans seeking autographs congregated behind a gate. The device exploded, injuring three people, including two-and-a-half-year-old Amanda Santos. Davis, Bonilla, and Van Go drove off, having no idea they had hurt anyone and leaving a bloodied Santos to be consoled by her parents, Marivel, an unemployed legal secretary, and Derrick, an architectural draftsman without health insurance. When the media got wind of the story, Van Go refused to comment, and Davis, the driver of the car, was incredulous that it was a big deal. "Yeah, he threw a firecracker out of the car," Davis told the *Daily News.* "He didn't throw no firecracker into a crowd of people. Those people were behind a gate 20 feet away from my car." Davis said Van Go intended it as a joke. "Everybody throws firecrackers. He threw it six feet from my car. We were laughing about it."[9]

But it was no laughing matter. As the story rolled in and the picture of what happened became clearer, the Mets were infuriated, putting Van Go on what would become permanent administrative leave. The Santos family was outraged by his lack of compassion, telling the *Sporting News* that he had promised to help pay their medical bills but had done nothing more than send a teddy bear and balloons to Amanda. Third-degree felony charges were later reduced to a misdemeanor (Van Go hired celebrity lawyer Robert Shapiro to defend him), and in November he pleaded guilty. The judge handed down a suspended one-year jail sentence, three years of probation, a $1,000 fine, and two hundred hours of community service. The Mets considered Van Go's $11.95 million contract one of the biggest busts in team history. They were so fed up that they cut him with a year to go on the deal. While he claimed to have learned his lesson, his actions said otherwise: when an ambitious reporter tracked him down the following winter near his custom-built fortress in Scottsdale, Arizona, Van Go refused to discuss the incident, other than defiantly saying, "All the facts aren't out. The people were 30 feet away. How could somebody 30 feet away be hurt? I wouldn't throw a firecracker at kids."[10]

His career and perhaps he would never be the same. He muddled through four more seasons with four different teams, suffering the indignity of many trips back to the Minor Leagues. The prince turned pauper, the denial grew deeper. He got divorced shortly after the firecracker ordeal. Although he returned to baseball for a few years in the mid-2000s as an instructor in the Cubs organization and resurfaced in 2013 with the Houston Astros, his true love, the team that once lionized him, the St. Louis Cardinals, never hired him back. It hurt Van Go deeply that he could not return home.

Given all that history, I didn't expect Vincent van Go to make time for me. When I had gotten him on the phone a few weeks ago he was as cordial as a marooned crab. I explained the project, throwing in that I knew all about his uncle Carter's sweet potato pies and planned on visiting his childhood home in Jacksonville, but he remained completely unimpressed. "Not interested," he said.

At least with Carlton Fisk I had a lead on where to find him; Van Go could be anywhere. So if I can't find the man in the present, my only choice is to travel to his past.

＝

Cloudy beads of sweat drip off my arm and onto my steno pad as I powerwalk down a sidewalk flourishing with weeds, causing the blue lines of the paper to smear. The air smells like rotting grass, punctuated by the strident chorus of unseen insects. I reach up and tamp down my damp black hair, hot to the touch.

The ranch-style homes of Moncrief Park are packed tightly together, many bordered by chain-link fences, many with rusted cars parked on the lawn. I walk by a neighborhood watch sign put up by the Police Athletic League with the slogan "Filling Playgrounds, Not Prisons."

All I've got is an address, 4103 West Leonard Court, pulled from a public records search for Van Go and his mom, Willie Pearl. (I could find no record of Van Go's father.) While I'm not 100 percent certain this is the house Van Go grew up in, it seems likely—I know that he attended Raines High School, only a couple miles away, and I could find no other address listed for Willie Pearl. I don't know what to expect—I don't have a plan beyond finding the house and ringing the doorbell. Even if it is the right house, I have no idea if any Colemans still live there.

As I pass two kids playing basketball in the street next to a lot bursting with tall grass, I imagine Van Go and his cousins playing baseball and football here until the sun dipped below the horizon. Retracing his steps, I walk down Leonard Circle West, turning left onto West Leonard Court. Four houses in different shades of pastel with wrought-iron bars over the windows border the half circle, ranch homes with chain-link fences. A red F150 truck is parked in the short driveway of the alleged Coleman homestead behind a fence held shut with a strand of wire. The shiny car belies the rundown appearance of the house, its white paint faded and peeled to reveal splotches of yellow. Stymied by the locked fence, I knock on a neighbor's door to ask if anyone in the Coleman family still lives next door. A large man with a graying beard wearing a Houston Texans T-shirt answers, greeting me with a smile. "It's too hot out here for me, buddy," he says, already wiping his brow.

"Are you a Texans fan?" I ask.

"Yeah. My son plays for them," he says, proud but not bragging.

What are the odds that an NFL player's dad answers the door? Perhaps I shouldn't be surprised—this is the same neighborhood that spawned many professional football players.

"Louis Nix III is his name. Nose guard for the Texans. They call him Irish Chocolate." (I later Google this, baffled by the nickname, and learn that he went to Notre Dame.)

I tell him why I'm standing on his doorstep wearing a backpack and looking like a lost college student, and he says he doesn't know who lives in the 4103 house, although he's pretty sure it's not the Colemans any longer. "Sorry I can't help more!" he offers apologetically.

I head back to the main street to look for any signs of life in the house other than the truck parked in the driveway. As I snoop, out of the corner of my eye I see a red car approaching to my left. I had noticed the same car circling the block a couple of times, inching along and clearly taking an interest in my presence. I doubt the neighborhood gets much tourist foot traffic, let alone visitors openly toting notebooks in the blistering heat.

The car crawls along, slowing to a stop next to me. The window rolls down.

No sense in hiding. I walk toward the driver's-side window. "Hi there!" I announce to the driver as if I was expecting her. She's wearing a wrap around her hair, and she has kind brown eyes. There's a kid in the backseat and a younger woman with dyed red hair riding shotgun. She leans forward, peering at me with curiosity.

"Who are you looking for?" she asks.

"Vince Coleman. He was a baseball player from here, and I think this is the house he grew up in."

Any trace of suspicion vanishes from her face. "I don't think the family lives there anymore," she says. "I believe the mom passed away. Her sister too."

Strike 1. I thank them and head back to my car, satisfied that I've done all I can. His alma mater, Raines High School, is only two and a half miles away, so I swig some coffee and work my way through the suburban streets. There are still so many unanswered questions: What-ever happened to his dad? How long ago had Willie Pearl passed? And where the hell is Van Go right now anyway?

Raines High, home of the Vikings, was founded in 1965 as School Num-ber 165, built after nearby Jean Ribault High School's all-white faculty and students rejected the inclusion of African American students. Renamed for local educator William Raines later that year, the school is now 97 per-cent African American and has sent twenty-one players to the NFL. Being the middle of summer, there's construction going on in the lobby, and I walk past a trophy case and up to the front desk to ask about Van Go.

"Are there any old yearbooks I could look at?" I ask the receptionist, a woman wearing a white sweater and blue-and-black dress.

"They're all in the library, and the library is being renovated," she tells me. A couple of construction guys march into the lobby covered in sweat, seeking the refuge of air-conditioning, followed by two police officers.

"You know, I went to high school with Vince," she adds.

"Wait, you *went* here?" I ask, shocked. She doesn't look old enough to be Vince's classmate.

"Yes, sir. Leila Robinson. I was in Vince's class." The cops suddenly take an interest, wandering over.

"What was he like? Tell me about him!" I say, getting excited and opening my notebook. But Leila wants no part of my inquiries.

"No, no, I don't want to be interviewed," she says politely.

One of the cops chimes in. "Wait, I thought you was twenty-five," he says to Leila.

"I *am* twenty-five," she shoots back, cracking everyone up.

"Class of '78," I say, remembering my research. Leila does not seem pleased by my contribution to the conversation.

"Shoot, you old enough to be my mama," the cop jokes.

"Hush," Leila replies.

Strike 2. My only other lead is the reference to Van Go's uncle Carter, a deacon at Abyssinia Baptist Church, in a 1985 issue of *Sports Illustrated*.

Back in the car, back to the coffee, back on the road. Several miles later, I arrive at a lavish drive-in church decorated with purple and white balloons, with a marquee out front advertising the upcoming vacation Bible school. I walk with purpose, striding past a group of children, looking for the minister's office. I find Minister Richard Black in sermon prep at his desk, which is cluttered with papers and books. His gray hair is pushed back, and he is wearing all black.

"Was there a deacon here named Carter?" I ask after introducing myself. I realize I don't even know if Carter is his first or last name. Minister Black nods his head slowly, the gears turning, faint recognition on his face.

"Yes, Robert Carter," he says. "I believe he passed about thirty years ago." He has no idea who Vince Coleman is but says he remembers Robert Carter talking about his nephew playing professional ball. But this faint recollection is all I'm going to get. Strike 3.

On the way back to the freeway and the solace of my hotel bed, I take out Van Go's 1986 baseball card, which pictures him in midstride. His elbows are slightly bent, his shoulders are drawn up toward his ears, his compact frame is puffed out to project as much swagger as possible. The photo says it all. He's always wanted to be something more, something bigger. He wants to be Vincent van Go instead of just being Vince Coleman.

"His problem is that he's a follower," his St. Louis manager, Whitey Herzog, once said.[11]

As I prepare to leave Florida I'm not disappointed, because I never expected much out of him to begin with. Expectations, after all, are a dangerous thing.

Vincent van Go is gone.

=====

Next up: New York, New England, and a return to Rhode Island for a reunion with my own father. Three Wax Packers condensed in a tight window and time frame and perhaps the biggest score of all: a date with Doc Gooden.

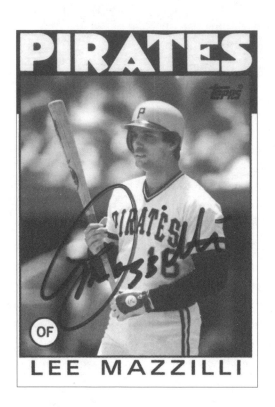

12

IS IT SEPTEMBER YET?

I think the hardest thing for any
player is to say no more.
—*Lee Mazzilli*

Days 28–32
July 16–20, 2015
Miles driven: 6,892
Cups of coffee: 76
Jacksonville FL to New York NY

When I left Oakland a month ago, I had no idea how important father
figures would be to this story. Of the nine Wax Packers I've covered so
far, only three had fathers who were reliable, positive influences in their
lives (Rance, Tempy, and Jaime); the other six dads ranged from alco-
holics to virtual strangers, with plenty of neglect and abuse in between.
As I leave the stickiness of Florida in my rearview mirror, I head up the
East Coast in pursuit of the next Wax Packer, Lee Mazzilli, and a visit
with my own father.

My dad took me to countless ball games as a kid. My memories of
those times are a collage of senses—the smell of sausage, peppers, and
onions from a vendor outside Fenway Park, a sandwich my dad had to
have before every game; his hairy legs outstretched next to me in the
bleachers; the steady calm of his voice as he explained how to score a
game. Whatever we lacked in common ground or understanding, we
made up for with baseball.

He showed me how to wrap tin foil around the antenna of my transis-
tor radio to get the Phillies radio station at night when the signal seemed
magically stronger. He threw Wiffle Balls to me in the backyard until

his arm felt like rubber. He came to every single Little League game I played and always, always told me how proud he was of me.

I idolized him. He was Google before the internet, his broad interests and voracious literary diet providing answers to any question I asked. And I delighted in the unwavering simplicity with which he explained the world to me.

"Who are the good guys and the bad guys?" I would ask when Tom Brokaw came on the TV to give an update on President Reagan's latest talks with Mikhail Gorbachev.

"The Russians are bad and we're good," he would say, rubbing his bushy black mustache. I became a little Republican, even dressing up one year as George H. W. Bush for Halloween. I sometimes miss that world, a clearly defined place of heroes and villains where my dad made everything feel safe and secure.

I imprinted on the outwardly perfect example that he and my mom set of their marriage, and I assumed that I too would grow up to meet a nice girl in college and have a family that went to church on Sundays. But as I grew into adulthood, developing my own set of beliefs and values and learning to think for myself, I had to deal with the challenges that we all face once the playing field is level with that of our parents. I began to see serious cracks in their marriage, the way that it was *too* traditional, too asymmetrical; they were stuck in the old-fashioned spheres of wife as homemaker and husband as breadwinner. My mom knew nothing of their finances, and while my dad was fair-minded and kind, he controlled all the purse strings. They grew apart, finding other partners for emotional support, and although my dad ultimately was the one who wanted a divorce, the foundation of their marriage had long since crumbled. The asymmetry of their marriage made the split harder on my mom, who suddenly found herself a fifty-eight-year-old single woman who hadn't been in the workforce in thirty years and had never paid her own bills.

The divorce, coupled with the demise of my relationship with Kay, left me hurt and angry. I had been a model teenager who had never given my parents any trouble, but in my twenties I lashed out at both of them for having built up an example that did not endure. But as Don Carman told me, when you're angry you're really just feeling sorry for yourself.

My mom now lives near me in California, thrilled to be a grandmother (my sister's two kids have taken the pressure off me to reproduce). My dad remarried and moved to Chicago, but I've struggled to acclimate to our new dynamic as adults. Our conversations, mostly done via phone these days, orbit around some emotional sphere, occasionally scratching the surface but never blasting into its core. We discuss business and politics and movies but rarely venture into the intensely personal territory where I like to be. When he asks about my life, which he always makes a point of doing, I hear myself parroting back to him, talking about everything except what really matters. I think I do this out of some deep-seated respect for the boundaries of our old relationship, because I still want to be the ten-year-old who thinks the Soviets are evil and the Americans are good and who idolizes his dad, not someone who makes him feel uncomfortable.

When I see him in a few short hours, I know we'll talk baseball. But this time, when he asks about my life, I want to blast into that emotional sphere, to honestly answer that most basic of questions: *What's new?* I want to tell him who I really am—a thirty-four-year-old liberal with Buddhist leanings who might not want to follow the seemingly preordained path of marriage and kids and who thinks Reagan wasn't that great a president after all. And I don't want his approval or even a response. I just want him to listen.

JUNE 5, 1973

Back behind the baseball field of Abraham Lincoln High, or rather the patch of dirt and weeds masquerading as a baseball field, Lee Mazzilli is hiding with his buddies. Although school isn't quite out yet, summer is here, and Maz can't be happier. The country may be in turmoil, haunted by Vietnam and the looming specter of Watergate, but for Maz, summer means nonstop baseball here in the working-class Italian neighborhood of Sheepshead Bay, Brooklyn, only a couple miles northeast of Coney Island.

Maz is a good student with a bad case of senioritis, seeing no harm in cutting class now and then to enjoy the sunshine, like he's doing now, sitting under a tree near home plate.

Across the field he sees a figure approaching and within moments recognizes the aggravated march of his baseball coach, Herb Isaacson.

"Shit," Maz says to his friends. "Coach sees me."

Isaacson stomps closer, stopping a few feet away and peering hard into Maz's face, turning Maz's olive complexion slightly pink.

"Hey, Mazzo, you hear anything?" he asks gruffly.

"What do you mean coach?" Maz musters.

Shit. I'm fucked, he thinks.

The old man's face breaks into a grin.

"Mets."

He puts up a single finger.

Once again: "Mets."

Maz's eyes grow wide. It finally registers.

He has just been taken in the first round of the Major League Baseball draft (the fourteenth overall pick) by his home team, the New York Mets.

He takes off running. He runs and runs and runs through the cluttered city streets, past local markets and street vendors, straight through blinking orange Don't Walk signs, dodging cars and smiling at the honks that follow. He doesn't stop until he reaches East 12th Street between Avenues Y and Z, dashing up to the second floor and bursting through the door of the three-room apartment he shares with his parents and older siblings, Joann and Freddy. It's a modest dwelling for the second-generation Italian American family, space at such a premium that the bathroom is located outside and down a hallway.

His father, Libero, hears him before he sees him. A welterweight boxer turned piano tuner, he knows nothing about baseball but everything about fatherhood, taking Maz to countless speed-skating practices and competitions in the winter and baseball games in the summer. Years from now, when Maz is an established Major Leaguer, Libero will frame each of his baseball cards as a reminder of his youngest son's success.

The whole family knows that Maz is going places, knows that he won't be in Sheepshead Bay long, not with that speed and athleticism.

Scouts have been over to the house for his mom June's famous chicken cacciatore, and multiple teams have shown interest. Maz just wanted to get drafted, let alone in the first round. But first round *and* taken by his home team? Too good.

"Dad!" he gasps, trying to catch his breath. "Mets! First round!"

His dad rushes forward and squeezes his son, kissing his cheek and telling him how proud he is. They hold each other, tears streaming down their faces.

═══

I've lived in or near cities all my life, but nothing compares to New York City. After having spent only $8.75 on tolls the entire trip, I drop $35.10 to get across the maze of bridges and expressways guarding the Big Apple. Driving one of the perilously narrow, perpetually-under-construction expressways choked with traffic, I pass old brick apartment building after apartment building stacked close together, dressed with steel fire escapes. I marvel at the mass of humanity contained within a single block, vertical row after row of windows and air-conditioning units. And this isn't even Manhattan. This is Staten Island.

Maz now lives in Greenwich, Connecticut, in a five-bedroom, four-bathroom Colonial with a large backyard perfect for Wiffle Ball games and Easter egg hunts. The wealthiest town in the state, Greenwich, a haven for hedge funds and private equity firms, is only forty minutes from the heart of Manhattan. This may be where Maz ended up, but it's not where he started. To trace his roots, my dad and I are staying in a Comfort Inn in Brooklyn's Sheepshead Bay, spitting distance from Coney Island.

Maz is now a spring training instructor and special advisor for the Yankees, and we've made plans to meet tomorrow night in the town of Rye for dinner. With his son, LJ, a prospect in the Mets' Minor League system, Maz spends much of his time watching him play, and since it's the heart of the baseball season, that time is limited. Still, I'm grateful that he is willing to set aside a couple hours for a complete stranger with no book contract or baseball writing credentials. After I left a few messages on his home answering machine, Maz had called me back right before the trip, deeply apologetic: "I really apologize. I know you called a couple of times. I'm not normally like that," he said in a thick Brooklyn accent, leaving me stunned that this ex-ballplayer would think he had anything to apologize to me for. His wife, Dani, a former broadcaster, was also super helpful in arranging our meeting. While I was in Florida a couple days ago, I reached her on the phone. "I'll help you set it up," she offered. "Lee's a private guy; if you want to know where he is at a party, look in the corner of the room," she said.

I meet up with my dad in our hotel room. I've conscripted him to be my research assistant for the next couple days, figuring this trip will serve as our annual father-son road get-together, a tradition that goes back several years.

I walk in the room and give him a big hug.

"Hey, big guy!" he says, his usual greeting for me. "How was the New Jersey Turnpike? Was it jammed?" he asks.

"Not too bad," I reply.

"I'm so glad I MapQuested my route," he says about his drive. "I would never have found this place. That MapQuest is pretty good."

Yes, MapQuest. He'll discover Google Maps in about 2020.

The British Open golf tournament is on TV (golf is his other favorite sport). "They had to delay the tournament due to high winds," he says as we sit on our respective beds, facing the tube. He's almost seventy but could pass for a decade less, his brown hair flecked with gray and cut short. Unlike Rance, his eighties mustache is long gone, and he's wearing a gray Duke shirt (my alma mater) tucked into dark blue jeans. We fall right back into our old pattern, talking about weather and traffic, circling that emotional sphere. And, of course, our ever-reliable go-to: baseball.

"I was trying to watch the Dodgers-Nationals game last night," he says, eyes on the TV. "They had to suspend it because the lights went out twice. The Dodgers were winning 3–2." He pauses, then continues: "I was watching this thing on 20/20 about this kidnapping in Vallejo. That's kind of near where you live, isn't it?" I nod, and we move on to a vast range of topics, from the odd shape of the state of Maryland to the paucity of black hockey players to the socioeconomics of Jacksonville. We don't talk about his relationship with my stepmom, Katina, or my dating life or how my mother is doing out in California. And I'm just as much to blame as he is, too uncomfortable with the thought of making him uncomfortable. I sip my hotel coffee and stare at the screen while we chat, our eyes in parallel.

Given that we have a job to do, I debrief my dad on Lee Mazzilli. Growing up in blue-collar Sheepshead Bay with two working parents, Maz was a natural athlete. He was ambidextrous, giving him the unusual talent of throwing equally well with both arms (although he wasn't particularly strong from either side—the "weak arm" label followed him throughout his career). When he was ten, he started fatiguing quickly and falling often when competing, and orthopedic surgeon Dr. Arthur Michele diagnosed him with a muscle imbalance caused by an atrophied left hip, affecting his balance. "I came to the conclusion that Lee possessed total physical unfitness," said Dr. Michele.[1] Maz learned an early and important lesson in humility. Accustomed to winning at everything, he suddenly had to undergo painful physical therapy sessions every morning and evening to strengthen his left side, a ritual that would last for eight years. By the time he was twenty-one, he was playing center field for the New York Mets, and a few years later, he was one of the best players in the National League and the sole bright spot on an otherwise pitiful Mets team. This is the Maz whom my dad remembers playing center field in the 1970s, winning the 1979 All-Star Game for the National League with a walk-off walk, of all things, which he accentuated with a spectacular bat flip, decades ahead of his time.

Every newspaper article from that era referred as much to Maz's good looks as to his baseball prowess; playing in New York meant constant media attention, and his tall, dark, and handsome profile made him a crossover celebrity. He signed a contract with the William Morris Agency, read for TV and movie parts, and was constantly compared to John Travolta; even Frank Sinatra brought him onstage during a show at Caesars Palace. But while the spotlight was flattering, Maz was never comfortable in its glare—he never stopped being the quietly confident, always generous kid from Sheepshead Bay. "I had a very hard time dealing with that [the fame]. I look at myself as just a guy from the streets of New York," he said.[2] When twenty-two-year-old clubhouse assistant Charlie Samuels needed a place to live in 1980, Maz, then a bachelor, invited him to crash at his house on Long Island. "I don't put myself on a pedestal. I am no better than the man cleaning the ballpark or the woman selling hot dogs. I just happen to be an athlete," he told the *New York Times*.[3]

Maz's time as baseball royalty was short-lived, however, as injuries slowed him down. He was traded to Texas, then to the Yankees, then to the Pirates within one season. He spent the rest of his career as a role player, albeit an important one, delivering key hits upon his return to the Mets in 1986 in their championship season. He retired following a stint with the Toronto Blue Jays in 1989 at thirty-four, the same age I am now.

═

My dad is not a shy man.

We're walking the cramped streets of Sheepshead Bay, the worn asphalt baking in the hot summer sun, passing row after row of old brick apartment buildings mixed with delis and small groceries. The diversity of the neighborhood resembles the United Nations chamber and reminds me of my home back in Oakland. We're outside for only a few minutes, my nose in my notebook, when I hear my dad mumble, "If I see somebody a little bit older . . ." Then I hear his voice: "Excuse me! Are you from this area?"

Here we go, I think, remembering all our family vacations, when my dad would talk to *everybody*, always super cheerful and positive.

I look up and see him in front of an older woman with dyed red hair wearing a sundress. She's carrying two plastic bags of groceries.

She stares at him with the compassion of a pitchfork. The look is so hostile, so truculent, that I wonder if I had misheard him. Had he asked what kind of underwear she had on? How much money she makes?

He repeats the question, and her face hardens more. She glares another instant, spins on her heel, and marches off.

"Dad, remember, we're in New York," I say.

He just laughs and looks for his next opportunity. We're now outside a supermarket, where he approaches another older woman, this one pushing a cart. She has bright blue fingernails and is wearing white pants. I stand to the side, half smiling, half cringing.

"Are you from this area?" he asks her.

"Yeah," she replies curtly. A large nose dominates her narrow face.

"Is this a big Italian area?" he asks.

"Used to be. Now it's Russians, Muslims, Jews, and some Italians," she says, all business. "It's changed a lot."

"My son here, he's writing a book on Lee Mazzilli, who grew up around here," my dad says proudly, motioning toward me. I give a meek smile.

"Oh yeah, his mom used to go to the beauty salon down there," she replies, her face softening. "I knew of her but didn't know her personally," she says. I'm amazed that the Mazzilli name is still known on these streets. I thank her for her time and ask her if there's any place to get lunch nearby.

"Yeah, Emmons Avenue," she says, launching into a long set of directions that has me reaching for my phone.

"Are there any places closer?" I ask.

"What's wrong with you? You're young, you walked all the way down here!" she says, then pauses and adds, "Go and call a taxi, or an Uber, whatever you kids use," before waving good-bye and walking away.

"You're right, we *are* in New York," my dad says once she's gone, cracking us both up.

A few hours later we walk through the turnstiles at MCU Park to watch the Single-A Brooklyn Cyclones take on the Vermont Lake Monsters. This is baseball at its roots, a sleepy game played on a languid summer night in front of a few thousand people with the Thunderbolt roller-coaster visible beyond the left-field fence. Twelve bucks gets us excellent seats down the first-base line, where we sit side by side reading our programs, studying the rosters like homework. It's hard to tell if the people are here for the game or the nonstop entertainment on the sidelines—it's YMCA Night, Fireworks Night, Princess and Pirate Night, *Honeymooners* Night (the TV show), and Bus Operator Sandy Bobblehead Night all in one, the last of which appears to be the Cyclones' seagull mascot, Sandy, dressed up as the Jackie Gleason *Honeymooners* character. Between innings, *Gong Show*–type entertainment distracts the crowd (the PeeWee dance crew! whack an inflatable baseball with a golf club!), and between pitches, the players lining the top step of the dugout peek back to scan the crowd for attractive women, as timeless a baseball tradition as the hot dog. My dad and I trade observations on the game, sprinkling the conversation with politics.

"What do you think of Bernie Sanders for president?" I ask.

"I think he's a good candidate if you like not having to work for a living," he says.

"Who do you think the Democratic nominee is going to be?"

"I think it's going to be Joe Biden," he says.

Baseball is a game like no other. It's my favorite for the same reason that it's many others' least favorite: it's long and ponderous. For those prone to boredom, baseball is excruciating; but for those who relish stillness, it is exquisite. Those long lulls, anathema to the always stimulated, provide the ideal setting for building relationships. Baseball is the backdrop for self-discovery.

Somewhere in there, the Lake Monsters beat the Cyclones 4–3, but the final score hardly matters. For three hours I am that ten-year-old in our living room again, and there are good guys (John Kasich, Jeb Bush) and bad guys (Bernie Sanders, Joe Biden). Three hours sitting side by side, and yet I still haven't worked up the courage to really talk to him.

Maybe tomorrow.

=

I'm sitting across from Maz in the back of Ruby's Oyster Bar and Bistro in the tony suburb of Rye. My dad sits to my left, and Maz is leaning over a plate of liver, bacon, and onions.

"My wife's liver is better," he says in that thick Brooklyn accent.

I now see what all those writers were talking about in the 1970s describing his "matinee idol looks." Even at sixty, Maz is debonair, his black hair slicked back, his tanned skin glowing from his six-foot-one frame. He's wearing a snug black T-shirt that conforms to his thick upper arms and chest and a pair of black jeans. As he talks, a tattoo on his left bicep peeks out from under the edge of his sleeve, but not enough for me to identify it.

Maz is an active listener, his dark brown eyes rapt, completely present in the moment. It's the skill that made him such a good coach and manager once he finished playing. For the first time on the trip, one of the Wax Packers seems as interested in me as I am in him.

"What made you decide to write this book?" he asks.

It's a simple and obvious question, yet I'm so accustomed to steering the conversation that it throws me a bit.

"As a kid, you know, my first baseball cards were around 1986. I'm thirty-four," I begin.

"That makes me feel old. I'm probably your dad's age, right?" he replies.

I explain the premise of the book and my experiences thus far.

"Are you surprised how big leaguers turned out?" he asks, flipping the script some more.

"It ranges a lot. One thing I've found interesting is that players aren't nearly as into baseball as the fans are," I reply.

"Why is that?" he asks.

I start to respond, and he adds, "I know why, but I want to ask you why."

"Don Carman considered it self-preservation. What is your take?" I ask.

"Yeah, you know, when we get to a certain age, there are things we can't do. But in my mind I think I can still do it. I think an athlete always has that competitive edge in him. Always. You never lose that," he says with the same look that Tempy and Randy had when discussing their desire to get back in the game.

My dad sips his glass of Cabernet Sauvignon, content to take a back seat and listen as Maz and I give and take. He occasionally asks a question or adds a comment but mostly just chuckles at Maz's dry humor.

"We're staying in Sheepshead Bay," I tell him.

"No offense, but that's not a very good area. I lived there," he replies. "We had five of us living in a three-room apartment, my brother and sister and my mom and dad. We didn't have much. But that's all we knew. It was normal to us," he says.

"Were you surprised when you got drafted in the first round?" I ask.

"Yeah. Absolutely. I just wanted to get drafted, I didn't care when. I had no clue where I was going to go," he says with a smile, flashing a set of bright white teeth.

During his couple of seasons in the Minor Leagues, he got a taste of a world much bigger than Brooklyn. In 1974 he played for the Anderson Mets in western South Carolina.

"When I went down there, you're down south, and you're talking the seventies, and it was chain gangs on the side of the road, KKK, all that stuff that I had not been privy to," he says.

"What was your manager there like, Owen Friend?" I ask.

"Miserable bastard," he says, cracking up my dad. "I'm gonna be very nice and say that."

Maz is quick-witted, direct, and honest. He sits with his back against the wall, relaxed and at ease. He tells me about the surreal nature of his relationships with Willie Mays, whom he idolized as a kid and who became his personal mentor during those early years when Maz was learning to play the outfield. We gloss over the highlight of his career, the Mets' dramatic comeback win over the Red Sox in the 1986 World Series, because what new could possibly be said about one of the most chronicled series in baseball history?

While many of his teammates were careless with their money, living in the moment a little too much, Maz was always smart and careful. He didn't rush into anything, equally patient at the plate (he excelled at drawing walks) and in his personal life. Enduring yet another question about his love life in a 1980 interview, he said, "It's tough being married when you play ball. You're always moving around. I'm not getting married to get divorced. Once I get married, I'll stay married."[4] A man of his word, Maz married Dani in 1984, and they're still married today.

I ask how his ride on the baseball carousel came to an end.

"In 1990 there was the lockout. That spring I still wanted to play, but I couldn't get to camp because of the lockout. And when they finally resolved it, there was a very short window for spring training, so there really wasn't an opportunity to get invited to spring training to see what you've got. And that was it," he says.

"What did you do that first year you were out?" I ask.

Like the rest of the Wax Packers, his memory of life immediately following retirement is a blur.

"I don't really know," he says. "We wanted to start a family [their eldest child, Jenna, was born in 1989]. The stars weren't lined up right to go back to playing."

Before long, he was busier than ever, trying on several new careers: he opened a restaurant, went to work with a friend at a mortgage bank, served as commissioner of an independent baseball league, and even starred in an off-Broadway play following a dare from buddy Dan Lauria (the father on *The Wonder Years*). But no matter what he did, none of it was baseball.

After Maz wandered in the wilderness for six years, Dani brought him home by making him leave home. "My wife, she basically pushed me out the door," he says, resting his elbow on the chair in front of him.

"Nothing ever fills the void," Dani said back in 2003, aware that her husband still had baseball left in his system.

"She just knew this was something I needed to do. I needed a push, and she pushed me," Maz says.

The hardest part was going back on the road, away from his family. Nothing is more important to Maz than family. He eased himself back in, managing the Single-A Tampa Yankees. He and Dani made a pact to never go more than three weeks without getting the family together. By 1999 Maz had graduated to Double-A Norwich, and from 2000 to 2003 he was the first base coach for the New York Yankees, winning another World Series ring in 2000. But he almost didn't get that far.

His twins, Laccy and LJ, were only seven when he decided to return to the game. LJ in particular was attached to his dad.

"I said to him, 'Remember in September, Dad's gonna be home, and I'm gonna take you to soccer and basketball, and I'll be with you every day,'" he tells me, his dark eyebrows slightly furrowed. I feel my dad shift next to me.

"One day I had an off day and flew home from Florida to surprise my wife," he begins. "I came home and said, 'Where's the big guy?' She said, 'He's in bed.' I went and surprised him, woke him up. The first thing he said was, 'Dad, is it September already?' And that just broke my heart. I went downstairs and told my wife, 'I can't do it.' It killed me," he says.

We all sit in silence for a moment, staring at our drinks.

"What's your tattoo about?" I finally ask, breaking the silence.

"That's me and my brother," he says, his eyes welling.

He pats his bicep.

"Me and my brother."

"How would you describe your relationship with your siblings?" I ask. I had read that Maz was the youngest, with Freddy seven and Joann three years older, but I know little else about them.

"I lost my brother," he says softly. "We were together for fifty-some years, and there wasn't one time where he and I ever had a fight. Not one time that he and I ever cursed at each other. Never. He was such a big part of my life, losing him—I had a tough time with that," he says, closing his eyes and reaching his hand to his forehead.

"I lost my best friend," he adds.

Maz and his wife, Dani, and sister, Joann, helped put together a small charity, the Fred L. Mazzilli Foundation, in his memory to raise money for lung cancer funding.

"It's just us licking the envelopes and putting the mailings out," Maz says.

We chat a bit more over coffee, but it's getting late, and Maz has to get back to Greenwich.

"Thank you for dinner," he says, gripping my hand tightly and looking me warmly in the eyes. "It's good to see you're going out and spending time with your dad. Enjoy your time together—it's precious."

My dad and I ride back to Sheepshead Bay together, saying everything by saying nothing at all.

═

The next morning, before parting ways, my dad and I sit at a Starbucks for our other favorite activity: Trivial Pursuit. He's strong in every category but entertainment, while my weakness is art. For years, although I came close, I could never quite beat him, but the torch has now been passed, as I win handily. He's got to head back to Chicago, and I've got an appointment in Doc Gooden's living room tomorrow, but I'm not ready to go. I feel that anxious pit in my stomach, that hollow feeling I experienced as my parents drove away after dropping me off for my freshman year of college, effectively ending my childhood.

"Dad," I begin. He turns his hazel eyes on me, bright but with slight circles underneath. They are the same eyes I have been looking into for thirty-four years. He raises his eyebrows.

"Dad, I want to tell you some things," I begin. "And I just want you to listen. You can respond if you want to, but mostly I just want you to listen. I don't need your approval or your opinion, I just want you to know certain things about me."

"Sure," he says, crossing his legs, folding his hands, leaning back the same way Maz did last night at the restaurant.

Once I start talking, I don't even pause to breathe. "I know you want me to find someone special and get married and have kids. I know you think I would be unhappy if I never did that, that my life would somehow be incomplete. You don't say that out loud, but I know you, I know how you feel. And maybe you're right, maybe I would be miserable if I was always alone. But I like my life. I'm happy being alone. I like my freedom. I'm not like you, I don't see the world through the same lens that you do. And I love you so much, you know that, and I am always so grateful for all the opportunities you and Mom gave me. But I'm different from you. I'm not a Christian. I don't believe in the same God that you do. I like to sit still and meditate and just observe my thoughts. My god is just trying to be as present as I can, which I think is what love really is, and being compassionate to other people, treating them well. I'm telling you all this because I want you to know that me having these beliefs and feeling this way is not out of some defiance of you, it's not some rejection born out of bitterness about what happened between you and Mom, because I accept all of that. I respect you and love you for who you are, but it's different from who I am. I need you to know that."

I ramble. I don't care. The whole time I look him right in the eye, feeling naked and vulnerable and exposed. When I finish talking, my whole body feels like an unclenched fist, tingling slightly. He looks at me with a look that only a parent can show to a child. After sitting and listening for several minutes, he opens his mouth to reply. "Brad, I know all that," he says, astonishing me. "And I'm so proud of who you are."

The world does have good guys and bad guys after all. Heroes do exist. And although he never had his own baseball card, my dad will always be one of them.

'85 RECORD BREAKER

DWIGHT GOODEN, NEW YORK METS
Youngest 20-Game Winner, Modern History

13

NOBODY HOME

When I was young, my neighbors had a
VCR tape of my dad, and I used to watch
that video. When the part with the drug
problem would come on, I immediately
would just start crying. Every time.
—*Dwight Gooden Jr.*

Days 33–35
July 21–23, 2015
Miles driven: 6,983
Cups of coffee: 84
New York NY to Westbury NY

"I think he's stoned," says the promoter, fiftyish, wearing a canary-yellow polo shirt tucked into khakis. He swings his gut around the bar, clearly agitated, trying to get the attention of an attractive woman in her forties who's standing nearby.

"I gave him quite a fee for this too," he says.

The woman, apparently a colleague, grips her cell phone tightly and glares straight ahead.

"Just tell me, Junior, be honest with me. What's going on?" she says, pacing around the bar and sounding like she knows exactly what's going on.

I've just walked into the Olde Stone Mill restaurant outside Yonkers, a leafy suburb north of the Bronx.

She pulls the phone away from her face and whispers to the promoter: "He says he has food poisoning." She's tall and attractive, with immaculate makeup.

Dwight "Doc" Gooden, one of only three players to ever appear solo on the cover of *Time*, is nowhere to be found. One of the most dominant pitchers of the 1980s, Doc, now fifty, still earns on the fumes of that fame, appearing at venues like this to meet and greet fans and sign autographs. For $100 you get a speech from Doc and an autograph while you nosh on the "ballpark menu" of hot dogs and hamburgers.

The "Junior" that the woman is talking to on the phone is Doc Gooden Jr., better known as "Little Doc" (he is a few inches shorter than his father), who also serves as his dad's agent.

I walk into the adjacent dining room, where the bulbs in the chandeliers splash bright light on the yellow walls. About thirty-five people, including a tableful of nuns and a kid in a wheelchair, are waiting and patiently eating their hot dogs.

Waiting for Doc to show up.

Doc Gooden, like Carlton Fisk, was the type of player I didn't care for as a kid simply because he was so good (and because he played for the Mets, the archrivals of my beloved Phillies). He burst onto the scene in 1984, winning the Rookie of the Year Award at age nineteen, and a year later had one of the most dominant seasons in baseball history, winning twenty-four games with eight shutouts and posting an anemic 1.53 ERA. He won the National League Cy Young Award before he could even legally drink a beer.

But the city of New York doesn't just venerate its stars, it devours them. Doc (a nickname he earned at age nine for his surgical dissection of hitters) owned the city, and it owned him; a 105-foot-high Nike ad of him covered the side of a skyscraper on West Forty-Second Street. By 1986, the year the Mets won the World Series, Doc was already starting to burn out.

Those who knew the real Doc, the Doc who had grown up in the working-class Belmont Heights neighborhood of East Tampa, Florida, were not entirely surprised. "Dwight shouldn't have been in New York," his high school baseball coach, Billy Reed, now eighty-three, told me last week when I was in Tampa. "He should have gone someplace like Minnesota. A low-key town." Although Doc's childhood seemed stable on the outside, beneath the surface lurked dysfunction that would haunt him his whole life.

Doc's mom, Ella Mae, was the disciplinarian who emphasized education, but working two jobs limited her ability to keep watch over Doc; his father, Dan, was an ex-semipro ballplayer who worked at the local Cargill plant and always wanted to be the good guy. He was also a philanderer. When Doc was only five, Dan would take him out to get a snack before the *Game of the Week* came on NBC, and on the way he'd stop at his mistress's house, leaving Doc in the car and saying he had to drop something off for a friend. One day when Ella Mae got wind of what was going on, she followed him to one of his trysts with a .38 and opened fire when he got to his lover's door, hitting him in the left arm. He wasn't critically injured, the police were kept out of it, and the whole thing was swept under the rug.

A short time later, Doc's half sister Mercedes was babysitting him when her husband, known for his violence, stormed into the house in a rage and shot her five times right in front of Doc and his eighteen-month-old nephew. Doc grabbed his nephew and bolted for the bathroom, locking them inside in sheer terror until he heard the police arrive. Mercedes survived but had permanent injuries.

All of this happened before Doc was six.

"For a long time, I buried most of these dark family memories," he wrote in his third autobiography, *Doc*, in 2013.[1]

Instead, Doc focused on baseball, and Dan was always happy to indulge. He spent hours and hours mentoring Doc, teaching him the fundamentals and strengthening his body to handle the punishment of pitching. He worked out Doc's abs until it hurt to laugh, made him stand on a board laid atop bricks just to get his balance. Dan saw potential and dollar signs in his son's blazing fastball, knowing he could go high in the draft. And while he spent time with Doc, he never disciplined him. When Ella Mae suggested Doc get a job, Dan would make the applications disappear. He'd give Doc money and tell him to go enjoy himself. Coach Reed observed all this from afar with a disapproving scowl but could only do so much. "I had to coach Dwight from the shoulders up," he told me.

Coach Reed wasn't afraid to lay down the law, no matter how good his pupil was. When Doc was a few minutes late to homeroom on Opening Day, the star player earned a ticket to the bench. Although Doc was offered a full ride to the University of Miami along with free housing, Doc and Dan had their sights on pro ball. After being drafted in the first round (fifth overall) by the Mets in 1982 (eventually negotiating an $85,000 signing bonus), an excited but naive Ella Mae asked, "Will the Mets let you go to college first?" "No, Ella," Dan said. "It doesn't work like that."

Only four years later and on top of the world, Doc was holed up in his apartment on Long Island while his teammates were being toasted by two million New Yorkers as they cruised down Lower Manhattan in the World Series victory parade. He had stayed up all night snorting cocaine and doing shots with friends and groupies, arriving back at his apartment in time for the rising sun to sting his bloodshot eyes. He was a world champion. He was in agony.

From there, the tragedy of Doc Gooden unfolded over three decades, with so many twists and turns and rehab stints that I gave up counting when reading the stack of books and articles meticulously documenting his plight. The cocaine addiction, which had begun in January 1986, culminated with a suspension in early 1987, and although he would remain clean for several years, resisting the white medicine would become a lifelong struggle. He was suspended for all of 1994 for failing too many drug tests and hit rock bottom in March 2006 when he was sentenced to one year and a day in a Central Florida prison for violating his probation. There were some highlights amid the wreckage—in 1996, after not playing the previous season, he threw a no-hitter, and despite all the career interruptions, he finished with 194 wins when he retired in 2001. While the sports world largely considered him a disappointment, he may have overachieved, given all his demons. Following his playing days, he served for many years as a special assistant to Yankees GM George Steinbrenner, who always had a soft spot for him.

Doc's family life was just as tumultuous. He had seven children with three different women, none of whom he is still with today (he is twice divorced). The sweet and loving boy never fully matured. Stunted by addiction and those long-buried childhood traumas, he reluctantly entered *Celebrity Rehab*, a reality show with Dr. Drew Pinsky, in 2011. Although he had no expectations, something about Drew's style clicked with Doc, and it actually worked in a way none of the previous programs had. In his 2013 book Doc wrote: "I am more than two years clean now . . . I don't drink. I don't use cocaine or any other recreational drugs." Rather than taking an absolute, black-and-white approach, he emphasized self-compassion and persistence: "I hope I never stumble again. But if I do, I promise to pull myself back up again and try some more."[2] Doc may finally have found the cure.

=

I'm standing in Doc Gooden's living room, but he is not home.

The house, modest and inconspicuous, is located in the town of Westbury on Long Island east of Queens. It's a family neighborhood of two-story brick or wood-shingled houses, basketball and hockey nets dotting the driveways. Casa Gooden is home to Doc and four of his adult children. Although they've been there for more than a year, they still haven't fully unpacked, the living room and hallways cluttered with framed photos and baseball mementos waiting to be mounted. In one room stands an old-school video arcade game (Multicade) next to a seat cushion standing on its side and an ironing board. There's an enlarged photo of Doc celebrating his no-hitter leaning against the wall.

I walk into the kitchen, which looks out onto the backyard pool, and sit down with Doc's oldest son, Little Doc. I hand him an envelope with $200 cash as promised, and he offers me a bottle of water. Earlier this morning, he texted me the bad news that while he was still available, his dad was called in to Citi Field (where the Mets play) for a last-minute charity event and that my meeting with Doc would have to wait until tomorrow morning.

A little girl walks by, chattering to herself.

"That's Milan," Little Doc tells me. "She's visiting from Maryland. She lives with her mom." Milan is the youngest of Doc's seven kids.

I'm just as interested in Little Doc as I am in his father. Like Carlton Fisk, Doc reached such a level of celebrity that his story is common knowledge. But I want to know what effect his troubled life had on his oldest son, born to a woman his dad had a brief fling with in 1985.

Wispy and wearing a backward hat loosely fitting his head, Little Doc has a polite and amiable demeanor. While his dad's narrow features convey a certain austerity, Little Doc's face is rounder, his smile bigger and more inviting. He's twenty-nine but retains a teenage innocence in the way he lights up as he talks, his dreadlocks falling past his shoulders.

"I feel as if I played baseball myself," he says. Every summer as a child he would join his dad on the road, where he experienced the royal treatment. It may have been because few of the other players had kids, or it may have been because he was Doc Gooden's son. He would do everything but play in the game himself: shag fly balls during batting practice, sign autographs, even sit in the dugout in uniform. "The other players would just take care of me, give me hundreds of dollars," he says with a big smile.

But he was living two lives. The summers were five-star hotels and first-class treatment with his dad. Then when the school year rolled around, it was back to East Tampa to live with his mom, who worked for a medical clinic serving disabled children. She raised Little Doc on a $25,000 annual salary.

"It didn't make sense. How is this possible? How could he [his dad] have all this money and my mom is broke?" he asks me. I can see the frustration gathering on his face. He goes on: "Mom didn't have much income. There was no man around. No one with *this*," he says, pointing sharply to his ample Adam's apple.

Kids at school teased him, envious of his dad. "Some people would say, 'Why do you go to school? You should have your own school. You should drive a limo to school!'" he says.

But it just made him madder and more confused. He wasn't some rich kid with a silver spoon, he was one of *them*. He was East Tampa, Hillsborough Avenue, and to prove it, he started spending more and more time in the streets, slinging dope.

"I was making thousands of dollars in high school. I ended up having $30,000 before I was a senior. It was like, 'I don't know what *you're* doing, but I got *me* some money.' You know?" he says. "I was in the streets, just selling drugs, smoking weed, hanging with lots of drug dealers in the hood. I was catching cases."

"Catching cases? Does that mean you were getting in trouble?" I ask, confused.

He laughs at my naivete. "Sorry, yeah, catching cases means I was definitely getting in trouble. I caught a cocaine charge when I was seventeen for possession and attempt to sell. I had three of those at seventeen, actually. I ended up doing thirteen months behind those charges," he says.

In a particularly sad turn, Little Doc was in Hillsborough County Jail in 2005 when he was awakened by someone throwing a copy of the *Tampa Tribune* in his face. His dad had just been arrested for driving under the influence, eluding police, and resisting arrest without violence, and according to the front page, he was being brought in to the same jail.

Little Doc discusses all this with a sense of calm and openness, his low voice even. It's when I start digging into the underlying relationship with his father that he gets quieter, his voice reduced almost to a whisper. They lived together before the jail time, but both were careening out of control. While Little Doc knew secondhand about his father's addiction, he had never witnessed it himself.

"I had never seen him like that," he says.

One day he came home to find a handwritten note on the counter. "He left a letter that said, 'Carry on the name, the bank people already know you, make sure your grandma and everyone is taken care of, stuff like that," he says. Little Doc rushed to the garage, terrified of what he might find, but the car was gone. When his dad came home hours later, they didn't discuss it.

"Why didn't you bring it up?" I ask, following his clouded gaze into the backyard, where the sun is shining brightly.

Without turning back to me he mumbles, "I don't think I had enough courage or heart to stop and say, 'What's this? What's going on?'"

To this day, even living under the same roof, their bedrooms right across the hall from each other, they rarely talk about what really matters. Little Doc wants his dad to know what he feels and who he is. "I don't even know if he knows how intelligent I am about real life. I'm big on facts, big on statistics. I'm a completer, a seeker. I love research. I don't know if he knows I have that type of passion and ambition about life," he tells me, his voice stronger again.

"Why don't you tell him?" I ask.

He shifts in his chair, looks around the room, a bit self-conscious. "I don't know. A little stubborn, I guess," he says. "I guess it's like, if you don't know [by] now, you ain't asked about me," he continues, his voice trailing off.

He gets up to check the chicken nuggets baking in the oven, lunch for Milan and her playmate who's supposed to come over anytime now. I take a sip of my water and change directions. "Tell me about your music career," I say. I had read about his work as a rapper.

"I started music back in 2007," he says, sitting back down. "I spent thirteen months in jail in '04, then was back in the streets, doing the same thing. I was actually bigger. 2006 was my peak. I was sitting in a trap house, weed everywhere, when my buddy Andrew comes in with headphones on and a CD player. I immediately tell him to get to work, and I sat down and put the headphones on. I was like, 'Who's this?' He says, 'That's me!' He was singing R&B. He was like, 'Yo, you can rap too.' He told everyone in the house why they can be a rapper, and we all started rapping. The next day he called me and said, 'Come over to the studio, I've got a beat for you.' I recorded a song called 'Head First.'"

Little Doc had stumbled on his passion. While he had grown up dreaming of being a ballplayer just like his dad, he was not his dad. Music was his calling.

"I said, 'This is my way out. This is it.'" Using the money he had saved up from dealing, he started his own label, DJR Records, hired an advisor, and gave himself the moniker Prince of the Bay. While the music never hit it big, he still has aspirations of greatness.

"I want to do something good enough to where I get recognized and then I give my story. I want to speak for kids who had successful parents. I'd like to talk to them. I know there's tons of them going through what I went through. All of them just want to feel normal. I don't want to be caught in what my dad did or didn't do. I'm me," he says.

The Grammys will have to wait for now. Little Doc has two kids to raise from two different moms, one in Atlanta and one in Tampa, and he serves as his dad's agent. He moved up here last fall to focus on the business and get his head straight, leaving behind the streets of Tampa. But it's still hard. His brain runs as fast as his dad's fastball once did, spinning in multiple directions that leave him both excited and anxious. He has never even tried the cocaine he sold for years, preferring the calming effect that marijuana has on his brain. And while he wants to get clean, it's hard.

In addition to booking his dad for personal appearances like the one I am attending tomorrow night in Yonkers, Little Doc has launched a clothing line, Gooden Brand, that he is currently modeling. He's wearing a loose-fitting black T-shirt with "Doc Gooden" in big gray letters and his dad's silhouette on the front, mid-delivery, his right arm cocked back and ready to strike. "The line's been out two months now," he says. "We've got T-shirts, hats, performance wear, hoodies, bags. We also have a rehab product," he says, making me do a double take. But Little Doc means rehab as in pitchers who are rehabilitating their arms from Tommy John surgery.

"I have a vision to do a more sophisticated product line called Dwight Gooden. It's going to be suits, high fashion," he adds, taking off his hat momentarily to reveal a retreating hairline.

Before I go, I want to nail down the plan to meet with his dad. "Tell me again what your dad had to do today?" I ask.

"It's a pitching camp. They bring kids and work on pitching at the stadium," he says.

"What time tomorrow would work to do the interview?" I ask.

"I would think noon. We have a car coming at five to pick him up for the event." We make plans to touch base later today to confirm. Once I'm back in my car, I open my phone and Google the pitching camp at Citi Field where Doc is allegedly working.

I find nothing.

=

At 7:02 the next morning I text Little Doc about the planned interview with his dad: "Hey Doc, just wanted to check in so I can plan the day."

At 7:21 a.m. he replies: "Hey buddy I'm working on it now. Give me a few minutes."

10:38 a.m., Brad: "What's the word Doc? Is there a problem?"

10:40 a.m., Little Doc: "Well he's not here and he said he won't be back till like 3. I'm trying to figure out the best time."

I drive from Brooklyn to Westbury, figuring I should be nearby if Doc surfaces.

12:18 p.m., Brad: "I'm in Westbury. Is your dad back?"

12:18 p.m., Little Doc: "He says he is at Sprint getting his phone fixed he dropped water on it."

12:18 p.m., Brad: "What do you suggest?"

12:19 p.m., Little Doc: "Can u come to the event?"

I tell him I'll go but will wait in Westbury this afternoon in case his dad shows up. I post up at a Starbucks for a few hours, drinking three dark roasts while compulsively checking my text messages. Finally at 4:00 I head west toward Yonkers, pulling into the Olde Stone Mill restaurant parking lot.

4:50 p.m., Brad: "What's going on Doc?"

4:55 p.m., Brad: "Square with me please. I am sitting at the event."

5:15 p.m., Little Doc: "I'm going thru that too bro he didn't make the event. Trying to figure out what's been going on with him. It really sucks bcuz I'm in the middle of something I don't have an answer for."

5:15 p.m., Brad: "I hope he's OK. I understand your situation. Do you have any clue where he is? Do you think he relapsed?"

5:16 p.m., Little Doc: "If it helps any u have my permission to work it how u like."

5:16 p.m., Brad: "Have you seen him today?"

5:16 p.m., Little Doc: "I honestly don't know if he relapsed or not he's been complaining a lot about all the working he has to do."

And with that I walk inside and find the man in the yellow polo shirt and his immaculately made-up partner stomping around the bar, livid at Doc's absence.

Around the perimeter of the dining room are several pieces of New York baseball memorabilia: autographed photos of Derek Jeter, Gary Carter, C. C. Sabathia, all up for auction to raise money for charity. At the front of the room is the rectangular table where Doc is supposed to sit and sign autographs, but the chair is empty.

Three generations of baseball fans crowd around plates of hot dogs and french fries, looking out of place in this fine dining setting. I walk over to a lively mix of middle-aged fans who came of age during Gooden's heyday.

"He had the best curveball I've ever seen," says Peter, a forty-year-old with black hair slicked straight back and tucked behind his ears. "That thing would just drop off the table."

His brother Mike starts rattling off the names of all the players on the '86 Mets, the last year they won the World Series, as if they're old high school buddies: Hernandez, Carter, Dykstra, Backman . . .

The group nods and smiles with increasing delight, and soon a chorus of laughs floods the table as everyone begins chiming in with their own special Mets memory.

"I met Keith Hernandez at a Who concert!" one yells.

"I had a friend who had Gary Carter leave a voice mail on my phone!" another boasts.

They regress in age before my eyes, shedding cynicism and gaining poise with each successive story.

I walk over to another table crowded with boys and their parents. The kids are too young to remember Doc as a player, but their parents remember his dominance. Donna, a Yankees fan on vacation from Houston, fondly recalls Doc's no-hitter in 1996. At the adjacent table sit a group of nuns who were bused in from the Marian Woods convent.

As everyone chews their food, keeping their eyes on the room's entrance, the man in yellow trudges to the front to address the group. "I'm sorry to say that Doc won't be here tonight," he says. "It's very sad. He's back on whatever he's on. Of course, we will refund you your money. I'm really sorry again." A small murmur of concern ripples through the crowd, then the chatter resumes.

The world is still waiting for Doc to show up.

=

A couple days later I email Jay Horwitz, the Mets' longtime PR guy, to ask if he has any photos from the pitching camp at Citi Field that Doc allegedly attended the day I was in Doc's house interviewing Little Doc.

It's the same Jay Horwitz who frantically called Doc the morning of the Mets' World Series parade in October 1986 when he shut himself in his apartment following that epic cocaine bender, refusing to answer the phone. Jay has always protected Doc as much as he can; as a PR rep it was his job, after all, for all those years.

"Sorry Brad there were no photos," comes his one-line reply.

What kind of event for kids doesn't have any pictures, especially from the PR department? I find myself wanting there to be photos, to find some shred of evidence that Doc really was there at the stadium that day and not off in a bathroom somewhere getting high. But nothing on the internet suggests that the event even took place.

I keep pressing Jay for answers, and he keeps giving me one-line replies. Finally, I write, "Did this event happen?"

"I checked. It happened but he was not in attendance," is all he says.

I think of Little Doc, wanting so badly to do the right thing, disappointed yet again by his dad. Will he say anything once his dad resurfaces?

"I have so many 'why' questions for everyone," he told me during our interview.

"Why not ask them?" I said.

"I think because I already know the answers," he replied.

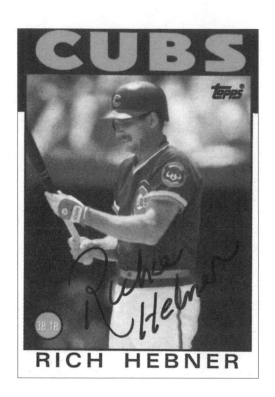

CUBS

RICH HEBNER

3B-1B

14

GONE FISHING

The semester ends for everybody.
—*Richie Hebner*

Day 36
July 24, 2015
Miles driven: 7,286
Cups of coffee: 90
Westbury NY to Norwood MA

"Where are you from?"

It's a question we get asked throughout our lives, but can the answer change?

I now consider California home. Every time I step off a plane back in the Bay Area and feel that crisp air in the jetway, I smile. But I will always be *from* Greenville, Rhode Island.

Everything in this part of the country is old and historic, the Europeans having settled Rhode Island as early as 1630. A suburb of Providence, Greenville is an old mill town dotted with oak and chestnut trees. In the years since my childhood, the town's name has become less and less apt as tracts of pristine forest have been converted into space for Applebee's and Target and Home Depot. But as much as the town's exterior changes, the soul of Greenville remains forever small town. Earlier this morning while eating a bagel at the town café, I overheard three wrinkly men bemoan the state of the world, including baseball: "I don't even watch anymore—the games take too damn long," one of them groused. I felt nothing in common with them, my life so far removed from this rural outpost, yet this place is a part of me. If I had a baseball card, this is where the writer would go to find my story.

The house I grew up in is a one-level stone cottage on a pond with meandering hallways resulting from multiple additions over the years. Lucky for me, it's still in the family, even though no one resides here year-round. I wander in and out of rooms as if I'm touring the house for the first time, picking up on small details I had always taken for granted—a vent here, a light switch there. All vestiges of my childhood bedroom, once a shrine to baseball players, have been replaced by the staid accoutrements of a guest bedroom save for a single piece of sloppy ceramic art I did in ninth grade, a green sculpture of a snake—or is it an earthworm? Art always was my worst subject. But no matter how many coats of paint or new color palettes are foisted on this room, these walls represent my childhood sanctuary, a place where I lost myself for hours amid nautical charts and baseball cards and science books.

I head outside to the backyard, along the shore of Slacks Pond, where I spent a good deal of my childhood fishing. I grab an old pole out of the tattered shed, bait the hook, cast the line, and then stare at the bobber on the pond's surface.

The yellow-orange-and-black orb dances along the water to the whims of the wind. Few things delight like the eruption of green in the heart of a New England summer, oak trees towering thirty feet above and casting dazzling reflections on the shimmering water. The air smells like damp leaves and mud, the boundary between earth and water. Slacks was built by the town in 1822 to provide a backup water source for the growing textile industry, but to me as a kid, it was simply "the Lake."

My eyes are locked on a fixed point, the bobber, which darts underwater if a fish grabs the worm squirming below. But for the most part the bobber just floats there, directing all my focus and attention to its slightest shift in direction. My breath slows, my body loosens, and the spaces between my thoughts grow larger, creating stretches of complete presence where the past is long gone and the future is still in motion.

Control what you can control, Rance told me.

Let it go, Steve Yeager said.

I don't get to write the script. Whatever it is, I just get to respond, Don Carman said.

I've been sitting here on the dock for an hour without having caught a single fish. I feel as content as I have since leaving Oakland.

Fishing isn't about catching fish.

⸺

"The price of freedom is eternal vigilance," reads the monument in the town square in Norwood, Massachusetts. Above the slogan is the town seal, depicting Revolutionary War patriot Aaron Guild, who, according to lore, left his oxen (also depicted in the seal) to fight the British in Lexington. Atop the monument base stand a man and woman cradling a toddler, with two soldiers standing guard below.

Patriotism is ubiquitous here. Across the street, in front of the Memorial Municipal Building, a sign with an American flag reads "Norwood Welcomes Home Lt. Col. David A. Doucette; Thank You For Your Service," which is also stamped with the town seal. The Municipal Building's steeple, granite rock, and stained-glass windows give the impression of a church, but the building is and has always been secular. Or as secular as anything gets here in Norwood.

Downtown's other corners are home to actual churches, the United Church of Norwood and St. Catherine's of Siena. I approach a town worker with green eyes and gray hair who's fixing yet another sign honoring veterans.

"Have you ever heard of Richie Hebner?" I ask him, holding my notebook at my side.

He studies my face hard with just a hint of suspicion, then breaks out into a huge smile.

"Richie *Hebnuh*?" he says in a heavy Boston accent, dropping the *r* just like his British ancestors. "Of *cawwse* I know Richie *Hebnuh*!"

Here in *Nahwood*, anyone over fifty knows the town's prodigal son. The worker leads me inside the Municipal Building and begins an impromptu guided tour: "The Memorial Carillon has fifty-one bells and weighs 43,076 pounds," he says. "The fifty-first bell is the fire bell. At Christmas they play some amazing carols. It's the biggest attraction in town. Do you want to go up and see it?"

I had forgotten that in small towns in this part of the country there are about six more hours in a day than everywhere else.

"Thank you, but I've got a meeting coming up," I say. "I'm actually wondering if you know of anyone who might know Richie personally," I ask.

"I didn't grow up here, but I can point you in the right direction," he says.

A few minutes later I'm knocking on the door of the assistant town manager, Bernie.

A rail-thin bald man wearing a bright yellow shirt and necktie, Bernie greets me warmly and offers me a seat. Every inch of his desk is covered with mountains of paper, several of them positioned at angles to each other.

"Nice filing system," I joke.

He is not amused.

Bernie grew up with the Hebners. "My brother-in-law played hockey with Richie," he says. "Richie came from a working-class family. No pretensions." He tells me about Richie's hockey heroics and launches into the history of Norwood, describing how many of the town's industrial employers have moved south or overseas, hurting the economy. "We had a few baseball players come out of Norwood. But Richie had the longest career of all of them."

Old ways of life linger in places like this. When I ask for more referrals to people who know Richie, Bernie rattles off landline phone numbers from memory.

I don't even know my mother's cell phone number.

As I've shared the Pack with each Wax Packer, no one has elicited a stronger reaction than Richie Hebner. ("Tell Richie we need to go chase some nurses," Steve Yeager said with an impish grin.) And that reaction was always overwhelmingly positive. By all accounts, Richie was born to do one thing: play baseball. Although he was an even better hockey player in high school, he knew that baseball players generally played longer and stayed healthier, so he spurned the Boston Bruins' advances in order to sign with the Pittsburgh Pirates as a number 1 draft pick in 1966. He chose wisely: he went on to play nineteen seasons before retiring in 1986 at age thirty-eight.

Richie was spoiled with success early. Fast-tracked to the Majors as part of the Pirates' youth movement in the late sixties, he found himself the Opening Day third baseman at age twenty-one, batting second ahead of Roberto Clemente and Willie Stargell. The Pirates won five National League East titles in six years, including the World Series in 1971. It was easy having fun with all that winning, but Richie brought the fun everywhere he went. He never got cocky, never forgot his modest upbringing here in Norwood. He would befriend everyone at the ballpark, from the team president to the ushers and clubhouse assistants.

"He loves to play, loves to have fun. After all these years, he's not doing you a favor to come to the ballpark. You can't have enough guys like him. A pro," said his manager, Jim Frey, when Richie was winding down his career with the Chicago Cubs in 1984.[1]

Nicknamed "the Hacker" for his free-swinging ways, Richie could flat-out hit. He racked up 203 home runs and 1,694 hits while playing third and first base. And starting at age fifteen, he dug graves with his father and brothers back in Norwood, where his dad was the foreman for a Jewish cemetery. Richie made sure to never let his pro baseball career get in the way of his gravedigging—every off-season he would return to Norwood, grab a spade or jackhammer, and start digging. He liked the workout and the extra money, and the manual labor was a good outlet for all his nervous energy. Richie never did like sitting still.

But did he love baseball too much? After being released by the Cubs in spring training in 1986, he coached American Legion ball and then returned to the pros as the manager for the Single A Myrtle Beach Blue Jays. From 1988 until now, he's been on the road every season but three, ranging from the low Minor Leagues to two stints as a Major League hitting coach. During his four kids' formative years, he was on the road. But at what cost? At the beginning of this coaching run, shortly after taking the job in Myrtle Beach, he told the *Pittsburgh Press*: "My wife is expecting again in September. We have two girls. Maybe we'll get a little baseball player. I get a call once in a while and the wife will say every time a truck comes down the driveway they [his daughters] think daddy is coming home. It ain't happening, Elizabeth [his oldest daughter, then four]."[2]

Elizabeth is now a teacher, thirty-one, with two kids of her own. Richie is still in uniform.

＝

"Ah, fuck!" Dennis Hebner yells, fumbling with the keys of his white rental car as the alarm wails. "How do you turn this fuckin' thing off?"

Richie is fast asleep at home a few miles away, having arrived at 1:30 in the morning on the team bus from Buffalo. He's the hitting coach for the Triple-A Buffalo Bisons, still enduring the long bus rides across small-town America. The Bisons are playing later tonight in Pawtucket, Rhode Island, where I'm scheduled to see Richie before the game. But to maximize my time, I've scouted out his younger brother Dennis, whom I'm now meeting in a Dunkin' Donuts parking lot.

Dennis is cut straight from New England cloth. "Ask me anything," he says, shaking my hand firmly. "My daughter tells me I talk too fuckin' much, but what the hell, right? I may say things I shouldn't, but I'll always be honest." He's wearing an army T-shirt and jeans, with a ball cap pulled over his gray hair.

"My son just turned twenty-one in February, and he's been in the *ahhmy* for three years," he says in that Boston accent, his light eyes brightening. "He was over in Afghanistan. He says, 'I can't wait to go back. It's such a fuckin' high.'"

Dennis finally silences the car alarm, and I climb in for a tour of the town. He opens up a canister of tobacco and packs a large wad under his lower lip, easing onto the road.

"You're a college professor?" he asks while he drives, making an unsafe amount of eye contact.

"Yeah," I reply, wishing he'd show more interest in the road.

"My god, how old are you?"

"Thirty-four," I say, gripping my seat.

"You look good for your age!" he says, spitting tobacco juice into a cup.

Dennis is the youngest of five, all boys. His dad came from a German family and grew up in the area, while his mom moved from Ireland in her twenties; together they raised the boys in the Catholic Church, Dad working as a foreman at the Jewish cemetery and Mom part-time as a nurse's aide. "We had food on the table, we had clothes, but we never had anything new, we never went on vacation. The first vacation I ever went on was my honeymoon," he says.

We drive past a senior living facility. "Believe it or not, this is the baseball field we first learned to play in," Dennis says, pointing out where the field used to be. "We lived right over there, and there was a hole in the fence we'd come through from our backyard to the field. There were so many kids around here. Back then everyone had four or five kids in the family."

All the Hebner boys were athletes, but Richie had the most talent. ("I had a better arm than him, but he'd never admit that," Dennis confides.) Despite being an alpha jock, Richie was quiet and introverted as a kid. "He was a real homebody. He never went out," Dennis says. "He never dated girls. But he made up for it once he left Norwood." Steve Yeager's comment about chasing nurses with Richie pops in my head.

We drive past the new high school, an impressive, beautifully landscaped campus that looks more like a college. "They ripped down the old high school where we went and put up a soccer field," Dennis says.

"Is there any chance we can go to any of the cemeteries where you would dig graves?" I ask, eager to learn more about the family business.

"Nah, it's about twelve miles from here," he replies, practically a day trip for New Englanders. Instead he explains the process of hand-digging graves: "It all depends on the soil. Some of it was easy stuff, some of it was hard, like gravel. It would take us two, three hours. We didn't use vaults."

"Must've been a lot harder in the winter, right?" I ask.

"Yeah, but what's good with the snow is that we could have a drink," he says.

"I've always wondered—do you really dig six feet down?" I ask.

"No. We'd try to go at least three and a half feet down," he replies. "Richie, he still works at a funeral parlor."

There's an undercurrent of melancholy as he talks. While Dennis is upbeat and cheery as he chronicles the family story, that story is heavy with misfortune. In under an hour, we've done a lap around the entire town, but Dennis isn't done talking.

"We can park the car over in that lot and chat some more," he says, packing more dip into his lower lip. "Wanna hear the weirdest fuckin' thing?" he asks. "This should be in Ripley's Believe It or Not. Within nineteen days in April of '06, my wife and two of my brothers' wives all died of cancer." Richie's wife, Pat, was not among them, but Dennis lost his love, Martha. He went into a tailspin, giving up his job in the cemetery and gaining fifty pounds in only a year and a half. But after four long years he pulled himself out of it and now is focused on a warehouse job and raising his twin girls. I notice that he's still wearing his wedding ring.

"I'm supposed to meet Richie at the ballpark at two," I say, changing the subject.

Growing up, Richie and Dennis were close but competitive, the way brothers close in age tend to be. Richie was older, but Dennis was more outgoing; he even taught his older brother how to drive. When Richie came home in the off-season they would drink pints and play darts at a bar called the Irish Heaven for hours at a time on Saturday mornings. They both had wood-burning stoves in their homes and would order a truckload of wood and make a weekend out of chopping it together. But now, despite living only ten miles apart, they barely talk.

"How would you describe your relationship with Richie now?" I ask as Dennis pulls back onto the street to drop me off at my car.

"I don't see him that much. It's a long story," he says. He doesn't want to talk about it, at least not on the record. I respect his wishes.

"Does Richie know you're upset?" I ask.

"I'm sure Richie knows. I know Richie has a feeling something's going on," he says. We drive past a long driveway dipping down to a house out of sight. "Richie lives down there. I don't want to stop," he says.

Here I am, 7,286 miles into the journey and right outside Richie Hebner's door, and I can't even knock. It's frustrating, but I'm not about to defy Dennis.

"Is Richie the kind of guy that doesn't like to talk about personal stuff?" I ask.

"Oh, he never talks about that, never. He never talks about anything he's done," he replies, misunderstanding my question.

"I mean more like his feelings, what's bothering him," I say.

"No, never," Dennis replies.

"You don't have heart-to-hearts, anything like that?" I ask.

"No," he says. Then again: "No."

≡

They don't build ballparks in towns like Pawtucket, Rhode Island, any-more. Driving through the modest neighborhood of family homes, past the Agnes E. Little Elementary School and Galway Bay Irish pub, I expect to see a Little League field around the next bend. Instead I find the last stop on Minor Leaguers' journey to Fenway Park, McCoy Sta-dium, home to the Triple-A Pawtucket Red Sox.

The PawSox were the affordable alternative to Boston when I was a kid, a place where big school groups could go for less than ten bucks to pass a low-key summer evening. I pull into the parking lot a bit early for my meeting with Richie and walk around the outside of the stadium, admiring the PawSox Walk of Fame banners along its edges. There's Marty Barrett, the handsome second baseman whom I looked up to as a kid. I chuckle when I see Carlton Fisk's ban-ner, his mouth wide open flashing his white teeth, looking happier than I've ever seen him. I walk toward the clubhouse entrance and see eight people milling about waiting for the team buses to arrive. A plus-size woman wearing a purple-and-white top and holding a cane sits near two younger, also overweight men clutching albums full of baseball cards. They appear to be her sons. I share the gist of my project with them, going through the list of Wax Packers. When I tell them about Vince Coleman, the bigger one laughs and says, "He's a dickbag."

When one of the buses pulls in, the woman in purple gets up and asks her sons, "Do you need me?," positioning herself in front with her cane. The players, wearing Bose headphones, backward hats, and street clothes, start to trickle out. As they walk toward the guardrail by the clubhouse entrance, the autograph seekers do their best to engulf them, thrusting forward Sharpies and baseball cards. Here in the Minors, most players are happy to oblige, muttering "thank yous" as they sign.

I stand off to the side and observe, fascinated and disturbed by the spectacle of grown men and women flocking to athletes for their signatures. Kids I understand, but adults with albums full of baseball cards and sleeves of Sharpies? Then again, I'm driving eleven thousand miles to meet the players in a pack of twenty-nine-year-old baseball cards; who am I to judge?

I tell the stadium security guard that I'm here to see Richie Hebner, the Buffalo Bisons hitting coach, and I'm surprised that he seems to be expecting me. As I walk into a stairwell and approach a simple white door with the PawSox logo, I realize this is the first time I've ever been in a baseball clubhouse. Feeling a frisson of excitement (and a bit of guilt for having judged the autograph seekers outside), I push open the door and emerge into a roomful of lockers with freshly pressed uniforms neatly hanging inside and a spread of food covered with foil lids. I immediately recognize Richie, who's still wearing his civilian clothes. He's got thin brown hair, green eyes, and ruddy cheeks and is wearing green cargo pants, a long-sleeve blue shirt, and sandals. He looks ready for a backyard barbecue in Norwood.

He leads me into the dugout. We sit on the green cushioned bench, spitting distance from the field, and, just like his brother earlier today, he packs a wad of tobacco into his lower lip. I've never been this close to the field, so close I can see the individual grains of clay of the infield dirt. I'm shocked by how red they are.

"How long was the drive from Buffalo?" I ask.

"Light for the *minuh* leagues, only seven *owuz*," he replies in the accent, his voice a bit stronger than Dennis's.

"What did you do on the bus?"

"I read James Patterson. I read a lot of James Patterson books," he says. "You got so much spare time in this game. A lot of kill time." Following this three-game series in Pawtucket, he'll hang back for a brief break at home while the team travels to Syracuse.

This is Richie's sixth decade in professional baseball. When he was drafted in 1966, LBJ was president and Richie's black teammates in the Minor Leagues weren't allowed to stay in the same motels as the white players. Now there's a black president.

"I believe some of this game has passed me by, to be honest," Richie, sixty-seven, says. "It's a friendly game now. Everybody's making the big money."

In Richie's day, you didn't fraternize with the opposing team. If a pitcher didn't like that a hitter was standing too close to home plate, he threw at him, knocked him down. "I got hit four games in a row in '74," he says. Now throwing at a hitter can get you ejected.

He can't help but wonder what it would be like to play in today's multimillion-dollar game. Notoriously thrifty, Richie still can't get over the money he lost during the player strikes. "I lost about $200,000," he says. "I mean, the money now is ungodly. I look at what some of these guys are getting paid, and it's mind-boggling." He gazes out at the field as he talks.

It's not just that. It's the watering down of talent. When he started, there were only twenty teams in the league; now there are thirty. "You know, I don't want to tell some of these guys, but twenty-five, thirty years ago some of these guys would never have been out of Double-A," he says.

The ground crew massages and waters the infield grass several yards away with the care of master gardeners. There's some inclement weather in the forecast, and an ominous gray cloud rolls around the sky in right field. The Bisons' manager, Gary Allenson, who's short with a purposeful stride, walks by and snips, "The guys are ready when you're done with your frickin' biography," producing a snicker from pitching coach Randy St. Clair, who's smoking a cigarette nearby. The three of them can't seem to flush the game from their system, preferring the grind of the road to returning home.

I ask Richie about being pursued by the Bruins, playing hockey in front of sixteen thousand fans in the Boston Garden while still in high school, and breaking in with the Pirates in the late sixties. "I graduated in '66, and two years later I was in old Forbes Field. I'm like two or three lockers from [Roberto] Clemente and [Willie] Stargell. I look at myself and go, 'What the hell am I doing here?'" he replies.

The comment sounds familiar. Later on I check my notes and find the same quote in an article in the *Buffalo News* from last year. This happens a couple more times in our interview, Richie giving the same rehearsed sound bites he's given a thousand times before, perhaps literally. With six decades in pro ball, how many times has he been through the mill of a journalist's questions? I want to push past the clichés, dig deeper, but Richie has his guard up. Maybe it's because he's got a game to coach in a few hours and can't give his full attention the way the other Wax Packers have, or maybe, like Dennis implied, he's just not one to open up.

Richie now claims it wasn't hard to stop playing the game. But when he was cut by the Cubs at the end of spring training in 1986, he told the *Chicago Tribune*, "I don't want to go back to digging graves just yet."[3]

"Did you have a hard time walking away?" I ask.

"I didn't. I really didn't. I played a lot of years in the big leagues. I got released, and just, you know, the semester ends for everybody. I just accepted it and went home," he says.

But he didn't stay home. Even now, Richie isn't sitting still. He's still coaching and working the funeral circuit. When the conversation turns to his family, he answers my questions but doesn't elaborate in any great detail. "My wife brought the four kids up, and she did a hell of a job, you know. I've played with some players, and the dads had to go home because the kids were on drugs or something. I never had to go home because of that," he says.

When I mention that I was with Dennis earlier today, a flicker of apprehension passes across his face. I want to ask him about Dennis, to tell him to give him a call, to go throw some darts at the Irish Heaven. But I know it's not my place. My hour is up—Richie's got to get to working with the Bisons hitters. They have a game to play.

Several hours later, I watch from the stands as the Bisons edge the PawSox 2–1 while Richie observes from the dugout where we sat earlier. Thirty miles away up Route 95, Dennis drives his twin girls to their theater class, so close to Richie but yet so far away.

=

Before getting back on the journey the next morning, I duck into the Greenville CVS and walk over to the greeting cards.

The chase for Carlton Fisk is back on. This weekend, Craig Biggio, Pedro Martinez, John Smoltz, and Randy Johnson will be enshrined into the Hall of Fame in Cooperstown, baseball's heaven. Every Induction Weekend, past Hall of Famers descend on the city to fete the newest members of their fraternity and make some pocket change by signing autographs. I find an ad online from MAB Celebrity Services for an autograph show featuring several ex-players; among them is Doc Gooden (time/day TBA—no surprise there) and Carlton Fisk, who for sixty-nine dollars will sign a flat up to eleven by fourteen inches or for ninety-nine dollars a bat or jersey.

If you can't beat them, pay them.

I scan the shelves for a card with an orchid, Carlton's favorite plant, and find one with a "Missing You" inscription on the front. On the way out, I stop by the photo department to pick up an eight-by-ten glossy color photo of my face that I've had printed.

Carlton may have evaded me in Florida, but I'm determined to get the last laugh.

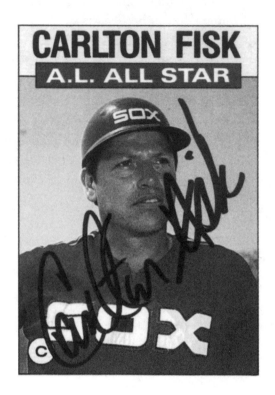

CARLTON FISK

A.L. ALL STAR

15

CATCHING CARLTON

Umm, thanks.

—*Carlton Fisk*

Days 37–38
July 25–26, 2015
Miles driven: 7,588
Cups of coffee: 93
Norwood MA to Cooperstown NY

Downtown Cooperstown, a two-block-by-two-block emporium of baseball nostalgia, is currently roped off from traffic and engulfed by a sea of orange and yellow, the colors of the Houston Astros. Fewer than two thousand people live here year-round, hardy souls willing to brave the upstate New York winters. But once a year, deep in the heart of summer, tens of thousands flock to this tiny outpost to venerate the game's greatest. An Astro his entire career, Craig Biggio is one of four players being inducted into the Hall of Fame this weekend, and the Houston fan base, while muted nationally, has turned out in droves to celebrate. I hear a dull sound overhead and see a blimp circling the downtown scene. I imagine what it must look like from up there, a colony of fire ants scurrying over asphalt.

I join the hysteria, walking down Main Street in search of the Tunnicliff Inn, a hotel hosting one of the weekend's big autograph shows. For eighty-nine dollars you can get Reggie Jackson's autograph; for eighty-five dollars, Robin Yount's; and for sixty-nine dollars, Carlton Fisk's, my archnemesis.

A throng is gathered outside the Tunnicliff's three-story facade of crumbling brick and black shutters. A sweaty, breathless man appears every few minutes in the inn doorway, addressing the crowd like an auctioneer teetering on a coronary as he tries to manage the traffic of people moving in and out. In one hand I have my notebook and in the other a paper bag with my surprise for Carlton. Little does he know how lucky he is—he's about to get my autograph.

Having already been rejected by Carlton and knowing that I'll have about thirty seconds with him while he signs the 1986 Topps baseball card I've brought, I've decided to have some fun. Athletes often add a flourish to their signatures commemorating their greatest accomplishments, which for Carlton might be "Hall of Fame 2000" or "ROY (Rookie of the Year) 1972." On the eight-by-ten glossy color photo of myself that I've had printed and signed, I add a personal inscription, which I plan to present as a gift. It reads:

> Dear Carlton,
>   All the best!
>   Brad Balukjian, Wheeler School Tennis Coach's Award, 1998.

I've also got the greeting card with the orchids on the front, inside of which I write the following:

> Dear Carlton,
>   I know you like orchids, which is why I picked this card. Steve Yeager, Garry Templeton, Rance Mulliniks, Randy Ready, Jaime Cocanower, Lee Mazzilli, Rick Sutcliffe, Richie Hebner, and the rest of the Wax Pack miss you, as do I—would have been great to have you as part of the project (not sure why you turned us down). But it's not too late—give me a call if you're so inclined.
>   Sincerely,
>   Brad Balukjian

I slide my business card inside.

There's something invigorating about being in a crowd that shares my zealotry for baseball. The sidewalks are stuffed with vendors hawking every bit of imaginable baseball paraphernalia, from the standard hats and jerseys to impressionist art of inductee Randy Johnson. It's like a small town in Iowa in an election year, its sleepy pace invaded by the bustle of not only fans but also major media outlets and illuminati. As

I shuffle forward in the autograph line, professional wrestler Ric Flair, here to capitalize on baseball fans' shared interest in wrestling, struts by in a suit, flanked by an entourage of attractive blond women. He walks fast, knowing that if he stops, he will be swarmed by the crowd like yellow jackets on a slice of watermelon.

I small-talk with the couple in front of me in line, Steve and Cheryl, from Monson, Massachusetts. They're draped in Red Sox gear, down to Cheryl's earrings. "This is my birthday present, to come here," Steve says. They've met Carlton before, at a similar event where they paid for his autograph. "He was very likeable," they say.

Well, who wouldn't be when you're paying sixty-nine dollars for thirty seconds of their time?

But I keep my thoughts to myself.

The drenched auctioneer reemerges from the shadows of the hotel and calls my ticket number, signaling that Carlton is ready to receive his audience. I'm directed to a small room with several long tables set up along the perimeter. Behind the tables sit a cheerful Jim Rice, an old Joe Morgan, my man Carlton, and someone I believe is Wade Boggs, although I can't quite tell if it's really him or a likeness borrowed from the Wax Museum down the street. He looks like he has done everything a scalpel and a bottle of red hair dye can do to preserve his appearance exactly as it was in 1986.

Carlton looks good, fit in a white polo shirt and gray slacks, and even—gasp!—smiling. He obliges fans' requests to take pictures with him after they fork over the price of a lobster tail / filet mignon dinner, even making small talk. ("You really ran across the Golden Gate Bridge?" he asks the woman in front of me, reading her T-shirt.)

When my time comes, I steel myself. Go time.

I slide the '86 Topps card in front of him, and while he brandishes a blue Sharpie, I spring into action.

"Carlton, since you're probably so tired of everyone asking for your autograph, I thought I'd give you one of mine," I say, unsheathing my eight-by-ten like a glossy Excalibur. "And since I know you love orchids, I got you a card of them," I say, handing the card across the table.

A girl in a blue dress seated next to him, presumably one of his representatives, giggles. He looks up at me, slack-jawed, baffled. "Umm, thanks!" he stammers, completely flummoxed by this turning of tables.

I don't want to make a scene any more than I already have (despite what I wrote in the beginning of this book, I really don't want to get arrested for accosting Carlton Fisk), so I collect the autographed card, thank him, and spin away.

Halfway out the door and sixty-nine dollars lighter, I glance back to see him flip open the card to scan the message inside.

Will he give me a call?

—

The next morning, while everyone else is at the induction ceremony, I have the Hall of Fame Museum all to myself, my first visit since a family trip in 1988. There's a picture of me from that trip, my shirt tucked into shorts hiked up too high, wearing a Phillies cap that flopped down over my ears as I stood in front of a display case for my favorite team looking as delighted as an eight-year-old can. I find that same case and take a picture, flooded by memories of all the baseball-related outings from childhood, my younger sister and mother patiently indulging me and my dad.

The literal hall is a high-ceilinged chamber with tall, rectangular pillars and a series of benches in a line in the middle of the room. All along the walls are the plaques of the Hall of Fame's members, each with a three-dimensional sculpture of the player's face and a one-paragraph description. I find Carlton's, which reads:

A commanding figure behind the plate for a record 24 seasons, he caught more games (2,226) and hit more home runs (351) than any catcher before him. His gritty resolve and competitive fire earned him the respect of teammates and opposing players alike. A staunch training regimen extended his durability and enhanced his productivity—as evidenced by a record 72 home runs after age 40. His dramatic home run to win Game Six of the 1975 World Series is one of baseball's unforgettable moments. Was the 1972 American League Rookie of the Year and an 11-Time All-Star.

He's wearing a Red Sox cap in his sculpture and has a lopsided grin revealing his top row of teeth. He looks content, no trace of bitterness.

As I wander the gallery of greatness, reading about the exploits of baseball's all-time best, I think about who's missing or, rather, who would be in *my* Hall of Fame. I've learned that the real greatness of a game that's supposed to be all about numbers has nothing to do with numbers, that all the home runs in the world can't replace the strength demonstrated when you're honest with yourself and deal with what's right in front of you. My Hall of Fame doesn't have Babe Ruth and Mickey Mantle and Carlton Fisk—it's got Garry Templeton, who spoke up when young black men weren't supposed to; Don Carman, who pursued a doctorate in psychology to exorcise his wounds from childhood abuse; Randy Ready, who was not afraid to love again after what happened to his wife, Dorene. These men, who were my childhood heroes, are still my heroes, but for entirely different reasons.

Yes, baseball is a game about failure, which you often can't control, but, more importantly, it's about how you *respond* to that failure, which is always in your grasp. And these men excel at that.

I think back to my childhood home on Slacks Pond.

Fishing isn't about catching fish. Baseball isn't about hitting home runs.

=

Somewhere around western Ohio, an unfamiliar phone number flashes on my screen. I pick it up, nursing a scalding hot cup of coffee, my ninety-third of the trip.

"Is this Brad?" a stern female voice says.

"Yes . . . ," I reply.

"Brad, this is Kim, Carlton Fisk's agent. I'm concerned about your blog post. What is the point of it?" she asks. My brain flicks in several directions—Kim, Kim, *yes*, this is the same Kim whom I had corresponded with months ago when trying to get Carlton to participate. Following my encounter with him at the Hall of Fame, I had blogged about the encounter, and word had apparently made its way back to his people.

"The point was just to tell what happened. What exactly are you concerned about?" I reply.

"I'm just kind of baffled by the whole blog. I thought I was very professional in responding to your request," she says, taking issue with my characterization of our past email conversation and sounding like a lawyer.

Oh wait. She is a lawyer.

"You were professional. I simply reported what happened. If Carlton doesn't like the way I am portraying things, tell him to give me a call. That's all I want, is to talk to him," I reply.

"Well, you have to understand, Carlton is at a different level," she says. I roll my eyes. "Some of these guys may want to relive their playing days, but Carlton has moved on to other things. He is always getting so many letters and requests, he can't possibly read them all. He's got ten grandkids, he's had some health scares lately, his mom is really elderly, he's got a grandson with Down syndrome," she adds.

I hold the phone away from my ear, getting annoyed by this laundry list of excuses. What does having a grandson with Down syndrome have to do with participating in an interview?

"Look, Kim," I say, the tension audible in my voice, "if he is so concerned, tell him to call me and tell me what he wants me to know about him."

"He doesn't even know I'm calling you right now," she says.

The conversation ends in a cordial stalemate. I doubt he will call but have made my final pitch for Carlton Fisk. Bottom line: Carlton has no interest in joining the Wax Pack, and there's nothing I can do about that.

Control what you can control.

I hang up and press on the gas, heading west. A few thousand miles and two Wax Packers to go.

CUBS

RICK SUTCLIFFE

16

CAPTAIN COMEBACK

But as good as I have it now, nothing comes
close to playing. Nothing ever will. Every
time I watch a pitcher go to the mound
to start a game, and he takes that toe hold
and digs that dirt out, right away I miss
that. I'll never get to do that again.
—*Rick Sutcliffe*

Days 39–46
July 27–August 3, 2015
Miles driven: 10,788
Cups of coffee: 118
Cooperstown NY to Las Vegas NV

Driving can be a meditative experience, especially when you've only brought six CDs on a seven-week road trip and can't stomach the idea of one more sing-along with Whitesnake. The plains of the central United States envelop the Accord as I press west past vast tracts of farm and pasture land, with only my random thoughts to keep me company.

During the long straightaways, I text with Jesse and the Kid, our adventures with Rance in Visalia feeling like years, not weeks, ago. I even correspond a bit with Sophia back in Naples, who writes, "Sick of old baseball players yet?" and says she is thinking about visiting the Bay Area for work. A rainstorm appears out of nowhere and pummels my windshield, heavy drops of water exploding on my hood like minigeysers as I squint to see the road, slowing down to avoid hydroplaning.

I'm tired, but I don't want to sleep. I'm lonely, but I don't want company. I want to get back to Oakland, but I never want this fantasy to end. There's a part of this whole thing that still doesn't seem real. Every time

I scroll through my phone and see "Don Carman" and "Lee Mazzilli" right alongside "Mom" and "Jesse" I have to pinch myself.

I'm now in the home stretch, having logged almost eight thousand miles to get across the country and now needing to get all the way back in just a few days. I'm due home in Oakland in a week, but first I'll be stopping in Kansas City to see the penultimate Wax Packer, Rick Sutcliffe, a dominant pitcher of the 1980s who's now a broadcaster for ESPN, and then on to California to resurrect Al Cowens, who passed away thirteen years ago. I worry that my leads on Al have run cold—his widow, Velma, hasn't returned any of my recent calls, and his oldest son, Purvis, said he may not make it down from his home in Oregon as originally scheduled. Without their help, it will be just me all alone in the streets of Watts and Compton, where Al grew up, chasing ghosts.

But Al's apparition will have to wait. First, I've got to find Rick Sutcliffe.

⸻

I park in front of Dixon's Famous Chili (*Since 1919!*) on Route 40 in Independence, Missouri, the hometown of Harry Truman and Rick Sutcliffe, known to most as "Sut." A suburb of Kansas City, Independence touts itself as "the Queen City of the Trails," the launching point for the California, Oregon, and Santa Fe Trails during frontier expansion in the nineteenth century. Right now it's the launching point for home, as I have a straight shot from here back to California.

From the looks of it, Independence peaked during Sut's childhood in the 1960s. Next to Dixon's is a storefront with a blank sign, and next to that is a place called Oddessy Martial Arts Supply advertising the following: pepper spray, stun guns, knives, and swords.

Since I'm all set on swords, I sit with the Accord's door open and wait for Sut to arrive.

The 1984 National League Cy Young Award winner, Sut beat hitters before they even stepped foot in the batter's box. At six feet seven on an already elevated pitcher's mound, he could wither hitters with his mane of bright red hair and no-nonsense glare. Intimidation and a nasty fast-ball/slider/curveball made him the highest-paid pitcher in all of baseball in 1985. Following his retirement in 1995 at age thirty-eight, he went to the low Minor Leagues to coach and eventually found a second life as a broadcaster. Now he's a staple on ESPN's *Wednesday Night Baseball* and *Baseball Tonight*.

A black Ford Expedition pulls up. The passenger-side window rolls down to reveal a pair of bloodshot green eyes.

"What's going on, man?" Sut says in a laid-back tone as I climb into the front seat. He's wearing a baseball hat with sunglasses perched on top, a black golf shirt, and white shorts. The man once nicknamed the Red Baron appears to be graying, judging by the fringe of hair peeking out below his hat, although his goatee is still ginger.

"Not much," I reply, shaking his massive hand. "Are you happy to be home?"

"Yeah, but it's just for a day," he replies. He tells me about his plans for tonight, which slightly exceed mine at the Comfort Inn in downtown Kansas City. "Kenny Chesney is hosting a dinner onstage tonight for his friends," he says. "I met him when I was finishing up playing with the Cardinals." Tomorrow, he'll watch him perform live at Arrowhead Stadium.

Sut's carved out a morning for me during his hectic, in-season schedule; as an ESPN commentator, he's responsible for about twenty-five games per year and another twenty-five appearances in the studio. He just got back from covering the Astros/Angels game in Houston.

"So what's your story?" Sut asks as we turn around to head toward his old high school, part of the tour of his hometown he has promised. Having been part of the media himself for the past twenty years, Sut isn't like the other Wax Packers—he's used to asking the questions rather than answering them.

I tell him about my hybrid career as a professor and writer and remind him of the premise of the book. He chuckles, amused. "You look like you could still be in college," he says.

Before I can even ask any questions, he starts narrating as we drive the leafy streets of Independence. "My parents divorced when I was eleven. My dad was a race car driver, so they were gone all summer, and we always stayed with my grandparents on my mom's side. When they got divorced, we just moved in with my grandparents," he says, pointing out their old home. Even before his parents split, his life was full of disruption. "We moved around a lot as a kid with my parents [he has a brother and sister]. We bought a house, bought another house, then another one. . . . I think I changed schools like seven times. My friends were always changing. It wasn't a lot of fun, really. I was always trying to fit in."

I instantly like him. He's open, introspective, thoughtful. I ask one question, and he carries on for several minutes, but not in a self-aggrandizing way.

Sut learned humility and hard work from an early age. When he was still a young child his dad put him to work in his grandpa's landscaping business. "From the time I was eight till I was fifteen, I worked in the fields. You'd get there when the sun'd come up, and you'd roll sod in the field and stack it on a truck, then take it to a house, lay it in the yard, and then you drive the truck back to the field, load it and unload it as many times as you could that day. You'd get a little bit of rain, and some of these rolls would be thirty, thirty-five pounds," he says.

It's a warm, sunny day, not overly hot. We park at Van Horn High School and vault out of the car for a quick visit. There's a lot of activity for a school in the middle of summer, and just inside the lobby I spot an entire display case dedicated to Sut. His 1974 yearbook, a plaque, his Chicago Cubs jersey (number 40), and his Van Horn High jersey (number 17) are all behind the glass. We don't linger long. Within just a couple of minutes, we've drawn attention to ourselves—it's not every day the school's biggest hero walks in the front door (who also happens to be six feet seven). As I take pictures of the case a woman walks over to chat with Sut, and as we walk out back down the steps he tells me she's the girls' basketball coach.

"When you're just walking around town do people recognize you all the time?" I ask.

"Yeah, well, basically. You know, I don't think there's anybody in town yet that I've not signed an autograph for," he replies.

"How do you feel about all the attention and autographs?" I ask. Unlike the rest of the Wax Packers, Sut is still in the limelight. But his attitude is the same as it's always been: it goes with the territory. "Sandy Koufax told me a thousand years ago when we went to lunch one day—it was my first year of spring training, and all these people were all over him for autographs—and he says, 'I will worry about autographs when they quit asking me.'"

Sut signs for free, and they still keep asking.

As we walk off the school grounds, a memory pops in his head: "I'll never forget this. I was a sophomore, and there was a girl that would sit in front of me [in class]. There was this senior, a big bully, and she wouldn't talk to him. Right as he's getting off from class he spits in the back of her hair. I see him coming down the stairs. He was a bigger senior, a football player. I smoked him, just knocked him out." For the first and only time in his young life, Sut found himself in the principal's office. "He says, 'You're suspended for three days. I just want you to know I applaud you for what you did. But we have a policy, and it's no fights.'" Sut has never understood cruelty.

As good as he was at baseball and basketball, he had his heart set on playing college football. Just like Garry Templeton, almost every Division I football program wanted him, penciling him in at quarterback. "The day my senior year ended my goal was to play football at Missouri," he says. But "it's like God had another plan for me," he adds.

Baseball players, already extremely superstitious, are known for their faith, often pointing skyward after a big hit. Even as the game's front offices have evolved to embrace data (the current analytics revolution is all about science trumping instinct), the men who play the game still trust their gut.

"So how did that go down, playing baseball instead of football?" I ask as we drive toward Independence's town square.

"I got drafted in the first round by the Dodgers," he replies. "It's kind of funny, the day of the draft, ironically, I also had to register for the military draft. I was working at a dog kennel cleaning cages every morning, five days a week. The lady that owned the dog kennel came out and said, 'Hey, you've got a phone call, it's your grandma.' I pick up the phone, and she goes, 'You've been drafted,' and I'm like, right when I think my life can't get any worse . . . so I say, 'What is it, army? Navy?' and she goes, 'No, you've been drafted by the Dodgers!'"

We turn onto a side street. I look up at the sign: Rick Sutcliffe Drive, which takes us to a baseball field without any grass in the infield. "This is the ballpark where our school played," he says, resuming his story. Although his grandpa was "a carpenter with a first-grade education," he shrewdly steered the Dodgers to offering an $85,000 signing bonus. "He says to me, 'Do you know how much money that is? I had the best year I've ever had in my life, and I made just under $6,000 this year.'"

Sut paid his dues over the next several years, spending most of the next five seasons in the Minor Leagues, poking his head up to the Majors for a single game in 1976 and two more in 1978. His breakout party was 1979, when he won seventeen games en route to the National League Rookie of the Year Award. But the success was short-lived: the sophomore slump bit him hard in 1980, resulting in exile to the bullpen, where he languished through 1981. His manager, the voluble Tommy Lasorda, promised Sut he would get to start a game late in the 1981 season but never followed through. Their relationship soured, culminating in an infamous confrontation right before the season's end: "He just snapped, said, 'You don't even fuckin' belong in the bullpen,' then he kind of came at me. That's when I grabbed him and put him up against the wall and said, 'If you weren't so fuckin' old . . .' You know, I cleaned off his desk," Sut says euphemistically.

Although he is known as one of the kindest and most generous men in the game, Sut's temper could be extreme.

"The funniest part was he had all these Frank Sinatra albums and pictures on his office wall, everything signed 'to Tommy, love Frank,' and I snapped and said, 'I'm gonna throw that chair right through that fucking wall.' I'm about to throw it, and standing in the door is Dusty Baker, and he grabs the chair and he's laughing and he says something like, 'Kid, you're in enough trouble. You don't need Frank pissed off too.'"

A few months later, he was shipped off to Cleveland, where he began anew, bouncing back to win the American League ERA title.

And then the year that changed it all: 1984. The Cubs began the season with expectations for yet another season in the doldrums but surprised everyone with a strong start. Sut was traded from the Indians to the

Cubs on June 13 and immediately put them over the hump, going 16-1 with a 2.69 ERA after joining the team and leading them to the playoffs for the first time since 1945. Only a startling comeback from the San Diego Padres kept them out of the World Series.

Decades of pent-up frustration were released in Chicago as the Cubbies became rock stars, with Sut as their lead singer. "It was like I was one of the Beatles," he says. "I got rushed by people."

The owner of a popular downtown bar called Murphy's set Sut up with a key to an apartment above the bar, complete with a deck, pool tables, and big-screen TVs. Whenever celebrities—think Bill Murray, Huey Lewis, Mark Harmon (remember, this was the 1980s)—came to see a Cubs game and needed a place to hide out, they'd call Sut and ask for the key to the apartment.

When the big money started rolling in, Sut gave it right back. In his early years with the Dodgers, he visited children's hospitals and got inspired, vowing to make charity work part of his mission. Once he was financially set, he and his wife, Robin, started the Rick Sutcliffe Foundation, setting aside $100,000 every year for the mentally disabled, the elderly, sick children, and the homeless. That altruism runs in the family. As we ride, Sut talks repeatedly about how proud he is of his only child, Shelby. "Our daughter, she works for World Vision," he says, referencing the Christian organization dedicated to humanitarian aid. "Even after she graduated from Harvard Medical School and all of the opportunities she had, she's, you know, she's adamant about trying to help those kids over in Africa. And our son-in-law, he's a preacher, and he got assigned to San Diego. His church is there, and we have a two-and-a-half-year-old grandson." *All good*, I think. *But did it have to be San Diego?*

Shelby takes after her dad in other ways as well.

When I ask Sut about what set him apart as a player, he says, "Brad, there were guys that threw harder, that were a lot more talented. But I'll go on the record and say, I don't know that anybody was ever more prepared." He pauses to lasso his thoughts, then continues: "It's kind of like my daughter. You'd love to have her as a student. She got all As, went to TCU [Texas Christian University] and Harvard. But she told me, she goes, 'Dad, these kids in school, they're a lot smarter than I am. But I learned how to study. I know how to prepare.'"

Sut's phone rings. I glance at the screen—Ryne S.

"Wait," I begin, "is that who I think it is?" Ryne Sandberg, Hall of Fame second baseman, Sut's ex-teammate, and one of the greatest Cubs of all time?

Sut lets it go to voice mail. "Sorry, dude, can't take it," he says out loud. Ryne Sandberg screened for me. Surreal.

"I want to show you the house," he says, picking up the phone and calling his wife. From his side of the conversation, I can tell that Robin wasn't expecting company. "She's like, the laundry's everywhere, the maids are coming, I'm not dressed," he recaps. "It'll be okay."

=

The downstairs of the Sutcliffe home is a shrine of hardware. Among the accolades are a replica of the 1981 World Series trophy won with the Dodgers; his 1984 Cy Young Award, which I find surprisingly unimpressive; and even an Oscar, given for his performance in the 1984 season. There's a framed *Sports Illustrated* cover from 1984 picturing the National League's dominant pitchers—Sut and fellow Wax Packer Doc Gooden, all of nineteen years old. One wall is covered with framed photos of Sut with celebrities from all sides of sports and entertainment—Dale Earnhardt, Charles Barkley, zz Top, and many others.

But only one memento is meaningful enough to make the more heavily trafficked upstairs part of the house: the Buck O'Neil Legacy Award, given for outstanding support of the Negro Leagues Baseball Museum, located here in Kansas City. O'Neil played for the hometown Kansas City Monarchs, became the first black coach in Major League Baseball in 1962, and was key to establishing the museum, which Sut counts as one of the most important sites in all of baseball. "It'll change you," Sut says of visiting the museum. "It's one of those moving experiences where you just don't realize how tough it was and how wrong it was."

Sut has always remained true to his midwestern values—decency, hard work, integrity. He's never understood the cruelty that humans are capable of. Every time he looks across the kitchen table and sees the O'Neil Award, he's reminded of why his work is so important and why it can never stop.

═

Sut has perfected the art of the comeback. Hamstring and shoulder injuries nearly ended his career twice—first in the hangover season of 1985, then again in 1990. Both times he was left for dead, and both times he came back, winning the Comeback Player of the Year Award in 1987 and 1992. In 1992, when he was coming off a subpar year with the Cubs and seemingly winding down at age thirty-six, the Baltimore Orioles took a chance on him, signing him as a free agent. After two bad years in a row, the team looked to the opening of their new ballpark at Camden Yards as a fresh start.

"I was not gonna sign with Baltimore," he says as we pull into a greasy-spoon diner called the Big Biscuit. The clatter of silverware and lively buzz of conversation, punctuated by the occasional yell from the kitchen, fills the restaurant as our waitress hurriedly seats us.

"I mean, I was a thirty-six-year-old guy coming off surgery. I didn't need to be in the American League," he says, ignoring his menu. (The American League is known for having more offense.) "But I fly to Baltimore to meet with Johnny [Oates, the manager, who had been Sut's catcher his rookie season], and Johnny walked me out to the mound and said, 'Nobody knows, but you're gonna throw the first pitch ever at this ballpark.' And Brad, something just came over me, you get these tingles and goosebumps, and I walked off the mound, looked at my agent, and said, 'Let's get something done. I'm gonna play here.'"

Unlike Tommy Lasorda, Oates was true to his word. Two weeks before the season started, he announced that Sut would be his Opening Day starter against the Indians. "I said, 'Johnny, you need to let Mike Mussina pitch that game. He's a lot better than I am,'" Sut says, sipping some coffee. "And Johnny goes, 'I know that.' And then he goes, '[Ben] McDonald's better than you too.' But he told me, 'The reason you're starting Opening Day is I wanna line you up against everybody else's ace, knowing you can hold your own, and I'm gonna put Mussina and McDonald up against their three and four guys, and that's how we're gonna succeed.'"

Sut more than held his own. He shut out the Indians on Opening Day 2–0, the first of sixteen wins he racked up that season. Baseball bard Thomas Boswell wrote in the *Washington Post*: "Sutcliffe is an anachronism—a pitcher who's all heart. He always takes the ball. He never confesses an injury. He pitches until his arm falls off. Then he expects you to wait until he's healthy and can ring up some more big numbers. Of course, nobody waits. And he returns."[1]

He played two more seasons, then shut it down in 1994 at age thirty-eight. Out of the game for a year, he got restless, wanting to give back. When Larry Lucchino, president of the San Diego Padres, called and offered him the Padres pitching coach job, Sut's response nearly floored him: "I don't want to go to the big leagues. I want to go to rookie ball." It was the equivalent of getting offered a full ride to Harvard and opting instead for Bunker Hill Community College. Sut reported to Idaho Falls, Idaho, as the team's pitching coach on a $15,000 salary for the 1996 season. "Honestly, Brad, I never enjoyed having a uniform on more." A couple years later, he joined the Padres and ESPN broadcasting teams and never looked back.

But his biggest comeback was yet to come.

"So, uh, you probably read it was seven years ago now I got diagnosed with colon cancer," he volunteers. "I had a routine colonoscopy. I didn't want to do it, but Robin forced me to. I had had no issues," he says. My thoughts drift to Gini and Jaime Cocanower.

Doctors removed a single cancerous polyp, and Sut endured chemo and five days a week of radiation. He ended up having to wear an ileostomy bag for eight months. "Radiation was the worst. That was unbelievable. I literally spent, a lot of times, half a day just sitting in a bathtub because the radiation was around my rear end," he says.

Sut faced his fears head-on. Before he got the biopsy results, he gathered Robin and Shelby together at home. "Somehow we ended up in a closet, and I said, 'If it's [the cancer] all over, I'm just telling you right now, it's not gonna be a lengthy deal.' We all started bawling, and I looked at my daughter, and I said, 'Hey, I know where I'm going. I know where I'm at. I know I have been so blessed. I've done more things than most people get to do, and I'm adamant about you introducing your mom to your stepdad.'"

It thankfully didn't come to that—Sut remains cancer-free—but he was ready no matter what the test results.

"I've got to run pretty soon. Have a tee time at 11:15," he says as I finish my Chicago omelet, in honor of the Cubs.

Still, I feel like something's missing.

We get back in the car and head back to Dixon's Famous Chili to retrieve the Accord.

"Tell me a little more about your relationship with your parents," I say. He had mentioned that they divorced when he was fairly young, but he had hardly spoken of them since. Everything was about his grandparents.

"Um, I don't know if my dad is dead or alive," he says softly. "He took off when I was eleven, never sent child support or alimony or anything. My grandparents raised me. My grandpa has always been my dad," he says.

His dad was a race car driver who went by the moniker Mr. Excitement. After he ran off with another woman, Sut and his siblings moved in with their grandparents. His mom remarried but died young, at fifty-five.

The more we discuss his dad, the more the hurt creeps back into his voice. I share Don Carman's story with him, about how Don still carries that trauma. I want Sut to know that his experience is sadly common in the baseball fraternity.

"I'm seventeen, eighteen years old, at my first big-league camp, and there are all these great players, Hall of Famers [Sandy Koufax, Don Drysdale, etc.], and I wasn't in awe of any of them. I wasn't afraid of any of them," he says. Just like Carman, Sut weaponized his anger. On the mound, the cheerful gentle giant transformed into a warrior, the hurt and pain from childhood channeled into every fastball.

"My dad, being Mr. Excitement, the great racer, my dad was my idol to begin with. I wanted to be just like my dad," he says, some moisture appearing in the corners of his eyes. "But I never looked up to anybody after what my dad did to me. I know what a piece of shit is. I know what not to be."

With Shelby, Sut has done everything his father never did for him. He clears his throat. "I tell her every time I talk to her that I love her," he says, pulling back into Dixon's.

Excitement, after all, is overrated.

=

Over a thousand miles later, Las Vegas gleams in the desert like a neon warning sign, a symbol of humanity's brutal dominion over nature. It is at once the loneliest and most connected place in the country. It was not on my original itinerary, certainly not in the last days of a forty-nine-day sprint across more than eleven thousand miles, when I figured I'd be dragging to the finish line.

Except here I am, standing on Las Vegas Boulevard, developing a kink in my neck from staring up at the Stratosphere Tower, a 1,149-foot poor man's Space Needle at the end of the Strip.

I plop down my credit card for $180 (so much for cheap Vegas hotels) and haul my suitcase up to the room. I have no interest in gambling, but the nightlife, the promise of adventure, calls to me like an old friend.

Speaking of old friends, my phone chimes with a text. It's Jesse, the same Jesse who was there almost seven weeks ago as I passed out on the side of the freeway in Visalia.

"Any shenanigans?" he asks.

"Getting ready in the hotel," I type, adding, "it's on," our signature phrase for mischief. I peel off the T-shirt I've been wearing all day and unfold the ironing board from the closet.

I stand shirtless in front of the bathroom mirror. My trim torso is now interrupted by a bloated gut, all definition gone from my abs. Small bulges of fat hang over the crease where my upper thighs meet my hips. I probably haven't gained more than ten pounds, but on my slight frame, it shows. I suck my stomach in, trying to remember what it used to look like.

Memories of past debauchery in Vegas flood back: waking up next to a woman I didn't recognize in a motel I didn't remember entering; trying cocaine for the first time in a hotel bathroom with people I had just met; having sex in a stairwell railed out of my mind. In our twenties, Vegas was the ultimate escape. But what is it now?

I finish getting dressed, rub some gel into my hair, and check myself in the mirror. My eyes are bloodshot and ringed with dark shadows. Who am I kidding?

I laugh and throw down my room key, face-planting dramatically on the bed, rolling around and laughing harder. The thought of going out right now, doing a bunch of shots, getting hammered, and hitting on girls couldn't be less appealing.

"*Fuck that*," I say out loud. All I want to do is lie in this bed and read my research notes on Al Cowens, the last of the Wax Packers, write in my notebook, and fall asleep with the lights on.

Tomorrow afternoon I'll be back in California (but not San Diego, thank God). I've got one card in the Pack to go, and in just under seven weeks, I've managed to retrace much of my life, from fishing in Greenville to driving in OCD-addled circles in LA to seeing the woman I once thought I'd marry. I've redefined what the word "hero" means to me and created some new villains in the process. And I'm not done yet.

Tomorrow, crossing the Golden State border, I'll recognize home; but will home recognize me?

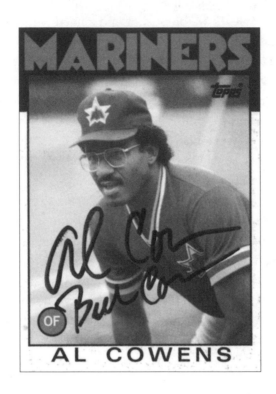

17

STRAIGHT OUTTA COMPTON

I'll never forget this. There were six of us,
six blacks, that went to this place that was
really close to the stadium in St. Pete. We
went over there because some of the white
players told us they had more rooms. We
introduce ourselves, say, "We're part of
the St. Louis baseball club and we heard
you have some apartments for rent." The
guy says, "We don't have no apartments."
We say, "One of our guys said you did." I
had never seen a Ku Klux Klan hood in
my life. He opens the door to show me.
—*Billy Cowens*

Days 47–48
August 4–5, 2015
Miles driven: 11,341
Cups of coffee: 123
Las Vegas NV to Compton CA

Everything changes.

In 1867 Griffith Dickinson Compton, a gold rusher originally from southern Virginia, led thirty pioneer families from Stockton, California, south into the coastal plains of Rancho San Pedro in search of a new start. The settlers purchased some land and began farming the area that later incorporated as the city of Compton. Two years later, the Los Angeles and San Pedro Railroad was completed, revolutionizing transportation and access to the area. Forty years of agricultural production ensued, with the railroad eventually yielding to the automotive and aviation industries in the early twentieth century, developing Compton into the Hub City for its geographically central location in Los Angeles.

During this period of growth, Compton was almost all white—in fact, in 1949 and 1950 the Bush family lived there (including future presidents George H. W. and W.). As the defense industry took off during World War II, Compton changed once again, with the population exploding from 16,198 in 1940 to 47,991 in 1950 to 71,812 in 1960. The demographics shifted dramatically during this time period as well; in 1948 there were only fifty African Americans in the entire city, but when LA's black population started gaining affluence and sought life in the suburbs, Compton's black numbers swelled. By 1960 blacks composed 40 percent of the population. The end of discriminatory housing laws led to massive white flight, and by the late 1980s, the city was almost three-quarters black, with its white population at a mere 3 percent. The once-lily-white city of Compton became a hub of black culture, spawning the West Coast hip hop movement and giving rise to such groups as the N.W.A.

But everything changes.

＝

I'm back in California, where it all started.

I walk into Centennial High School, the alma mater of the last Wax Packer, Al Cowens, on Central Avenue. A black iron fence rings the campus's perimeter, and above the entrance a bright white sign reads "Home of the Apaches." There are a couple of desks set up in the lobby and plenty of foot traffic for the teachers' summer professional development activities, branded as "Taking Action on Academic Literacy." Centennial has produced many star athletes over the years, several of whom are commemorated in yellowed photos on the walls, but there's no sign of Al. I linger for several minutes and notice that not only are there no black people, I am the only non-Latinx person in sight.

Inside the school office I approach an older Latina. "I'm writing a book about one of your alums. Is there an administrator I might be able to speak with?" I ask. A few moments later, a black man wearing a gray Apaches T-shirt and jeans emerges from the bank of offices in the back and introduces himself as Doug, the new school principal.

"I'm writing a book and doing some research on one of your alums, Al Cowens," I say.

"The O.J. guy?" he asks. I laugh. It isn't the first or last time someone will confuse Al Cowens for Al Cowlings, the driver in the infamous white Bronco chase. I correct the record.

"Oh yeah, sounds familiar. Did he play with the Royals?" He walks me back to the front of the high school, telling me he's only been on the job for seven months.

"Is the school mostly Latinx?" I ask.

"It is now," he replies. "This school used to be 99 percent African American."

"What changed?" I ask.

"People moved," he says with a shrug.

I ask if he knows of anyone who might have known Al, and it turns out I'm in luck.

"You know what you should do; the alumni association is meeting here at six, and a lot of guys from his time will be there. Come on by," he says.

Back out on the street, I'm surprised by how spacious Compton's main drag is. I had expected bleaker, cramped streets based on its reputation for crime; in a city of fewer than one hundred thousand, there were eighty-seven homicides in 1991. But crime has dropped, and Central Avenue is a wide thoroughfare, two lanes in each direction, with single-family homes set back from the road without fences. *Straight Outta Compton* movie posters are everywhere, promoting the release of the N.W.A. biopic in just a couple of weeks. It's a gorgeous summer day with a light breeze tickling palm fronds overhead, the perfect temperature for maximum comfort.

Al went to high school in Compton but lived in nearby Watts, a neighborhood of Los Angeles. He was the oldest of four; his parents, Peggy and Al Sr., met in the LA projects when they were in high school, and both became school janitors. He spent his childhood walking everywhere, even as the social upheaval that roiled the country in the 1960s made the streets unsafe—Al was thirteen when the Watts riots tore through his neighborhood, destroying many businesses that would never return. Baseball was his outlet and his ticket out. A third baseman through high school, he was converted to the outfield for his strong arm when the expansion Kansas City Royals drafted him in the seventy-fifth round in 1969.

Although his high school sweetheart turned wife, Velma, had to talk him out of quitting a couple times (she knew he would always regret it if he quit too soon), Al worked his way through the Royals farm system, debuting with the big club in 1974. Three years later he was one of the best players in baseball, the runner-up for the American League MVP Award after crushing 23 home runs and 112 RBIs and posting a .312/.361/.525 slash line. His manager, Whitey Herzog (remember him from the Garry Templeton incident?), loved him, calling him "the ideal player."[1] Respected by his teammates, Al kept his head down and went about his business. "Quiet" was the adjective always used to describe him in media accounts. In the 1977 playoffs against the Yankees, his teammate Hall of Famer George Brett said Al should be the MVP. "But he won't be, for three reasons: He's black, he's married, and he plays in the Midwest."[2] Brett was right.

But Al was unable to sustain his play at that level, and his career took a sharp turn in 1979 when pitcher Ed Farmer hit him squarely in the face with a pitch, breaking his jaw and causing him to miss three weeks. Farmer claimed it was unintentional, but the circumstances were fishy: Farmer hit the first batter he faced, Frank White; he had been knocked around by the Royals hitters; and he had already given up a run-scoring single to Al before he beaned him in the fifth inning. Following the incident, Al ate through a straw for three weeks, quietly seething. Things turned even uglier when he sought a dish of chilly revenge more than a year later. Now playing for the Detroit Tigers, Al came up to face Farmer in the eleventh inning. He hit a ground ball to shortstop, and rather than run to first, he bolted for the pitcher's mound, where he greeted Farmer with a right hook. Al was tossed and suspended for seven games, and a warrant was even issued for his arrest. Some say he was never the same after the incident.

But he did come back, playing several more years of productive ball with the Seattle Mariners before being iced out in the collusion scandal in the mid- to late eighties that similarly victimized Wax Packer Steve Yeager. Released by the Mariners in 1986, Al was done at age thirty-four.

Later that evening I return to Centennial High, where I meet a friendly group of alums, most of them from Al's era, just as Principal Doug had suggested. A woman named Vivian tells me she knows Al's brother Billy and will have him give me a call. It's the best lead I've got so far on finding Al.

═══

The phone rings at 8:00 a.m. It's from a 310 area code. Los Angeles.

"Hello?" I say, willing the grogginess out of my voice.

"Hey, is this Brad? I was told to call you. This is Billy Cowens."

"Oh hey. Thanks for getting back to me, Billy. I'm writing a book that includes a chapter on your brother Al, and I was hoping I could talk to you about him today if you're around," I say.

"Well, first off, he's not my brother. He's actually my first cousin," Billy replies.

Apparently Al and Billy duped the baseball world for years, telling everyone they were brothers. When I met Garry Templeton at the start of the trip and showed him Al's card in the Pack, he said, "I roomed with his brother Billy in the Minors!"

I get dressed and meet up with Billy at the Elephant Bar in Torrance, near Compton. Recently retired from the Compton Fire Department, Billy's about six feet tall, with a thin white beard. He's wearing a plain red hat and red shorts. He's fresh from a water aerobics class, rehab for his second hip surgery which needed to be replaced after years of pounding on the job. We ride together through the streets of Watts, Billy navigating and pointing out the projects where he grew up.

"I was raised on welfare as a kid," he explains. "I have a deaf sister a year younger than me. My mom couldn't go to work because there was nobody else to take care of her. She had a lot of medical issues. And my dad, he was a sanitation worker, but he didn't support the family. He had another wife."

I've become sadly numb to the stories of negligent fathers.

Billy was three years younger than Al and looked up to him.

"What would you guys do together?" I ask as we pass by row after row of automotive repair shops where the steel industry used to be.

"Throw rocks," Billy replies.

I laugh, not expecting that answer and not sure if he's being serious. "Rocks?" I ask.

"We just liked throwing rocks, man. We'd go down by the railroad tracks and throw rocks. Al, he had an accurate arm too," he says. Everywhere they went, school, baseball practice, friends' houses, they would walk and throw rocks, testing their arms by making targets out of trees, signs, each other. The buses were too expensive.

"What he got into, I got into. What helped us out was sports. We were athletes, and for some reason gangs didn't bother athletes," Billy says. Toward the end of their high school days, gang warfare laid siege to Los Angeles as the Bloods and Crips rose to prominence. Although the Cowens boys were generally able to avoid that scene, they were still in South-Central LA, and fights were part of life. Although he was always quiet, Al was never afraid to defend himself: "Al was the best fighter. He didn't pick fights. But he could fight." When Ed Farmer beaned him in 1979 Farmer had no idea who he was messing with. "That's the only time I ever saw him really angry. That summer [following the incident], that's all he talked about. He said, 'I'm gonna get him,'" Billy says, limping along with his cane for support.

Billy was a ballplayer himself. Not quite as good as Al, but still very good. He was drafted by the Minnesota Twins in the eighth round in 1972 but declined to sign, wanting more money. It was a mistake. When he signed with the Cardinals two years later (the same year Tempy was drafted number 1), he had dropped all the way to the nineteenth round. He played in the Minors for a couple years but never made it past Double-A. Just like Tempy, he felt the squeeze of racism, sometimes overtly, like when a landlord refusing to rent a room to him showed him his KKK hood, sometimes more subtly in the competition with white ballplayers.

"You just had to be much better [than the white players]." He points to me: "If you and I were playing the same position, and let's say you hit .310 and I hit .310, and you steal twenty bases and I steal forty bases, and your fielding percentage is .960 and mine is .970, you get the job," he says.

Al, it turns out, is a fitting player to end the Pack. As I retrace his upbringing and his career with Billy, multiple connections to the other

Wax Packers come out: Billy was roommates with not only Tempy but also Scott Boras, Don Carman's boss; Billy now helps out at Major League Baseball's Compton Youth Academy, where inner-city kids get baseball coaching for free, and is friends with Rod Davis, who is friends with Stacey Pettis, Gary Pettis's brother; in 1979 Al was traded from the Royals to the Angels as part of the deal that included Rance Mulliniks. The baseball world is small, its inhabitants closely interconnected. Al has brought my journey full circle.

Given their similar skills and upbringing, I'm curious why Billy thinks Al made it where he did not. Based on how quickly he replies, Billy has clearly thought about this before: "Nothing ever fazed Al. He didn't get rattled. Some people have bad days, and they bring it back the next day. He would never do that," he says.

"How did you deal with failure?" I ask Billy.

"I was not like that," he replies. "It would bother me."

As we walk around the Compton Youth Academy grounds where Billy volunteers, past baseball fields ranging in size from Little League to Big League, I ask him, "What else did Al like to do?"

He pauses to think it over. "Man, Al loved to fish. Just loved it," he says. Because Al knew fishing isn't about catching fish.

===

I want to talk to Velma, Al's widow, to hear what happened to Al. I had read in the papers that he was diagnosed with congestive heart failure in 1999 and that he died at home of a heart attack on March 11, 2002. He was fifty. But beyond that, there's little known about the story.

I had written Velma a letter explaining the project but had had only one phone conversation months ago in which she expressed reservations about being interviewed. Billy told me she is a very private person, and she hasn't replied to any of my voice messages. But her eldest son, Purvis, who lives in Grants Pass, Oregon, suggested I drop by her house, since he couldn't make it down himself due to work obligations. I have an address for Velma in Downey, one of the many suburbs of eastern LA County, and Billy told me that Al's daughter, Trinetta, still lives there with her mom.

After leaving Billy back at his car, I head for Downey. I find a Toyota Avalon and Nissan Altima parked in the driveway of the modest ranch-style house. The neighborhood is silent, and the green of the well-kept lawn looks dull in the light of dusk. Two plastic chairs sit on the lit porch along with small statues of elephants and a dog with a bone in its mouth.

Cradling my notebook and with my backpack slung over one shoulder, I ring the doorbell. A moment later, a young girl, no more than seven or eight, answers with a cautious look on her face. *This can't be Trinetta. Maybe it's Trinetta's daughter?* I smile, trying to reassure her that I'm harmless.

"Hi, I'm Brad Balukjian, the writer." (I hate saying my last name; even I struggle to pronounce it.) "Is your mom or grandma home?"

She immediately turns and calls for someone. A moment later, a young woman in her twenties appears in the doorway. I presume she must be Trinetta.

I introduce myself and explain the book project about her dad; she says that she wasn't aware of it and that her mom is still at work but should be back around 8:00. I tell her I'll come back later.

When I return an hour later, the cars are gone from the driveway, and the porch light is off. The house has gone completely dark, the message clear—leave us alone.

I have one play left. Pulling out my phone, I dial Purvis and fill him in on what just happened.

"I don't know why my mom is being so fucking stupid," he says, clearly agitated. "She's so close-minded. This is bullshit. I want you to go back there and knock on that fucking door with me on the phone!"

I pace the street in the darkness.

"I'm not gonna do that, Purvis. But why don't you just tell me your dad's story?" I suggest, sitting on the curb under a streetlight. For the next hour, Purvis vents and then relaxes, running the full gamut of emotion. He has got a lot to say and seems grateful to have the opportunity.

Now forty-three, Purvis was the only one of the Cowens kids who was old enough to appreciate his dad's time in the big leagues. He would shag balls in batting practice with the other players' sons and videotape his dad's at bats so he could analyze them with him later. Once Purvis was older and playing baseball himself, Al taught him everything he knew about the craft of hitting. "My dad was a family guy. He was a quiet, quiet man," Purvis says, echoing everyone's favorite descriptor for Al. "But if he said something, it was meaningful," he adds.

There was a lot going on beneath the surface throughout Al's life. When I had asked Billy about Al getting drafted by the Royals, he was matter-of-fact, saying it was a great day and that the family celebrated. Purvis, a much more open book, has a different version of the story: "The night he got drafted, he got shot. One of his friend's brothers shot him."

My mind flashes through all the other Wax Packers' draft stories— Lee Mazzilli running home to hug his dad, Rick Sutcliffe's grandfather haggling with the Dodgers for $85,000. And Al Cowens got shot.

"Was it an accident?" I ask.

"I mean, it may have been an accident. But I don't know how you accidentally shoot your brother's friend," Purvis replies.

"Where was he shot?"

"Somewhere in the stomach. He was okay, he just had to wear something to protect his stomach. They told him not to slide headfirst," he says.

Until the family moved to the quieter suburb of Cerritos, Purvis grew up in the same streets as his father. "I got jumped every day at school because the kids knew who my dad was, and they wanted to take my stuff," he says.

The most important lesson Al taught him was to always have his guard up, to always be vigilant. "My dad was a fighter, a warrior," he says proudly. "He came from the ghetto. And he instilled that in me."

Purvis looked up to his dad, but he also clashed with him. When he was still living at home, attending Compton College, he got a girl pregnant. Al wasn't happy. He told him he had to leave. "That was just my dad. He said I couldn't bring a kid there. He loved his granddaughter, but he wasn't taking care of her," Purvis says.

About a year before he died, Al found God. He and Velma had grown up religious, but for that last year of his life, Al was on a crusade. A quiet man most of his life, he suddenly spoke out, heard a calling to tell people, especially kids, what he felt baseball was all about. He would give talks and presentations to inner-city kids about the cruel nature of baseball, about a game that he loved more than anything but that chewed him up and spat him out when it was done with him. He talked about the heartless side of the game, the way players were pressured to take amphetamines and steroids and then, once their careers were over, *boom*, they were done, it was over, like being thrown into a freezing cold shower. He was angry with the game, with the struggle to find life and meaning after his career ended, and he encouraged people to always make God and family priorities in their lives.

In the weeks before his death, Velma noticed him grow quiet and distant, as if he knew something bad was coming. Two weeks before he died, his behavior turned downright scary and irrational.

"Me and my dad had a fistfight," Purvis says. "I don't even remember what it was about. He got into an altercation with my brother. And he had his baseball ring on, so he sliced my brother's head with the diamond of the ring. He told my mom, 'Purv's next!'"

I watch as a car drives by, so riveted by the craziness of this story that I forget I'm sitting on a curb in East LA.

"We went out in the street. It was raining, and the neighbors came out to watch. I had no shoes on. I busted his glasses and bloodied him up. I was tired. He was like, 'What's wrong, son?' I told him my feet hurt, and he said, 'Okay, let's take it to the grass.' So we went to the grass and kept fighting. It was crazy," he says.

"How did it end?" I ask.

"When he saw that he wasn't going to whoop my ass, he went into the house and grabbed his gun. My mom stepped in front of him. The cops came and told me to leave. He told me, 'Don't ever come back to my house.' Two weeks later, he was gone."

The intensity that defines the father-son relationship can take many guises. For Purvis and Al, all the unspoken raw emotion that had existed between them erupted like a volcano into the open that day and then was left to dissipate in the streets where they came from.

"How did you find out about him passing?" I ask.

"My grandma called me and told me to come over to the house. And I knew instantly," he says. When he got there, Al was lying in bed, having already passed. "I just stayed in the room, hugging him and crying, trying to wake him up until the coroners came," he says, his voice still steady and calm.

"After that, I would write letters to him every day, and then at the end of the week I would go to Huntington Beach Pier and rip them up and throw them in the ocean. I was writing him shit that I didn't tell him," he says, choking back tears.

Purvis never figured out what made his dad so mad that day, mad enough to threaten to kill his own son. He has some ideas that sound a bit out of left field, deep-state conspiracy-type stuff. But stranger things have happened. "Once he started speaking out, something happened," he says, referencing Al's evangelism about the dirtiness of baseball. "Something happened, man. Somebody killed my daddy. And I would take that to my grave. My daddy did not have a heart attack."

Purvis doesn't know who or how, but he remains convinced that the kind, gentle man who was his father was punished for being too real, too honest, *too black*. He has seen too much ugliness, too much racism, to believe his dad just got sick one day.

When Al signed with the Mariners in 1982, he traded in his number 18 jersey for number 16. An eight-year-old Purvis was confused: "Why didn't you get number 18? Why did you get number 16?" he asked his dad in the clubhouse. Al grabbed the new jersey and threw it to his son: "That's for you," he said, walking away to the trainer's room. "When he came back I said, 'Dad, I don't understand.' He goes 'P. That's the sixteenth letter in the alphabet. That's for you.'"

=

On my final day there is only one thing left for me to do: find Al. I locate his grave online—it's in the Inglewood Park Cemetery, Acacia Slope Plot, Lot 432, Grave F. But when I get there, I find acre upon acre, row after row of headstones without any guide or map. I think of the final scene in *Raiders of the Lost Ark* when the Ark of the Covenant is wheeled into a warehouse with thousands of identical-looking boxes. After spending way too long driving around at five miles per hour scanning the plot names painted on the sides of the curb, I finally find Acacia. But that still leaves me with at least a couple hundred yards of headstones to search, each row with maybe fifty to sixty graves. I'm fighting daylight.

As I watch the sun dip toward the horizon and I start to think about giving up, I spot it, a simple slab on the ground: "Cowens, Husband, Father, and Grandfather, 1951–2002," the gravestone reads.

I rest his baseball card on top and take a picture.

Most people have one life to make it count. On my journey, I've learned that baseball players have two. Al's first headstone might have read "1974–1986," along with this John Updike quote: "The little death that awaits all athletes."

A player's baseball life is built in the James Dean mold—live fast, die young. It is marked by dramatic peaks and valleys, the home runs and the strikeouts. That life brings incredible fame, even for the most marginal of Major Leaguers. But it's a mirage that comes at a steep cost—broken marriages, estranged children, substance abuse.

Although Al was gone too soon, most ballplayers get a redo. And in that second life, the challenge is to learn to live like the rest of us, to understand that most of life is not a home run or a strikeout but a line-drive single to left or a groundball to second. Coming down off the high of their baseball lives is an excruciating hangover that for some players, especially the biggest stars, lingers. Those who made the adjustment realized that they were just people like you and me who happened to be good at baseball and that the key to contentment was something inside them all along, the same skill that enabled them to reach the highest level of their craft—the ability to accept whatever is right in front of them, good or bad, success or failure, without resisting.

I sit down in the grass next to Al and look around. I sit completely still. The air feels warm and comforting, the sun filtering through wispy clouds and a nearby tree to illuminate the frenetic dance of a swarm of insects looking like wisps of confetti. I hear the dull roar of jet engines at nearby LAX and the chirps of unseen birds surrounding me. I look down and see a single maroon ant probing my feet with its antennae.

The lesson I learned in dealing with OCD has been reaffirmed throughout this journey, that we overvalue our thoughts and feelings, which are out of our control and ephemeral and often illogical, and undervalue the importance of our behavior, which we *can* control. And if we change our behavior in a positive way, our thoughts and feelings will follow.

Everything changes, except for this one constant: as long as you're breathing, you will always have whatever is right in front of you. Make it count.

I think about what it means to be a fan, about the millions of people who idolize Major Leaguers, going so far as to wear jerseys with strangers' names on the backs. We make assumptions about the fame and fortune that big leaguers experience and fantasize about what it would feel like, even for one day, to share in that.

But here's the thing: we already know. Once the novelty wears off, what it feels like to be a Major League ballplayer isn't that much different from what it feels like to play softball on your Sunday morning beer league team. Which is why Don Carman, standing on the dugout steps of Veterans Stadium, could not for the life of him understand why thirty-five thousand people had given up their Sunday and paid good money to watch him throw a baseball.

As I watch the ant at my feet, thoughts arise and form like single drops of water, then just as quickly are absorbed again in the sea of my mind. I shuffle the Wax Pack in my head, each card conjuring up memories in a disjointed stream—Randy Ready's chatter, the infinite grass of Camargo's prairie, Sophia's smile.

Sophia. I almost forgot that she'll be in San Francisco soon, temporarily relocated for work. I think back to the yoga studio in Naples, her easy laugh and big smile, and my irrational impulse to run away from it all, to think in terms of absolutes, all or nothing, home runs or strikeouts.

But most of life is just a line drive to left.

I pick up my phone and bring up her number to send a text.

The screen shines brightly against the dipping sun. I start tapping away with my thumbs.

"What time does your flight get in?"

1 ☐ PETE ROSE	33 ☐ JEFF LAHTI
2 ☐ ROSE SPECIAL: '63-4-5-6	34 ☐ KEN PHELPS
3 ☐ ROSE SPECIAL: '67-8-9-70	35 ☐ JEFF REARDON
4 ☐ ROSE SPECIAL: '71-2-3-4	36 ☐ TIGERS LEADERS
5 ☐ ROSE SPECIAL: '75-6-7-8	37 ☐ MARK THURMOND
6 ☐ ROSE SPECIAL: '79-80-1-2	38 ☐ GLENN HOFFMAN
7 ☐ ROSE SPECIAL: '83-84-85	39 ☐ DAVE RUCKER
8 ☐ DWAYNE MURPHY	40 ☐ KEN GRIFFEY
9 ☐ ROY SMITH	41 ☐ BRAD WELLMAN
10 ☐ TONY GWYNN	42 ☐ GEOFF ZAHN
11 ☐ BOB OJEDA	43 ☐ DAVE ENGLE
12 ☐ JOSE URIBE	44 ☐ LANCE McCULLERS
13 ☐ BOB KEARNEY	45 ☐ DAMASO GARCIA
14 ☐ JULIO CRUZ	46 ☐ BILLY HATCHER
15 ☐ EDDIE WHITSON	47 ☐ JUAN BERENGUER
16 ☐ RICK SCHU	48 ☐ BILL ALMON
17 ☐ MIKE STENHOUSE	49 ☐ RICK MANNING
18 ☐ BRENT GAFF	50 ☐ DAN QUISENBERRY
19 ☐ RICH HEBNER	51 ☐ BOBBY WINE
20 ☐ LOU WHITAKER	52 ☐ CHRIS WELSH
21 ☐ GEORGE BAMBERGER	53 ☐ LEN DYKSTRA
22 ☐ DUANE WALKER	54 ☐ JOHN FRANCO
23 ☐ MANNY LEE	55 ☐ FRED LYNN
24 ☐ LEN BARKER	56 ☐ TOM NIEDENFUER
25 ☐ WILLIE WILSON	57 ☐ BILL DORAN
26 ☐ FRANK DiPINO	58 ☐ BILL KRUEGER
27 ☐ RAY KNIGHT	59 ☐ ANDRE THORNTON
28 ☐ ERIC DAVIS	60 ☐ DWIGHT EVANS
29 ☐ TONY PHILLIPS	61 ☐ KARL BEST
30 ☐ EDDIE MURRAY	62 ☐ BOB BOONE
31 ☐ JAMIE EASTERLY	63 ☐ RON ROENICKE
32 ☐ STEVE YEAGER	64 ☐ FLOYD BANNISTER

EPILOGUE

I'm back in a car again, back on the road. But this time the car is a rental and I'm playing Whitesnake on my phone's Spotify app instead of on a CD.

Everything changes.

Sleet, which I haven't seen in years living in California, smears my windshield as the wipers struggle to keep up. I blast the heat, fighting to stay warm as I watch clouds of my breath dissipate in the air in front of me.

I've flown back east for another college buddy's wedding, this one in Philadelphia, and have absconded for the afternoon to drive two hours northwest to Duryea, just outside Scranton. The Topps factory is long gone, having closed in 1996, but its spirit endures in the former employees who still live in Duryea. Forget about the players; the last piece in the Wax Pack puzzle is to meet the people who actually made the cards.

Which brings us full circle, back to Mary Lou Gula.

Space is plentiful in the town of Duryea. The grounds are wide open around the old Topps factory at 401 York Avenue, now occupied by Pride Mobility, a company that manufactures scooters and other mobile vehicles for seniors. The softly undulating hills nearby create a pleasant landscape for a town that has experienced a lot of change since the 1980s. Topps closed its doors in 1996 ("outsourcing," one former employee tells me), and other companies, such as RCA, took their manufacturing elsewhere.

Even the parking lot at Mohegan Sun Pocono Casino Resort in nearby Wilkes-Barre, where I'm scheduled to meet Mary Lou and several other former Topps employees, is vast. I pull my jacket collar as high as it will go and scrunch my neck down like a jittery turtle, protecting my bare skin from the bite of late winter cold as I walk into the casino. The smell of smoke smacks me as I enter the lobby and hear the assault of money, shrill slot machines mixed with thumping music and a too-loud emcee making announcements no one even tries to understand. I walk to a central bar area and spot what must be the crew—three old friends laughing hard, happy to interrupt each other and to be interrupted.

Tom, Mary Lou, and Mary Lou's daughter Chris shared many years and laughs on the Topps factory floor. Tom is the elder statesman, an older man with glasses and a white beard extending to his sternum whose Facebook page identifies him as "Former MR. TOPPS." He talks sparingly, standing off to the side while the ladies describe the card-making process to me in exquisite detail, but when he does speak, it's in a measured, nasal voice in which every word seems important.

Topps was his life; "I met my wife there," he tells me.

Chris, now a flight attendant in her late forties, got into the family business right out of high school, working the DF line, card cutting, and card slitting in the factory. A few minutes later, Kim, around Chris's age, joins us.

"We were just talking about card cutting!" Chris says.

"I hated card cutting," Kim shoots back with a grin.

Ten days after graduating from the local high school, Kim joined the rest of the town and started working in the factory. At seven dollars an hour back then, you couldn't beat the pay.

As the four of them reminisce, long-buried memories burst to the surface, the souvenirs of a shared experience. The same joy ballplayers experience at team reunions is on display here in a smoky casino near Duryea. They may not have played the game, but these people are a part of the game's larger community. No matter how much baseball changes— and it has changed exponentially in the past few years with the influx of analytics and Big Data—what always remains the same is its unique role as a catalyst for building relationships. No other sport has the kind of down time that baseball has, the pauses that lead its detractors to call it boring but that are actually its greatest strength, providing the time needed to build relationships with the people around you.

In 1992, at the height of America's baseball card collecting obses-sion, Topps stopped putting sticks of gum in packs (collectors complained that the gum stained the cards) and abandoned its trademark wax paper. It also began printing cards on white cardboard rather than the traditional brown. A few years later, the baseball card bubble burst due to overproduction, a crippling players' strike, and the rise of the internet.

And then there's Mary Lou, the same Mary Lou who bundled our Wax Pack back in the factory in November 1985. She has done many jobs since, but nothing compares to those twenty-five years she put in at Topps.

"Brad, listen to me," she says, moving closer to my face to make sure I have her attention.

"The day the factory closed in 1996, we knew it was going to be the last day. I worked second shift," she says, recalling it as if it was yesterday. The workers walked outside the factory doors and faced the same decision they always faced after work: Town Tavern or Litzi's Lounge? But this time they did something different.

"We all walked outside, took our hats off, and tossed them in the air," she says, evoking a graduation.

"Wherever they landed, that was it."

JUNE 2019

Rance Mulliniks closed down his baseball academy in 2018 but still gives the occasional lesson to young ballplayers. Twice a month he goes to El Paso to do baseball clinics for a nonprofit that emphasizes education. He and Lori still live in Visalia, where he continues to dabble in real estate. His son, Seth, graduated from high school this year and will attend Olivet Nazarene University in Illinois in the fall; he will major in mechanical engineering. Rance's daughter, Shaylee, just finished the seventh grade and wants to be a nurse.

Steve Yeager quit smoking, but not the way he expected to. He was diagnosed with lung cancer in 2016, had surgery to remove part of a rib, and added a fourteen-inch scar to his collection of baseball battle wounds. He underwent chemotherapy and is now cancer-free. Following the 2018 season, he retired from his post as the Dodgers catching instructor but still goes to spring training and chips in whenever the team needs him for an appearance. His son Evan transferred from Pierce College to Cal State Dominguez Hills, where he played baseball and earned his degree in business. Steve and Charlene still run the Jersey Mike's sub shop in Granada Hills.

Tragically, Glenda Templeton, *Garry Templeton's* wife, passed away in 2018 from pancreatic cancer. "We took her to the hospital February 26th, and she died March 11th," Tempy tells me on the phone. He is still running Camp Templeton, running around with the grandkids, but is looking to downsize from their home in San Marcos. He can't put a knee replacement off much longer and has cut his golfing down to once per week. He'd still like to coach in professional baseball, but the game today barely resembles the game he played in the 1970s and 1980s. "They said they're not hiring the old guys," he says.

Gary Pettis is still the third-base coach with the Houston Astros. In 2017 he finally got his World Series ring, helping to lead the Astros past the Dodgers for the team's first world championship. I never heard back from him.

Just as promised, *Randy Ready* went back into baseball in 2016, landing a job managing the Class-A Advanced Jupiter Hammerheads, in the Florida Marlins organization. He moved on to manage the Jacksonville Jumbo Shrimp in 2017 and 2018 before parting ways with the Marlins last fall. Following his divorce from Tracy, he met a woman named Hope (not on Tinder!), whom he married earlier this year. When his son Mark graduated from high school, he moved to Grand Junction, Colorado, where he lives on the farm he bought back in the 1990s. Dorene is still living in Tucson; their oldest son, Andrew, an ER doctor, recently took a position nearby and is involved with her care.

Jaime Cocanower still hasn't retired from Tyson Foods even though he and Gini are still enjoying their retirement home in northwestern Arkansas. They bought the pontoon boat they had always wanted and regularly cruise Beaver Lake. Gini retired in June 2017 and remains cancer-free.

Carlton Fisk still hasn't called me, and I doubt my autographed photo is framed on his wall. He emerges from seclusion for the occasional autograph signing or public appearance. The Pawtucket Red Sox inducted him into their Hall of Fame in 2017.

Don Carman has put his doctorate in psychology on hold to follow in my footsteps (kidding) as a writer. He still works for Scott Boras but has the material for multiple self-help books drawing on his years as a sports psychologist. Don's old coach Bob Ward had a heart attack a couple years ago followed by open-heart surgery and is now in better shape than he has been in years.

After years of lobbying and cajoling, *Vince Coleman* finally got elected to the St. Louis Cardinals Hall of Fame in 2018. Grinning from ear to ear, Vincent van Go gave an acceptance speech in which he celebrated his favorite person: himself. "Now that I'm back, I'm back politicking, because I'm my biggest advocate. I would love nothing more than to be able to share my craft, my knowledge, and my skill set and to be an inspiration to every kid that walked through your locker room door."[1] The Cardinals haven't called.

A year after my trip, ESPN released a documentary titled *Doc and Darryl* (part of the network's *30 for 30* series) chronicling the ups and downs of *Doc Gooden* and Darryl Strawberry. Doc appeared jittery and gaunt throughout the program (which was filmed shortly after my visit), leading many to suspect that he had relapsed. While not saying it outright, the film strongly implied that Doc was not clean. Codirector Judd Apatow said, "As it went along, I think we became more and more aware of how recent some of their troubles were, so it changed the documentary in a big way."[2] Right before this book went to press, on June 7, 2019, Doc was pulled over at 1:00 a.m. by police in Holmdel, New Jersey, and was arrested for driving under the influence, possession of a controlled substance, and possession of drug paraphernalia. Police found him with two baggies of a substance suspected to be cocaine.

In March of this year, a headline on my phone took my breath away: "Yankees Guest Instructor Mazzilli Hit in Head by Batted Ball." *Lee Mazzilli* was hit in the head by a line drive in center field during batting practice and ended up in intensive care with bleeding in his brain. Fortunately, he made a full recovery. His son LJ is playing baseball for the Long Island Ducks.

The semester finally ended for *Richie Hebner*, who coached his final season with the Buffalo Bisons in 2016. He now spends most of his days driving the hearse and helping wherever he can at his friend's funeral parlor near Norwood. His brother Dennis left his job at the warehouse and now works as a driver for O'Reilly Auto Parts. He and Richie still aren't as close as they used to be.

Rick Sutcliffe keeps on going, earning a contract extension from ESPN in December 2018 to continue broadcasting games. His beloved Chicago Cubs finally won the World Series in 2016.

Billy Cowens bowls twice a week and continues to enjoy retirement. Purvis Cowens moved back to the LA area to be close to the rest of his family and now helps out at the Compton Youth Academy, coaching baseball. He is also a special education teacher and varsity baseball coach at Cerritos High School. *Al Cowens* was nominated for the Kansas City Royals Hall of Fame this year.

And as for me, I'm still renting a room in Oakland, still single. Things with Sophia didn't work out, but just because something ends doesn't mean it was a failure.

I sometimes take out the Pack and shuffle through the cards and smile. Several people have asked me if I would consider writing a sequel, getting another pack and getting back out on the road.

But the answer is no. I've already lived my dream. I'm awake now, and as Don Carman told me, "I don't get to go back to sleep and dream again."

One pack. No turning back.

ACKNOWLEDGMENTS

I want to start by thanking the Wax Packers. I am still in awe that so many of these men who occupied such a vital part of my childhood were so generous with their time when they really had nothing to gain. I had little more than an idea and the passion to see it through, and this book could not exist without their cooperation. Thank you.

For five years I worked part-time making about $30,000 a year in the Bay Area so I could have the time to dedicate to a project of this magnitude. There was lots of rejection and adversity, and I could not have made it through without the support and love of a tight group of friends and family: my sister, Lauren, whose courage and resilience are always an inspiration; my three nieces, Stacia ("the whorl tooth shark"), Olivia ("the Bat"), and Bianca ("the Inuit"), and my nephew, Chase ("Ponda Baba"), who bring such joy through their curiosity and innocence; my hockey buddies, the Flying Moth, H. Ash Brown, Cabbage, Gonzo, Cataldo (who gets extra props for giving feedback on the entire manuscript), and Treasure Island; my colleagues at Merritt College, Jason Holloway, Rick Ramos, Monica Ambalal, Nghiem Thai, Laura Forlin, Chris Grampp, Mario Rivas, and Arja McCray, who were always supportive; my two brothers-in-spirit, Adam and Jesse Brouillard, who are so important that they are in this book; and of course my parents, who also play an important role in the book itself.

Ever since taking my first journalism class from Bob Bliwise at Duke University, I have dreamed of having the space and time to truly practice the craft of literary nonfiction. Professor Bliwise, Professor Susan Tifft, and Professor Christina Askounis were my writing mentors, and I will always be grateful to them. My first job out of college as a fact-checker at *Islands* magazine also laid the groundwork for this book, training me in the trade. I'd like to thank my colleagues there, especially Allison Joyce, Lisa Gosselin, Nick Robertson, and Melissa Wilbanks, for teaching me how to write, fact-check, and edit.

Without the help of some very important people, this book would never have come to fruition: Greg Veis reminded me of the book's larger meaning; Andrew Eil convinced me to stay true to my vision and convictions; Rebecca Kyles refused to let me give up, saying this book was inside of me and had to come out; Deborah Davis gave an outstanding read early on that may have saved the book.

To my writers' group, Laird Harrison, Staci Hobbet, Robert Luhn, and Terry Shames, thank you for your careful edits and emotional support.

Thanks to Susan May, Jessica Kraft, Zara Stone, Jesse Brouillard, and Ali Fearon for their feedback on the manuscript.

I'd like to thank Jerome Petit, Ele Avagliano, Caroline Faua, and Joseph Faua for hosting me in Tahiti while I wrote sections of this book.

Bill Francis at the Baseball Hall of Fame kindly provided research files on all the Wax Packers from the hall's prolific archive. I am also grateful to the Society for American Baseball Research (SABR) and Newspapers .com as research sources.

I have to thank many people in the publishing industry for their time and assistance: Ken Ilgunas, Jason Turbow, Mark Weinstein, Doug Grad, Mychael Urban, Jeff Deck, Dan Epstein, Dave Jamieson, Doug Wilson, Ellis Henican, Tyler Kepner, Nick Diunte, and Graham Womack.

On the road trip and in my reporting, I spent time with several sources who were generous with their time: Glenn Carman, Bob Ward, Jerry Luzar, Stacey Pettis, Mary Lou Gula, Kim Litchkofski, Chris Giguere, Tom Hamilton, Bob D'Angelo, Rob Rains, Terry Kibler, Dana Mulliniks, Jorge Ramos, Tom Pearse, Herschel Musick, Billy Reed, Arthur Carman, Bob Kendrick, Betty Walker, James Carman, Steve Grande, Melanie Mulliniks, and Ganell Mulliniks.

I'd like to thank my editor at the University of Nebraska Press, Rob Taylor, for believing in me when other publishing houses would not. For that, I will always be grateful. At UNP, big thanks to my publicists, Anna Weir and Rosemary Sekora; marketing manager Mark Heineke;

project editor Sara Springsteen; copyeditor Mary Hill; and contracts expert Leif Milliken. You are consummate professionals.

I'd also like to thank my initial agents, Peter and Amy Bernstein, for doing more to improve this book than anyone else by pushing me so hard. Without their critical eye, this would never have been as good.

Topps generously gave permission to use images of the cards from the Wax Pack. Thank you Hadley Barrett and Michael Brandstaedter.

Finally, thank you to every utility infielder and middle reliever from my childhood (especially those whose names started with *F*) for inspiring me to believe in the underdog. This book began there.

P.S. I don't really have anything against San Diego.

NOTES

1. WARMING UP

1. In the spirit of full disclosure, I did open up multiple packs, just in case I ended up with too many dead players. The integrity of the pack I chose remains intact—there was no mixing and matching.

2. HAPPY MEALS

1. Dick Miller, "Angel Voices Sing Mulliniks' Praise," *Sporting News*, August 20, 1977.
2. Dave Perkins, "Mulliniks Always Talked .300," *Toronto Star*, March 18, 1993.
3. Hal McCoy, "Dayton's Yeager Guides All-Star," *Dayton Daily News*, July 14, 2015; Alan Greenberg, "Yeager Still Ducks When a Bat Breaks," *Atlanta Constitution*, April 25, 1977.

3. YEAGER BOMBS

1. Bob Oates, "Yeager: I'm Better Than Bench," *Los Angeles Times*, February 9, 1975.
2. Mike Littwin, "Lasorda Sure Had That Fella Yeager Rested for Series," *Los Angeles Times*, October 26, 1981.
3. Technically, the Sheik gave me three options: shoot me with his .38 Magnum, stab me with his butcher knife, or simply break my leg. Suffice to say it was awhile before I felt ready to return to the literary theme of childhood heroes.
4. Bob Oates, "Yeager's High School Football Coach Was Impressed," *Los Angeles Times*, May 29, 1983.

4. CAMP TEMPLETON

1. Neal Russo, "Templeton Apology Demanded," *St. Louis Post-Dispatch*, August 27, 1981.
2. Jeff Pearlman, "From Mad Dog to Mentor," *Sports Illustrated*, June 26, 2000.
3. Gary Smith, "The Other Side of Second Base," *Inside Sports*, June 1982.
4. Thomas Boswell, "Irate Herzog Awaits Templeton Apology," *Washington Post*, August 28, 1981.
5. John Feinstein, "Teammates Back Templeton as He Returns to 'Scene of the Gesture'; Templeton Now Has Team Backing," *Washington Post*, September 23, 1981.
6. Roy S. Johnson, "A Welcome for Templeton," *New York Times*, September 17, 1981.

5. HOUSTON, WE HAVE A PROBLEM

1. Brief time travel note: the Astros actually did end up winning the World Series in 2017, beating the Dodgers in seven games.

6. RANDY IS READY

1. Bill Plaschke, "Padres' Ready Handles Horror of Wife's Tragedy," *Los Angeles Times*, September 30, 1988.

9. CHASING CARLTON

1. Pat Jordan, "Conversations with the Dinosaur," *Men's Journal*, March 1993.
2. Doug Wilson, *Pudge: The Biography of Carlton Fisk* (New York: Thomas Dunne Books, 2015), 310.
3. Wilson, *Pudge*, 81.
4. Jordan, "Conversations."

10. LEADER OF THE PACK

1. Peter Pascarelli, "Phillies Pounded by Cubs," *Philadelphia Inquirer*, August 12, 1989.
2. But it's still more charming than San Diego.

11. VINCENT VAN GONE

1. Franz Lidz, "Invincible," *Sports Illustrated*, April 15, 1991.
2. Craig Neff, "In-Vince-Able Man of Steel," *Sports Illustrated*, June 17, 1985.
3. Cathie Burnes Beebe, "In-Vinceable Thief Coleman Elevates Art of Stealing," *St. Louis Post-Dispatch*, July 12, 1989.
4. Rick Hummel, "'Egotistical' Coleman Quiets Critics," *Sporting News*, August 13, 1990.
5. Juan Williams, "Jackie Robinson Fought for Justice in Baseball and in America," *Washington Post*, May 3, 1987.
6. Wins above replacement (WAR) is an advanced metric that represents the number of wins a player adds to his team's total above a replacement player at that same position; it is meant to capture the overall contribution of a player.
7. Bob Klapisch and John Harper, *The Worst Team Money Could Buy* (New York: Random House, 1993), 93, 258.
8. Dwight Gooden with Ellis Henican, *Doc: A Memoir* (Boston: New Harvest, 2013), 122.
9. Steve Serby, Miguel Garcilazo, and Corky Siemaszko, "Mets' Coleman Tagged as Firework Hurts Fans," *Daily News*, July 26, 1993.

10. Steve Marantz, "Royal Reckoning," *Sporting News*, February 14, 1994.

11. Marantz, "Royal Reckoning."

12. IS IT SEPTEMBER YET?

1. Jack Lang, "Lee Mazzilli: Portrait of a Loving Family," *1981 Mets Scorebook*.

2. Steve Serby, "Serby's Sunday Q&A with . . . Lee Mazzilli," *New York Post*, June 17, 2007.

3. George Vecsey, "Mazzilli's Rude Awakening," *New York Times*, August 18, 1981.

4. Dick Young, "Mazzilli Ready to Switch-Throw for Mets," *Daily News*, March 8, 1980.

13. NOBODY HOME

1. Gooden with Henican, *Doc*, 19–20.

2. Gooden with Henican, *Doc*, 276–77, 271.

14. GONE FISHING

1. Bob Verdi, "The Cubs Dig Hebner's Wit," *Chicago Tribune*, April 2, 1984.

2. Gerry Dulac, "New Digs," *Pittsburgh Press*, April 17, 1988.

3. Fred Mitchell, "Cub Veterans Wait Nervously by Phone," *Chicago Tribune*, March 16, 1986.

16. CAPTAIN COMEBACK

1. Thomas Boswell, "Heart on His Sleeve, Good Stuff Inside," *Washington Post*, April 7, 1992.

17. STRAIGHT OUTTA COMPTON

1. Sid Bordman, "Royals Find Jewel in Steady Clouter Cowens," *Sporting News*, October 8, 1977.

2. Allen Abel, "Cowens Now a Villain," *Globe and Mail*, June 28, 1980.

EPILOGUE

1. "Vince Coleman's Cardinals Hall of Fame Speech," YouTube, https://www.youtube.com/watch?v=SnPpW3KwVkE.

2. Graham Winfrey, "Judd Apatow on the Surprise Outcome of His First Documentary, 'Doc and Darryl,'" *IndieWire*, June 30, 2016, https://www.indiewire.com/2016/06/judd-apatow-espn-30-for-30-documentary-doc-and-darryl-strawberry-dwight-gooden-1201701325/.